Historical-critical
Introduction to the
Philosophy of Mythology

Jon Berry
June 2021

SUNY series in Contemporary Continental Philosophy
Dennis J. Schmidt, editor

Historical-critical Introduction to the Philosophy of Mythology

F. W. J. Schelling

Translated by
Mason Richey
Markus Zisselsberger

With a Foreword by
Jason M. Wirth

State University of New York Press

Published by
State University of New York Press, Albany

© 2007 State University of New York

All rights reserved

Printed in the United States of America

No part of this book may be used or reproduced in any manner whatsoever without written permission. No part of this book may be stored in a retrieval system or transmitted in any form or by any means including electronic, electrostatic, magnetic tape, mechanical, photocopying, recording, or otherwise without the prior permission in writing of the publisher.

For information, contact State University of New York Press, Albany, NY
www.sunypress.edu

Production by Marilyn P. Semerad
Marketing by Anne M. Valentine

Library of Congress Cataloging-in-Publication Data

Schelling, Friedrich Wilhelm Joseph von, 1775–1854.
  [Historische-kritische Einleitung in die Philosophie der Mythologie. English]
  Historical-critical introduction to the philosophy of mythology / F.W.J. Schelling ; translated by Mason Richey, Markus Zisselsberger ; foreword by Jason M. Wirth.
      p. cm — (SUNY series in contemporary continental philosophy)
  Includes bibliographical references and index.
  ISBN-13: 978-0-7914-7131-9 (hardcover : alk. paper)   1. Mythology.   I. Title.
  ISBN-13: 978-0-7914-7132-6 (pbk. : alk. paper)

BL314.S3413 2007
201'.3—dc22
                                                                2006024606

10 9 8 7 6 5 4 3 2 1

Contents

Foreword *Jason M. Wirth*	vii
Translator's Introduction *Mason Richey*	xv
Author's Outline of the Content	3
Lecture 1	7
Lecture 2	23
Lecture 3	37
Lecture 4	51
Lecture 5	69
Lecture 6	85
Lecture 7	103
Lecture 8	123
Lecture 9	139
Lecture 10	159
Author's Notes	177
Translators' Notes	189
English-German Glossary	221
Index	231

Foreword

The great Walter Otto once lamented the eventual failure, despite their initial excitement, of Schelling's Berlin lectures on the Philosophy of Mythology and Revelation (1841–1854). Schelling spoke at a time in which the "spiritual world was at the point of fully losing the sense for genuine philosophy" because "*mythos* remained in an age in which poesy was lost."[1]

Schelling, after a meteoric but tumultuous early career, had largely retired from a prominent role in public life. His career as a philosophical *Wunderkind* had been tempered by scandals, betrayals (especially by his ascendant former roommate and philosophical companion, Hegel), and tragedies, including the devastating death of his first wife, Caroline, in 1809. The period after his masterpiece, the 1809 essay on human freedom, included repeated announcements of the imminent appearance of *The Ages of the World*, which, despite many drafts and intense activity, was never finished. Indeed, of its three proposed divisions (the past, the present, and the future), it scarcely escaped the past. "Perhaps the one is still coming who will sing the greatest heroic poem, grasping in spirit something for which the seers of old were famous: what was, what is, what will be. But this time has not yet come. We must not misjudge our time" [XIII 206; works cited at end of foreword].

Schelling published little after the 1809 *Freedom* essay. There were a few small articles and the confrontation with his Munich colleague Friedrich Heinrich Jacobi, which resulted in the 1812 appearance of Schelling's unjustly neglected defense of his own thinking again Jacobi's vicious and belligerent attack. This was the last book that Schelling would publish in his lifetime. Nonetheless, Schelling's ensuing period of long, elected silence was not a period of inactivity. Quite the opposite. This time of reclusion included a series of remarkable lecture courses and public addresses, beginning with his stunning 1810 private lectures in Stuttgart, then the October 1815 public address *The*

Deities of Samothrace (effectively beginning the work of positive philosophy via the project of a philosophy of mythology), through to his remarkable lecture courses in Erlangen on his own thinking, on the history of modern philosophy, and including early courses on the philsophy of mythology. In 1826 he received the call to teach at the newly founded Munich University, where he gave several important courses, including those on the General Methodology of Academic Study (continuing to work on themes going back to his early career, including the call for a reinvigoration and enlivening of our approach to studies), the philosophy of mythology, the philosophy of revelation, the foundations of positive philosophy, and the remarkable 1830 *Introduction to Philosophy*.[2]

A decade after the death of Hegel, who had held philosophical court in Berlin until his death in 1831, Schelling received the call to come to Berlin, in part to counter Hegel's enormous shadow. The initial lectures courses, as Mason Richey reminds us in his fine introduction, attracted the likes of Kierkegaard, Engels, Bakunin, and Ruge. The lectures were a kind of celebrity event—or perhaps a circus event—as Schelling returned to the limelight supposedly to take on his former friend. However, Schelling had not come to destroy but, as he said in his opening lecture, "to heal." He then began to unveil the fruits of his active but reclusive years.

The lectures largely fell upon deaf ears. Walter Otto was right to insist that in an era when mythology was considered a science, and when science itself was becoming increasingly alienated from its own philosophical grounds, the lectures were doomed to be virtually inaudible, as if Schelling were speaking an unknown language. The lectures were not intended to be a contribution to either theology or the burgeoning discipline of mythology, but, as Schelling claimed at the conclusion of these present lectures, they sought to "expand" both "*philosophy* and *the philosophical consciousness itself*" [XI 252]. As such, Schelling's questions and philosophical sensitivity were utterly out of sync with his time. In fact, in many ways, the lectures still retain their strange, unique voice and concerns, although, in their own unprecedented way, they address the question of difference at the heart and the ground of all history. They are one of the most radical reconsiderations of the nature of historical time, and they anticipate some of the twentieth century's most penetrating investigations of this question. The inscrutable past—escaping the triumph of the idea—nonetheless lives as the groundless ground of the present. Schelling once addressed the living opacity that is the ground of the present: "*O Vergangenheit, du Abgrund der Gedanken!*" ("O the Past, you abyss of thoughts!").[3]

I think that it is fair to say that there has been a resurgence of interest in Schelling in the last twenty years in the English-speaking philosophical world. Nonetheless, virtually no material from the Berlin period has ever appeared in English. I have long regretted this, and in a conversation about a half-decade ago, my good friend and colleague Mason Richey agreed to do something about this lacuna. I am proud to offer these few prefatory words to and gratitude for both this fine translation and its insightful introduction. Along with the recent appearance of Bruce Matthews's fine edition of the *Grounding of Positive Philosophy* (SUNY 2007), we can at last begin to explore this remarkable crepuscular contribution to the philosophical discussion of the nature of philosophy itself.

Schelling's middle period, beginning with the 1804 appearance of *Philosophy and Religion* and culminating in both the *Freedom* essay and the various drafts of *The Ages of the World* (1811–1815), marks his attempt to articulate what Jeffrey Bernstein has aptly called an "interval" between what Schelling dubbed negative and positive philosophy. The former not only characterizes Schelling's earlier work but culminates in the 1807 appearance of the grandest monument to negative philosophy, namely, Hegel's *Phenomenology of Spirit*. In a manner of thinking, one could say that Hegel helped reveal to Schelling the limit of negative philosophy not by merely stealing it but also by perfecting it. Negative philosophy ascends to the absolute, revealing the absolute as the living ground of being. Hegel, however, does not, Schelling argues, fully confront the problem of time. Hegel's idea of history ascends to the idea and all of the past stands in service to this culmination. In a way, all of history is a grand march to the revelation of the dialectic, and in this way the end of history can be understood as a theodicy that justifies the slaughter bench of the past. Schelling never dismissed Hegel or his own earlier negative philosophy but argued that negative philosophy cannot proceed from existence itself. Rather it transcends existence to reveal the free ground of existence. It begins with necessity and culminates with freedom. Positive philosophy, however, reverses the direction, beginning with freedom as its starting point. This was decisively announced in the 1809 *Freedom* essay, which, although Hegel's name is never mentioned, is in a way the first text to struggle with the immense shadow of negative philosophy.

Martin Heidegger once made a decisive claim about the *Freedom* essay that he designated as a key sentence of his own reading. "Key sentence: Freedom not the property (*Eigenschaft*) of the human but rather: the human property of freedom."[4] Debates about human freedom have long oriented themselves around the extent to which freedom can or cannot be predicated of the human. Determinists eliminate freedom as a compelling predicate, while voluntarists celebrate it. For Schelling, the question has nothing whatsoever to do with the nature of freedom as a predicate. Freedom is not a property of the human subject. Freedom is not even a property of nature. Rather, it has everything to do with the nature of the human as a predicate of freedom. *If the human were a predicate of freedom, what then?* Of course, this assumes that freedom itself is a subject, but, while freedom first appears in the subject position, it is a false subject, a dissembling and ironic subject. It is not οὐσια construed as that which receives all predicates but which has no predicates of its own, as when Aristotle argued in book *Zeta* of his *Metaphysics* that being is a pure subject, "being not what is said of a subject, but being the subject of whatever is said" [1029a].[5] It is rather an *infinite lack* that is, as such, the infinite power otherwise than every beginning and ending but given within and thereby dis-completing every beginning and ending. "It must be before every ground and before everything that exists and therefore must be a *Wesen before* any kind of duality whatsoever. How could we call it anything else other than the primordial ground or better so the non-ground? [*Es muß **vor** allem Grund und vor allem Existierenden, also überhaupt vor aller Dualität, ein Wesen sein; wie können wir es anders nennen als den Urgrund oder vielmehr **Ungrund**]*" [I/7 406].

Positive philosophy, which is, in its way, always historical philosophy—or more radically, all history is natural history—descends from freedom to the brute facts of existence. As Karl Jaspers felicitously articulates it:

> A schematic comparison of negative and positive philosophy shows: negative philosophy is the science of essence (*Wesenswissenschaft*) while positive philosophy is the science of existence; negative philosophy is in regards to the Ideal while positive philosophy is in regards to the Real. Negative philosophy thinks that which is "not not to think" while the positive takes an actuality. Negative philosophy concerns itself with necessity while positive philosophy concerns itself with freedom; the former proceeds in dialectical movement while the latter is non-dialectical, narratival. The former is rational *a priori* science while the latter is an *a posteriori* science of actuality. In negative philosophy we proceed to the ascent of the highest idea and we attain it only as an idea. Positive philosophy leaves us in actuality and proceeds from actuality. In negative philosophy God is treated as the end while in positive philosophy he is treated as the beginning. In the former God is treated as a mere concept, an immutable God, while in the latter God is treated as an existing God, an acting God.[6]

I regard these lectures as among the most successful of the Berlin lectures. In a sense, they deliver on the 1797 *System* fragment promise for a new mythology and a sensuous religion. "Monotheism of reason and the heart, polytheism of the imagination and art, that is what we need!"[7] If negative philosophy ascends via reason through the many, through the others of nature, to the one (*über x hinaus* as Schelling was wont to say), then positive philosophy descends from the one to the factual lives of the many. Negative philosophy unifies nature in the idea of the absolute, while positive philosophy disperses, multiplies, fragments, and becomes many, heterogeneous.

Hence a philosophy of mythology is indeed just that, "a philosophical investigation of mythology. For a *philosophical* investigation is in general every investigation that proceeds beyond the mere fact (here the *existence* of mythology) and inquires about the nature, the essence of mythology—while merely scholarly or *historical* research is content to find and state the mythological facts" [XI 5]. In pursuing the nature of mythology, in delineating what it is, Schelling attempts to proceed from the fact of mythology to the ground of mythology. He is not attempting to proceed in arrears to the ground of a particular mythology but to the mythological as such.

Of course, the philosophy of mythology unites what are otherwise antonyms, for "nothing is more opposed than philosophy and mythology. But precisely in the opposition itself lies the definite challenge and the task of uncovering reason in just this which is apparently unreasonable, of uncovering meaning in just this which appears meaningless" [XI 220]. To put it more directly: Schelling proceeds from the fact of mythology, a fact that is in itself non-philosophical and whose givenness could not have been deduced as something necessary within the domain of philosophy, and attempts, using mythology's antithesis, to delineate the ground of what is otherwise factual but meaninglessly so.

It is right to speak of Schelling's method as a negative dialectic. He examines every possible explanation for the fact of mythology, excludes what, upon closer analysis could not be true, but saves (in the sense of sublation or *Aufhebung*, XI 8) what is true within every otherwise erroneous view. He proceeds backward, as this translation's introduction admirably details, until the truth of the ground of mythology emerges, beyond imputation, by "inducing it to giving itself to be known" [XI 4]. I think that one could also speak of this method as *genealogical* in the Nietzschean sense, that is to say, Schelling begins from the fact of the mythological and attempts to retrieve what is unthought—and in some sense inherently unthinkable—at its ground. Schelling retrieves genealogically not more myths about mythology. He establishes that mythology is neither the mere poetic fancy of humans nor a feeble attempt at protophilosophy or proto-science. Mythology is not a human invention. Furthermore, mythology has dispersed into the heterogeneity of peoples and languages. Mythology founds a people (and the dispersion of humankind into peoples is the dispersion inherent within mythology itself). It belongs to the ground of the multiplication of languages. "One is almost tempted to say: language itself is only faded mythology; what mythology still preserves in living and concrete differences is preserved in language only in abstract and formal differences" [XI 52].

Mythology is in fact the very fact of the multiplication of humanity, the tower of Babel's confusion of languages. These differences—the very heterogeneity of humanity—are not human inventions any more than language is simply a tool at the disposal of humanity. Mythology is subjective in the sense that it happened within humanity as its multiplication, as the dissemination of the One (difference) into Many (the heterogeneity of identities). But this dissemination was not the result of the agency of humanity.

> The theogonic process, through which mythology emerges, is a *subjective* one insofar as it takes place in *consciousness* and shows itself through the generating of representations: but the causes and thus also the objects of those representations are the *actually* and *in themselves* theogonic powers . . . The content of the process are not merely *imagined* potencies, but rather the *potencies themselves*—which create consciouness and which create nature . . . The mythological process does not have to do with natural *objects*, but rather with the pure creating potencies whose original product is consciousness itself. [XI 207]

And hence we come to Schelling's boldest claim, and one of the boldest claims of the nineteenth century, a claim whose strangeness no doubt still abides. One does not explain the fact of mythology philosophically by arguing that mythology is really something otherwise than what it purports itself to be (the infancy of reason, proto-science, archetypes, the despotic musings of power hungry priests, the overarching ambitions of a poetic instinct, culturewide delusional thinking, etc.). Rather the fact of mythology is the fact of what Schelling elsewhere calls the *tautegorical*. Mythology is the fact of the history of the coming of the Gods and the Gods come as themselves.

Schelling attempts to get to the primordial matter, the *Urstoff*, at the ground of mythology, and he discovers at the ground of the history of peoples something otherwise than the human, something "essentially split off from it and proper to itself: *the world of the gods*" [XI 7]. For at the basis of mythology is "something into which human invention will have not reached, which is not made by *humans*" [XI 222]. Schellingian philosophy expands into the ecstasy of the fact of a history of divine heterogeneity. No doubt the more than a century and a half that have passed since Schelling first gave these lectures enables us to disagree with the specifics of some of Schelling's understanding of other cultures, especially non-Western ones. Our knowledge of the historical facts of mythology now allow us to see that creation myths extend to virtually all cultures of the world and at levels of heterogeneity that Schelling, who argued that a people is the result of its respective mythology, did not and perhaps could not anticipate. And no doubt Schelling's regard of some of the peoples of South America as animals, incapable of community, is offensive, but nonetheless, Schelling brings thinking into contact with the vast and divine forces of difference at the ground of all of our mythologies. Schelling brings us before "the in themselves God-positing potencies" [XI 208] whose history has been the history of dispersal, of the ongoing splendor of the many. "The same potencies, which in their collective effectivity and in their unity make consciousness into what posits God, become in their divergence the causes of the process by which gods are posited" [XI 208]. Schelling brings us to the doorstep of the possibility of a philosophical religion.

Jason M. Wirth
Seattle University

Notes

1. "Der Durchbruch zum antiken Mythos im XIX. Jahrhundert," *Die Gestalt und das Sein* (Darmstadt: Wissenschaftliche Buchgesellschaft, 1955), 221.

2. This course has appeared in the Schellingiana series published by Frommann-Holzboog. Holger Zaborowski and Alfred Denker have also published an important collection of companion essays, *System—Freiheit—Geschichte: Schellings* Einleitung in die Philosophie *von 1830 im Kontext seines Werkes* (Stuttgart-Bad Cannstatt: Fromman-Holzboog, 2004).

3. See Manfred Schröter's introduction to his edition of *Die Weltalter in den Urfassungen von 1811 und 1813* (Nachlaßband) (Munich: Beck'sche Verlag, 1946), xviii.

4. Martin Heidegger, *Schellings Abhandlung Über das Wesen der menschlichen Freiheit* (1809) (Tübingen: Max Niemeyer Verlag, 1971), 9. [*Schelling's Treatise on the Essence of Human Freedom*. Trans. Joan Stambaugh (Authors: Ohio University Press, 1985), 11.]

5. This is Richard Hope's translation (Ann Arbor: University of Michigan, 1960), 133.

6. Karl Jaspers, *Schelling: Größe und Verhängnis* (Munich and Zurich: Piper, 1986), 98. This study first appeared in 1955 as part of a resurgence of interest in Schelling in the German-speaking philosophical world.

7. "The Oldest Systematic Program of German Idealism," trans. Diana Behler, in *Philosophy of German Idealism*, ed. Ernst Behler (New York: Continuum, 1987), 162.

Works Cited

[editions cited with standard pagination]

F. W. J. Schelling, *The Ages of the World* (1815). Trans. Jason Wirth (Albany: State University of New York Press, 2000).

———. *Schellings Werke: Nach der Originalausgabe in neuer Anordnung*. Ed. Manfred Schröter (Berlin: Beck'sche Verlag, 1927–1959 and 1962–1971).

Translator's Introduction

I. Describing Friedrich W. J. Schelling's thought is a tricky enterprise. A pedigreed and clichéd philosophical tradition holds that philosophy is "the love of wisdom and knowledge," by which one generally means the pursuit of things true and rational by the philosophical bureaucrats of knowledge, by those dedicated to rendering their domain truly academic. Stubbornly, love and her promiscuous cousin passion seldom buckle to knowledge, truth, and rationality, and only a few philosophers equal the attention Schelling lavishes on the *love* of and *passion* for knowledge.

One result of embracing this juxtaposition of affect and intellect is that his thought often travels the road of excess leading to the palace of wisdom. Although Schelling's road of philosophical excess leads him astray at times, it is obvious from meticulous weighing and adducing of evidence, factual and historical erudition, and stringent argumentation that his thought's refusal to sacrifice feeling for knowledge does not indicate that he abandons rationality, truth, and knowledge. Rather, as the living principle of the objects of inquiry animates his investigations, this entails that Schelling's philosophical thought is related to its object such that thinking "not so much forces, but induces it to open the sources of knowledge that are hidden and still concealed in itself. For our endeavor to discern and be alive to an object must (one still has to repeat it) never have the intention of imputing something to it, but rather only of inducing it to giving itself to be known" [XI 4; works cited at end of introduction].

Schelling, alternately branded a mad Rationalist, Idealist, or—worse still!—a Romantic, demands a research program whose empiricism and materialist aspects attracted Kierkegaard, Engels, Bakunin, and Arnold Ruge (who attended at Marx's prodding) to his Berlin lectures, among which is this *Historical-critical Introduction to the Philosophy of Mythology* (1842). Already in the first lecture this disposition has methodological consequences, in that the philosophical views are required to erect themselves in light of the nature of the objects, not to the contrary. Those methodological consequences are still fully manifest in lecture 10, where Schelling chides his era's version of the world's Francis Fukuyamas, the purveyors of a simplified, extorted, pre-arranged philosophy of history: "Nothing is accomplished with the empty and cheap formulas of Orientalism, Occidentalism . . . or in general with a mere application to history of schemas taken from elsewhere" [XI 232]. Indeed, these mythology lectures not only are rich in concepts and their development but also offer a full engagement with both the ancient mythological world's historical detail and a broad swath of the scholarly literature available during Schelling's era. Precisely Schelling's rigorous conscientiousness of balance among passion, conceptual abstraction, and factual detail led the underappreciated Argentinian philosopher Enrique Dussel to remark pithily—when he was guest lecturing at the State University of New York-Binghamton, and on the occasion of his preparation for an article on Schelling's late works—that for Schelling "life is the criterion of truth."

Now, paradoxically, life can display severe obstinacy and even an antithetical relation to truth, a situation deriving substantially from the fact that life is alternately messy, abject, exhilarating, beautiful, fun, boring, not easily classifiable, sublime, unpredictable, flabbergasting—that is, alive. On the other hand, truth is purported to be clean, demarcatable, digestible, and comprehensible—at least in the mode of the correspondence theory of truth, or in truth's classificatory mode, or as viewed through the prism of its logical underpinning. For Schelling, life being the criterion of truth is another expression of the embracing of the juxtaposition of affect and intellect. This expression manifests Schelling's assimilation of Spinoza's own claim about the union of affect and intellect: "[H]e who increaseth knowledge increaseth sorrow." Schelling absorbed this contention but augmented it by claiming that pain and suffering are universal, the point of passage to freedom, and the "path to glory." This potent mixture endows his thought with a most unusual philosophical comportment toward error. "Error . . . is not a complete lack of truth, but rather is itself simply the inverted truth" [XI 74]. If the motto and foundational principle of the terrorism and absolutism of the Grand Inquisition was that "Error has no right!" then the philosophically unusual generosity of Schelling's thought counters with a vigorous defense of error. Hence the trickiness and difficulty in explaining his thought.

With respect to his thinking, one should not mistake the defense of error as capitulation to stupidity, ignorance, fanaticism, or madness; indeed, albeit in a slightly different context, he claims in the lecture "On Fichte" that we have a duty to counter untruth always, and more so when it is witnessed to by silence. That a dedication to what is considered true is no criterion for fending off fanaticism and madness Torquemada and his small-minded henchmen proved precisely by the prosecution of the brutal Inquisition, in all its astonishing stupidity and ignorance. "Error has right!" but Schelling vindicates it in its role in the service of truth, knowledge, and goodness. Perhaps this disposition in his work in part derives from the aftermath of the unique situation in the Tübingen *Stift*, where he roomed with Hegel and the poet Hölderlin. Propelled to fame as the philosopher of the Prussian state, Hegel's later work represented to Schelling the cold, rationalized mechanism of the state apparatus; Hölderlin simply went insane, marching off alone on foot, on a snowy winter night, from Württemberg toward Bordeaux. Stemming from discontent both with Hegel's mechanically formulaic epistemological fundament and the poet's surrender to madness, the vitality in Schelling's thinking is the search to hold these opposites together in their many permutations. For example, his thought is supple enough to assert in lecture 1 that poetry (= potentially error, untruth, the expression of the mad) and truth are utterly opposed, yet that philosophy (= truth, knowledge, rationality) and poetry share the closest of affinities. In contending that poetry and philosophy are less separated than one assumes and that between the two there is an apparently necessary affinity and mutual attractive force, he remarks that general validity and necessity are as inherent in truly poetic forms as in philosophical concepts; but it is also true that philosophical concepts "should be actual, determinate essentialities. And the more they are . . . endowed by the philosopher with actual and individual life, then the more they appear to approach poetic figures . . . [H]ere the poetic idea is included in philosophical thought" [XI 49].

Insanity is just insanity, and to claim (as Hegel did) the real as the rational and the rational as the real is in Schelling's estimation just another form of madness. His philosophy recognizes that the condition of possibility of truth is error. Error is productive. Thus his thought seeks the creativity, expressivity, and lifeblood of error and false starts, whether their form be in poetry or, as the case may be, mythology; simultaneously he attends to the philosophical requirements of rigor. The synthesis of these dispositions and projects carves a path in his thought that might fruitfully be described as that of the knight errant. He is the Don Quixote of nineteenth-century German philosophy; his philosophy is not beholden to a rule. This has positive and negative effects: when his work succeeds it does so spectacularly, and when it fails it does so spectacularly. Particularly after the discrediting of the ontological proof, is it not mad as a hatter to deduce the existence of divinities, which after all is a task of these lectures? Are these mythology lectures a star-crossed late attempt to synthesize philosophical, discursive knowledge and its other, in this case theology, much as Schelling attempted to synthesize art and philosophical knowledge in the *System of Transcendental Idealism*? Why and how does Schelling continue to insist on thinking systematically about that which undermines systemization: freedom, historicity, temporality, and in particular the gods? Availing oneself of a non sequitur, one might perhaps think of a line from David Lynch's *Twin Peaks* as a guide for reading

Schelling's work: "I have no idea where this will lead us, but I have a definite feeling it will be a place both wonderful and strange."

II. As a way of more explicitly introducing the parameters of these lectures, it is fitting to discuss briefly a sense in which Schelling's project is tilting at windmills. He considered erroneous the content of the historical mythological systems and beliefs that are the topic of these lectures, yet his intent to trace philosophically the paths of errors until revealing the truths buried in them is indicative for the modes of production of knowledge and truth he might have envisioned these lectures exhibiting. Truth and knowledge are not *simply* the resultant matter of the activity of ferreting out what is incorrect, error prone, and mistake laden, in that even the mistake free—particularly if it is known only as static and out of relationship to other entities that mediate its existence—can be banal and lifeless to the point of irrelevance, to the point of anaesthetizing the capacity for contact with the multiplicity of the affections of experience. Dovetailing with this variation on the way life is the criterion of truth, it is a key trait of Schelling's grasp of philosophical "science" [*Wissenschaft*], that is, philosophical knowledge-producing activity, that the error of banality and lifelessness is a more cardinal sin than misunderstanding a doctrine. To a significant degree this is because for him philosophical science qua *Wissenschaft* includes the distinctive modality of *Wissenschaft* as history, and indeed history in the senses of both a) *historia* (historical narratives, accounts of historical events) and b) historical events (the German *Geschichte* and *Ereignisse*, events that have happened). To wit, already in *The Ages of the World* he lays his cards on the table in a meditation on *Wissenschaft* and history as related speculatively, that is, related speculatively in the sense of displaying an interpenetration of each other, of subject and object: "Therefore, all knowledge must pass through the dialectic . . . Can the recollection of the primordial beginning of things ever again become so vital that knowledge, which, according to its matter and the meaning of the word, is history, could also be history according to its external form?" [XIII 205].

To start with the most general scope of the temporality at stake in this philosophical modality, one can turn to some of Schelling's most specific statements on the speculative relationship of *Wissenschaft* and history, statements whose epistemological-methodological background appropriately is found in the introduction to a set of 1833–34 Munich lectures on the *history* of modern *philosophy*. Asserting that *science is a constantly developing product of time* and that those positioned to advance science do so in part by elucidating the connection to what is preceding, he remarks that "if it is also necessary, in order to learn to value and judge the truth, to know error, then such a presentation [of the preceding] is the best and most gentle way to show the beginner the error which is to be overcome" [HMP, 41]. The claim to necessity of error in this sense is not obviously true, and the question is how it is the case, especially with respect to the speculative relationship of *Wissenschaft* and history. In the *AW* Schelling affirms rather uncontroversially that "[p]ain is something universal and necessary in life" [XIII 335], but more similar in opacity to the claim about error in the Munich lectures, he connects this statement on the necessity of pain to the Spinozist linking of the increase in sorrow to that of knowledge—thus, from this starting point, which is further synthesized with the understanding that knowledge and freedom are inextricably linked, the entire claim runs: "Pain is something universal and necessary in life, the unavoidable transition point to freedom . . . It is the path to glory" [ibid., 335]. The commonality coursing through these contentions regarding the historical, speculative unity of knowledge, error, freedom, and pain is that the element of progression is coupled ineluctably with an element of regression. These lectures are conceived in part as an extended reflection on this thought, as it plays out in a concrete context.

Given Schelling's insistence on detail, fact, and evidence, it should not be surprising that the key to reliability of these abstract formulae lies not in some putative calculus of validity, and even less in a supposed immediate insight into the nature of things. Rather, it is at this stage that history itself begins to step forward. The moments of history largely comprise a *series* or *succession* of—at least partially—necessary mistakes, errors, painful experiences, setbacks, *and their overcoming*. Schelling is clear about this in the *AW*: "But when one time is compared with another time and one epoch is compared with another epoch, the proceeding one appears decisively higher. Hence, such seeming regressions are necessary in the history of life" [ibid., 313]. *Sans* elaboration this is a sheer platitude, but it is in fact here where the speculative unity of a dynamic history and *Wissenschaft* begins to take shape.

First, given that acquisition of knowledge qua *Wissenschaft* is the successive overcoming of pain and sorrow qua error, but thus also the transition to freedom and glory, and given that historical progression is grasped in the facticity of history as a series or succession of life-world events that require regression (the historical equivalent of error), setback, painful mistakes, and the proceeding or progressing beyond them, the speculative concurrence of these movements of the human project leads Schelling to the consideration in the mythology lectures that both *Wissenschaft* and history share the fact that "liberation is measured according to the reality and power of that from which it frees itself" [XI 247]. One of the central scientific [*wissenschaftlich*] tasks of the lectures is to add meat to this claim, to flesh out its empirical aspect, to clarify the relations between the varying mythological systems in their integrity as embodying moments of history. The contents of mythological systems qua error are vital because their linked relations circulate the productive and expressive capacities of human being in specific times and localities. Indeed, bitter is the ascent to Golgotha; yet, taking into account Spinoza, sorrowful though the history of *Wissenschaft* and the *Wissenschaft* of history may be, the obliteration of vital error would be a still grimmer fate precisely because it would mean the clotting, stoppage, and becoming static of the circulating forces, potencies, and dynamism of history, of the successive alteration of meaningful events, of life itself.

Second, with respect to the speculative nature of *Wissenschaft* and history, Schelling performs a reversal of epistemological perspective quite remarkable for a philosopher so closely associated with German idealism. In the *AW*, during the middle period of his career, Schelling observes with regard to the phenomena being investigated that "[m]ovement is what is essential to knowledge . . . [W]here there is no succession, there is no science" [XIII 208/209]; it is *not* the case that Schelling prioritizes the Rationalist or Idealist statement to the effect that where there is no science, there is no succession. Certainly the aspects of knowledge in play here are reflexive, but what is central, and unorthodox for his contemporary milieu, is the foundation from which he derives the notion that scientific [*wissenschaftlich*] principles related to a field of knowledge are locally relevant, positionally significant, temporally limited propositions that are distorted and badly (dogmatically, contradictorily, nonmeaningfully) determined when absolutized or when the method is separated from the being or essence of the matter itself that is at stake.

From the time of the *AW* to the mythology lectures there is an increasing crystallization of the extent to which the scientific concept and the historical material—that is, description and event, or the discursive subjective and material objective—are simply a unified complex of different forms of the same content. Schelling is also quite clear with reference to the fact that thorough conceptual development and empirical precision march in lockstep: "Whoever wants knowledge of history must accompany it along its great path, linger with each moment, and surrender to the gradualness of the development . . . [The world's] history is too elaborate to be brought . . . to a few short, uncompleted propositions on a sheet of paper" [ibid., 208]. Just as the natural scientist performs indispensable trial and error in the search for success, so philosophical *Wissenschaft*—to abstract for a moment from the speculative identity of subject and object—comports itself nondominatively to its object *because* the object is itself so unruly, and, in so doing, *Wissenschaft* respects the vitality of error, both its own and that of the historical life-world itself, precisely because not to do so would rob itself of its ownmost material, and thus of its ability to thrive.

In this sense Schelling shares an orientation with Theodor Adorno. Not least is this so because both philosophers were concerned to do justice to Hegel's dialectic precisely by dispensing with its totalizing character and prefabricated historical categories. In this vein, Adorno suggests that "[t]he history locked in the object can only be delivered by a knowledge mindful of the historic positional value of the object . . . Cognition of the object in its constellation is cognition of the process stored in the object" [*ND*, 163]. This means submitting to the qualitative moments of the object itself and immersing philosophical thought in the unruly heterogeneity of those objects. The mythology lectures do precisely this by means of attending with stunning attentiveness both to the mythological systems' content in themselves and to their interrelations—for example, lecture 7's analysis and reading of the intricate, complex, volatile, and unruly relationship between polytheistic mythology and Jewish monotheism is one of the finest exemplars of comparative study in any era or place.

This unruliness manifests itself in a temporal dynamism. Both in general and in the specific case of mythology this is marked by the succession of moments. It is equally the case with history and science that what is authentic, what is propositionally expressible in truth, is so essentially with respect to its affirmation as a moment contextually vouchsafed by the circulation of which it is a part. Thus the occasion for Schelling's declaration in the *AW* that there are "no assertions that would have a value or an unlimited and universal validity in and for themselves or apart from the movement through which they are produced. Movement is what is essential to knowledge" [XIII 208]. That is, already in 1815 Schelling announces the speculative identity of the ontologico-historical and methodological parameters for such a project as the mythology lectures, a project of elaborating the dynamic reciprocity of "proceeding" and "regressions" yielded by viewing historical phenomena in an equally dynamically philosophical way (that is, in a way that is *wissenschaftlich*, scientific). The lectures are devoted to tracing the path of the relevant movement, succession, and development of the concrete religious consciousnesses of various peoples. Just as an element of a system has its integrity by virtue of its positional significance and in a specific temporal order, Schelling observes that the moments and principles of the various mythologies are true to the extent that they are comprehended as part of an advancing movement and false or regressive to the extent that they are abstracted from this movement: "No single moment of mythology is the truth, only the process as a whole. Now, the various mythologies themselves are only different moments of the mythological process. Indeed to this extent every individual polytheistic religion is indeed a false one . . . but polytheism considered in the entirety of its successive moments is the way to truth and to this extent truth itself" [XI 211/212].

With the affirmation of the priority of the mythological process as a whole, and particularly with regard to emphasis on historical theogonies unfolding as related moments in this process, there is visible a Hegelian dimension to the Schellingian comprehension of mythology; nowhere is this more manifest than in the fact that in these lectures mythology in part functions in conjunction with a developing odyssey—a phenomenology, if you will—of human religious consciousness. This contributes significantly to the identity of *Wissenschaft* and *Geschichte* (history) as *historia* in terms of the speculative identity of subject and object, and is an acknowledgment of the inexorable narrative thread—and thus possibility for mistakes—running through true knowledge and the human history of regression and progression. "The theogonic process, through which mythology emerges, is a *subjective* one insofar as it takes place in *consciousness* . . . The content of the process are not merely *imagined* potencies, but rather the *potencies themselves* . . . The mythological process does not have to do with natural *objects*, but rather with the pure creating potencies whose original product is consciousness itself. Thus it is here where the explanation breaks fully into the objective realm, becomes fully *objective*" [XI 207]. The mythology lectures are an attempt to reanimate this spiritual odyssey; as historical presentation they propose to fulfill the task of knowledge (qua *historia*) treading the path of the gods—a task broached in the *AW*, initiated explicitly in the *Deities of Samothrace*, refined in Schelling's intervening quiet years, and delivered to the public in Berlin.

III. Having covered partially the background, methodological parameters, and conceptual content of these lectures, it is worth providing briefly a perspective on the role they play as a philosophical launching point for other endeavors and investigative forays that Schelling envisioned. To this end, one would be well instructed to remember the character of what one now is reading in the form of a discrete text. The *Historical-critical Introduction to the Philosophy of Mythology* has the character of publicly and orally delivered *lectures*—it was and is not a definitive treatment of the topic, but rather an *introductory* way of locating it historically and of employing a critical analysis (in both the broadly Kantian and polemical senses) for clearing the ground on which would be erected its exposition proper. It is creditable of Schelling that his plan for a philosophical exposition and elucidation of mythology deposits into philosophy the riches of mythological thought, while also lavishing on mythology the time, attention, and energy to understand it under the aspect of discursive thinking.

As with genitive phrases generally, there is an ambiguity in the Philosophy *of* Mythology. Here, on the one hand, this plays out in terms of philosophy's enrichment by a set of ancient ways of being; on the other hand philosophy endows mythology with a consciously comprehended significance for contemporary history, culture, religion, philosophy, and thinking in general. So, initially, one notices in lectures 9 and 10 that the preliminary conclusions about the contents, paths, and processual development of mythologies bear the fruit of establishing an orientation for research into mythology's place in the philosophies and content of history, art, and religion.

This set of directions takes up form and content as Schelling weaves them into an interdisciplinary fabric of knowledge in the *Philosophy of Mythology* lectures 11–20, which contain stunning philosophical engagements with a swath of thinking extending from Hume to Hinduism. Just as an example, it cannot be emphasized enough that Schelling's comprehension of

Greek mythology (particularly in terms of Homer and Hesiod) and philosophy (particularly Plato, but also Parmenides) places them in their contextual trajectory of development as integrally indebted to Indian mythology and philosophy (particularly in terms of Brahmanism as a living theory of the divine Godhead qua interrelationship of universal and particular and ideal and real, as well as the Vedic commentaries on the religious scriptures of the Upanishads, and the Bhagavad Gita's explanation of human purpose and the good life). The further reach of this connection to Jewish, Christian, and Islamic monotheism (dealt with here in lecture 7, in particular) is a matter of almost incalculably significant cultural, economic, and political importance in the contemporary world. Finally, then, with respect to the admittedly fitful and fragmented nature of Schelling's corpus, one notes that there is a way in which these lectures were to fit into a system that was to localize living temporal moments. The *Ages of the World*, for instance, quite provocatively suggests this system under the auspices of an extravagantly ambitious relationship of mythology, revelation, and pure rationalism, the contours of which were to fit together conceptually the occurrence, in general, of events in the past, present, and future. Others have performed various and variously successful attempts at the task of making Schelling's partial versions of this system fit together, so this task rests with their labors. Suffice to say that these lectures marked an opening elucidation of mythology (continued more substantively in lectures 11–20) and that mythology in its entirety was to be considered as comprising a significant aspect of the foundation for the revelation later handled in the lectures on the *Philosophy of Revelation*.

This introduction has endeavored to indicate how Schelling's philosophy attempts to hold together a series of opposites: truth and poetry, monotheism and polytheism, history and science, subject and object, knowledge and error, affect and intellect. This is possible because he is not a slave to a rule, yet this road of excess leading to the palace of wisdom sometimes leads Schelling far astray, down a sad and terrible path. He can tend to ignore Kant's admonition that philosophical thought requires self-consistency and thinking from the position of others. If he is all too often branded unfairly as seeking flight to the Other of Reason, then it is the case that Schelling does not always attend to the Reason of the Other. As the reader will soon gather, he finds the expressions of subcontinent Indian mythology as exquisite as he finds South American religion and thought abhorrent. He is simply wrong on his own terms, and being a product of his era in Europe cannot excuse his outrageous racism. The select passages where Schelling expresses this aspect of his thinking serve for headshaking and shame to those interested in his work—they also serve as a reminder that among the philosopher's greatest tasks is the sharpening of a critical faculty wielded to weed out prejudice in one's fundamental presuppositions and assumptions.

As a note on translation, there was no highly developed "translation theory" in operation—other than trying to "get it right." The translators, however, did profit from a tension created by the fact that one of us favored literal translations that sacrifice readability, while the other bridled that instinct and insisted on fluidity of expression. On many levels Schelling deployed German in a way difficult to translate. Thus, in addition to notes on variegated arcana, the rationale for the translation decisions for many words are given in the translators' endnotes, and several words with multiple translation possibilities are accompanied consistently by the bracketed German word. The reader is also advised that there are two sets of endnotes for this translation. The author's endnotes are indicated with superscript letters and the translators' endnotes are indicated with superscript numerals. The standard pagination has been employed. For readers desiring to compare the translation with the German original, the source text is the Manfred Schröter edition (taken from K. F. A. Schelling's editions), chosen because of its accuracy and ubiquity.

WORKS CITED

[Schelling editions cited with standard pagination, excepting *HMP*]

Theodor Adorno, *Negative Dialectics*. Trans. E. B. Ashton (New York: Continuum, 2000). [*ND*]

F. W. J. Schelling, *The Ages of the World (1815)*. Trans. Jason Wirth (Albany: State University of New York Press, 2000).

———. *On the History of Modern Philosophy*. Trans. Andrew Bowie (Cambridge: Cambridge University Press, 1994). [*HMP*]

———. *Schellings Werke: Nach der Originalausgabe in neuer Anordnung*. Ed. Manfred Schröter (Berlin: Beck'sche Verlag, 1927–1959 and 1962–1971).

Historical-critical Introduction to the Philosophy of Mythology

(Lectures 1–10)

Outline of the Content

First Book. Historical-critical Introduction to the Philosophy of Mythology
Outline of the Content

First Book

First Lecture: Title and object of these lectures (p. 1*). Course of development (p. 5). First method of explanation of mythology as *poesy* (mythology has no truth). Development and critique of this view (p. 10). Consideration of Herodotus's passage, II, 53: out of which is established the relation of Greek mythology to poetry (p. 15). Relation of the other mythologies, namely the Indian, to poetry (p. 21).

Second Lecture: The allegorical interpretation of mythology (truth is in mythology, but not in it as such): the various types of the same, the eumeritic, moral, physical (p. 26); the cosmogonial or philosophical (according to Heyne) (p. 30); the philosophical-philological (according to Hermann) (p. 34).

Third Lecture: Attempt of a synthesis of the poetic view and philosophical view (parallel between the co-effectivity of poetry and philosophy in the emergence of mythology and of that in the formation of languages). Result: mythology is, in any event, an organic product (p. 47).—What is explanatory lies in a third, which is above poetry and philosophy (p. 54). Transition to the examination of the historical presuppositions of mythology (p. 55). Critique of these presuppositions in the types of explanation heretofore: 1) that

---

*Pagination corresponds to the German original standard pagination

mythology was invented by individuals (p. 56); 2) from the people itself (p. 59). Primary authority against this latter, apart from the affinity of the various mythologies—that a people first emerges with its system of the gods (p. 61). Result: mythology is not an *invention*.

Fourth Lecture: The *religious* explanations of mythology (truth is in mythology as such) (p. 67). Various types of this, which cannot yet count as actually religious (*D. Hume's* assumption. *J. H. Voss*) (p. 68). Explanation that proceeds from the religious instinct, whereby either nature is used as an explanation (the deification of nature) or polytheism is derived solely from the *notitia insita* (p. 76). Assumption of a preceding, formal doctrine of God, disputed by Hume (p. 68). Explanation from out of the distortion of the revealed truth, a monotheism (Lessing. Cudworth. Eumeritic employment of the O.T. by G. Voss. Assumption of a primordial revelation. William Jones) (p. 83). *Fr. Creuzer's* theory (p. 89). Transition to the question of the causal connection between separation of peoples (= emergence into being) and polytheism.

Fifth Lecture: The physical hypotheses on the emergence into being of peoples (p. 94). Connection of this problem with the question of the difference of the races (p. 97). Cause of the separation of the peoples in a spiritual crisis, proven from out of the nexus of the separation of the peoples with the emergence of language —*1. Mos.* 11— (p. 100). Explanation of that crisis and of the positive cause of the emergence into being of the peoples (p. 103). Means to find the dissolution into peoples, and to preserve the consciousness of unity (Pre-historical monuments. The Tower of Babel) (p. 115).

Sixth Lecture: The principle of the original unity: a universal God common to humanity (p. 118). A closer investigation of this, in the course of which a transitional discussion over the difference between simultaneous and successive polytheism (p. 123). Decision over the primary question: who was that common God. Concept of relative monotheism and out of this the explanation of mythology as a *process*, in which peoples and languages, simultaneously with the system of the gods, emerge in lawful order (p. 126). Comparison of this result with the assumption of a preceding, pure monotheism (p. 136). Relation of relative monotheism to revelation (p. 140).

Seventh Lecture: Confirmation of the foregoing through the Mosaic writings (p. 144). Meaning of the Great Flood (p. 149). The monotheism of Abraham not an absolutely unmythological one (p. 161).

Eighth Lecture: Further determinations about the God of the pre-historical time in his relation to the true God (p. 175). Application to the concept of revelation (p. 179). Exposition of the relationship of the pre-historical to the historical time; out of which the conclusion that polytheism has no historical beginning, which agrees with David Hume's claim (p. 181). Supra-historical process, through which relative monotheism has emerged, and the last presupposition of mythology in the (by nature) God-positing human consciousness (p. 184). Result: mythology is, subjectively considered, a *necessary* (proceeding in consciousness prior to it) *theogonic process* (p. 193).

Ninth Lecture: On Ottfried Müller's apparently analogous view of mythology (p. 199). What properly remains to the Philosophy of Mythology (p. 202). Herewith, an excursus on the proprietary right of the author to his thoughts. Continuation to the question of the *objective* meaning of the theogonic process (p. 204).

Tenth Lecture: Connection and interrelation of the Philosophy of Mythology with other sciences and its importance for them: 1) for the Philosophy of History (p. 228), 2) for the Philosophy of Art (p. 242), 3) for the Philosophy of Religion (p. 244).

Lecture One

Gentleman, you rightly expect that I explain, above all, the title under which these lectures are announced. Indeed, not on account that it is new and that, in particular, prior to a certain time, it has scarcely been included in the lecture register of a German university. For whatever concerns this state of affairs, if one wanted to draw an objection from it, the admirable freedom of our universities would already put us in good stead, a freedom that does not restrict the instructors to the realm of certain once-recognized courses of study handed down under old titles, a freedom that also permits them to extend their knowledge over new domains, to draw near to themselves objects that have remained distant and foreign to them until now and deal with them in particular, freely chosen lectures. In so doing, it will seldom occur that these objects are not elevated to a higher significance and science[1] [*Wissenschaft*] itself not expanded in some sense. At any rate, this freedom permits the scientific spirit to be stimulated not simply more generally and manifoldly but rather more deeply than is possible in schools where only the prescribed is taught and only lawful necessity heard. For if in the sciences that have for a long time enjoyed general recognition and approbation the result is for the most part delivered only as material, without the spectator being shown at the same time the way that it was achieved, then in the presentation of a new science the spectators themselves are called upon to be witness to its emergence, to see how the scientific spirit initially takes possession of the object [XI 4], and then—not so much forces, but induces it to open the sources of knowledge that are hidden and still concealed in itself. For our endeavor to discern and be alive to an object[2] must (one still has to repeat it) never have the intention of imputing something to it but rather only of inducing it to giving itself to be known. And the observation of the way the resistant object is brought to self-disclosure through scientific art might enable the spectator, more than any knowledge of mere results, to himself in the future take active part in the continued formation of science.

It is equally unlikely that it could lead us to a preliminary explanation if one were to perhaps say that no two things are as foreign and disparate to each other as philosophy and mythology. Precisely that could entail the demand to bring them nearer to each other. For we live in a time where even in science what is most isolated comes into contact, and at perhaps no earlier time was a living feeling of the inner unity and affinity of all sciences more uniformly and generally widespread.

Indeed, however, a preliminary explanation might be necessary because the title *Philosophy of Mythology*—to the extent that it recalls similar titles, like the *Philosophy of Language*, the *Philosophy of Nature*, among others—lays claim to a status for mythology that does not yet seem justified. And the higher that status is, the deeper the substantiation [*Begründung*] it requires. We will not consider it sufficient to say it is founded on a higher viewpoint, for with this predicate nothing is proven—indeed nothing is even said. The views have to establish themselves according to the nature of the objects, not the other way around. It is not written that everything must be explained philosophically, and where more modest means suffice it would be superfluous to summon philosophy: for which, in particular, Horace's law is supposed to be in force[3]:

Ne Deus intersit, nisi dignus vindice nodus Inciderit.

[XI 5] Accordingly we will also attempt just this with respect to mythology; that is to say, if it does not admit of an even more modest viewpoint than the one that the title "Philosophy of Mythology" seems to express. Of course, all other and more obvious views must first be explained as *impossible*, and it itself must have become the *only possible* one, before we can consider it as grounded.

Now, however, this end will not be attained by means of a merely random enumeration. It will be in need of a development that does not only simply include all those views actually advanced but rather includes all those that can be advanced at all, a development whose method prevents that no view that generally can be explained is neglected. Such a method can only be the one that arises from below, namely, the one that proceeds from the first possible view, through sublation of the same attains to a second, and in this way, through sublation of each preceding one, lays the ground for one that follows, until that view is reached that has no other outside itself into which it could sublate itself and thereby no longer merely appears as what can be true, but rather as what is *necessarily* true.

At the same time, this would also already mean to pass through all levels of a philosophical investigation of mythology. For a *philosophical* investigation is in general every investigation that proceeds beyond the mere fact (here the *existence* of mythology) and inquires about the nature, the *essence* of mythology—while the merely scholarly or *historical* research is content to find and state the mythological facts. This research has to establish the existence of matters of fact, which consist here of representations, through the means that are supplied to it in surviving deeds and customs—or in the case they do not survive, through historically evinced deeds and customs, mute monuments (temples, visual works), or speaking testimonies, writings, which themselves move in those representations or reveal them as readily available.

The philosopher will not engage directly in this business of historical research; rather, presupposing it as in the main completed, he himself will at the most take it up in those places [XI 6] where it seems to him unsuitably executed or not completely finished by the researchers of antiquity.

In addition, working through the different possible views will accord still another advantage. Mythological research too had to go through its years of apprenticeship. The entire investigation has expanded only gradually, as the various sides of the object only became visible[4] to the researchers one after another. Just like the fact that to speak not of this or that mythology, but rather of mythology as such and as a general phenomenon, presupposes not merely the knowledge of various mythologies, which only very gradually came into our possession, but rather also the obtained insight that there is something in common and in agreement in all of them. At the same time, in this way the various viewpoints will not pass us by without all sides of the object thus revealing themselves one after the other such that we will properly know only at the end: what *mythology* is. For the concept from which we proceed at first can of course only be an external and merely nominal one.

Meanwhile, it will belong to the preliminary understanding to note that mythology is being thought as a whole and that what is sought is the nature of this whole (thus, at first, not the individual representations). And, for this reason, only the *prima materia* comes into consideration in all cases. As is known, the word comes to us from the Greeks; for them it designated in the broadest sense the whole of their own particular tales,[5] legends and stories, which in general go beyond[6] historical time. However, one quickly distinguishes two very different components in the whole. For some of those legends and fables do transcend historical time, yet remain in the pre-historical; that is, they still contain acts and events of a human race, albeit one superior to the talented and well-disposed [*geartet*] race now living. Further, some things are still included in mythology that are manifestly poesy [*Dichtung*][7] that is only derived from it or founded on it. But the core, the primordial material onto which all of this crystallized, consists of occurrences and events [XI 7] that belong to an entirely different order of things (not only than the historical, but also the human one), the heroes of which are gods, an apparently indeterminate lot of religiously venerated personalities who form amongst themselves a particular world—one standing, to be sure, in multiple relation with the common order of things and of human existence, yet essentially split off from it and proper to itself: *the world of the gods*. To the extent that it is then seen that there are many of these religiously venerated beings, mythology is polytheism, and we will name this moment that initially offers itself for contemplation the *polytheistic* moment. By virtue of this, mythology is in general the *system*[8] *of the gods.*

However, these personalities are at the same time thought in certain natural and historical relationships [*Beziehungen*] to each other. When Kronos is called a son of Uranus, then this is a natural relation [*Verhältnis*]; when he castrates the father and deposes him from dominion over the world, then this is a historical relation. Because, moreover, natural relationships are in the broader sense also historical, this moment will be sufficiently designated if we name it the *historical* moment.

However, it is also immediately necessary to recall that the gods are not somehow just present abstractly and outside these historical relations: as mythological, they are by their nature, from the beginning, historical beings. The full concept of mythology is for this reason not to be a mere system of the gods, but rather the *history of the gods*—or, as the Greeks say in simply accentuating what is natural and obvious: *Theogony*.⁹

Thus we face this peculiar whole of human ideas [*Vorstellungen*], and the true nature of this whole is to be found and mediated and grounded in the manner indicated. However, because in doing so we are to proceed from a first possible view, we will not be able to avoid returning to the first impression that the whole of mythology produces in us. For the more deeply we begin, the more certain we will be to have not prematurely excluded a view that can possibly be advanced.

So, in order to begin completely at the beginning—as we tend to say [XI 8]—let us imagine ourselves in the position of someone who has never heard of mythology and to whom the Greek history of the gods, or a part thereof, would now be presented for the first time; and let us ask ourselves what his feeling would be. Without question, a type of alienation [*Befremdung*] that would not stop betraying itself through the questions: How am I to take this? How is it meant? How has it emerged? You see that the three questions ceaselessly pass over into each other and are basically only one. Through the first one, the questioner merely demands a point of view for himself; only, however, he cannot *take* mythology differently—that is, he cannot claim wanting to understand it in any sense other than that in which it is understood *originally*, the sense, then, in which it has *emerged*. Accordingly, he necessarily proceeds from the first question to the second, from the second to the third. The second (how is it meant?) is the question about the *meaning*, but about the *original* one. The answer must therefore be formed such that mythology could emerge into being in the same sense. The *view* that refers to the *meaning* is necessarily followed by the *explanation* that refers to the *emergence*. And if, perchance, in order to let mythology emerge in some sense—that is, in order to ascribe to it a certain meaning as originary—presuppositions are necessary that can be proved as impossible, then thereby the explanation cannot be upheld, and along with the explanation neither can the view.

Actually, not much is required to know that every research proceeding beyond the mere facts, research that is for this reason somehow philosophical, has since time immemorial begun with the question of meaning.

Our preliminary task is, through the elimination and sublation[10] of all other views (and thus generally speaking in a negative way), to ground the view expressed by the title. For its positive demonstration can in the end only be the announced science itself. Now, we have just seen that the mere view as such is nothing, and thus also allows no judgment for itself, but rather only through the *explanation* bound up with it or corresponding to it. This explanation itself however will not be able to avoid making certain presuppositions that [XI 9], as unavoidably contingent ones, can be judged entirely independent of philosophy. So, through such a critique—which by itself does not yet bring along a viewpoint prescribed and, so to say, dictated by philosophy—it will obtain in setting those presuppositions of every single type of explanation into a comparison either with that which in itself is thinkable or believable, or even with the historically knowable, such that the presuppositions themselves are forced to prove themselves as possible or impossible, each according to how they agree with one or the other or stand in contradiction to it. For some things are already in themselves unthinkable, others actually thinkable but not believable, still others perhaps believable but contradictory to what is historically known. For according to its origin mythology indeed loses itself in a time into which no historical tidings reach. Yet from that which is still attainable for historical knowledge, conclusions can be drawn about that which can be presupposed as possible and impossible in the historically inaccessible time. And another *historical dialectic* than the one that earlier (mostly based on mere psychological reflections) has tried to deal with these times so far removed from all history lessons might still let more be known of a very dark pre-antiquity than caprice—with which one is used to conjuring ideas about this—imagines. And precisely by removing the false historical garb with which the various historical explanations have attempted to cloak themselves, it cannot fail to appear that simultaneously everything that is still to be historically determined about mythology, and the relationships in which it has emerged into being, becomes knowable. To that end at least one monument is preserved from that time, that which is least objectionable: mythology itself. And everyone will admit that presuppositions that mythology itself contradicts cannot be other than untrue.

After these remarks—which trace out the path of the succeeding development, and which I ask you to hold firmly as guiding threads because it cannot be avoided that this investigation entangles[11] itself in many ancillary and marginal discussions [XI 10] in light of which it would be easy to lose from view the main path and context of the investigations—after these remarks we thus go back to the first question, to the question: How am I to take this? More precisely, the question is: Do I take this as truth or not as truth?— As truth? If I were able to do that, then I would not have asked. If a series of true events was told to us in a detailed and understandable lecture, then it will occur to none of us to ask what this story means. Its meaning is simply that the narrated events are real ones. We presuppose in him who tells it to us an intention to inform us; we listen to him with the intention of being informed. For us, his story undoubtedly has a *doctrinal* meaning. In the question of how I am to take this—that is, what is mythology supposed to be, or what does mythology mean?—it is thence already recumbent that the questioner feels himself incapable of seeing *truth*, actual events, in the mythological stories as well as in the mythological representations themselves because what is historical is here inseparable from the content. But if they are not to be taken as truth, then as what? The natural antithesis of truth, however, is *poesy* [*Dichtung*]. I will therefore take them as poesy; I will assume that they are meant as poesy and for this reason also have emerged into being as poesy.

This would therefore be indisputably the first view, because it emerges from the question itself. We could name it the natural view or the guileless view to the extent that, as we grasped it in the first impression, it does not go beyond that impression and consider the countless serious questions that attach themselves to every explanation of mythology. The difficulties present themselves to the more experienced almost immediately, difficulties that would be bound up with this viewpoint if one wanted to take it seriously. It is also not our intention to maintain that it has ever actually been advanced. After the given explanations it is enough for us that the view be a possible one. Granted as well that it has never attempted to make itself valid as an explanation, still there was no lack of people who at least wanted to know of no [XI 11] other view of mythology than the poetic one and who displayed a great aversion to every research into the *foundations* [*Gründen*] of the gods (*causis Deorum* as old writers express already themselves), and to every investigation at all that wants a sense of mythology other than the ideal one. We can see the reason for this antipathy only in a fond concern for the poetic of the gods, the poetic that, however, is captured by the poets alone. One fears that that poetic could suffer impoverishment or even disappear under research aiming at the foundation—a fear that would, by the way, be unfounded even in the worst case. For the result, however it may turn out, would always relate only to the *origin* and establish nothing about how the gods are to be understood with the poets or vis-à-vis pure artworks. For even those who see in the myths some sort of scientific meaning (for example a physical, natural one) do not want or claim that one thinks of just this meaning in the case of the poets also, and for this reason: as in general the danger does not seem great that in our time—extensively learned about everything aesthetic, and at least better learned than about quite a few other things— still many could be inclined to spoil Homer for themselves through such ancillary ideas. In the most extreme case—and if our time would still be in need of such a lesson—one could indeed refer to the well-known book by Moritz,[12] that, for its purpose, is still highly recommendable. Everyone is free also to contemplate nature merely aesthetically, without therefore being able to prohibit natural science or the philosophy of nature [*Naturphilosophie*].

Likewise, everyone may, for themselves, take mythology purely poetically. However, whoever wants with this viewpoint to say something about the nature of mythology must assert that it has also emerged into being purely poetically and must allow all the questions that emerge with this assertion to present themselves.

Taken without qualification, as we cannot take it differently before a reason for limitation is given, the poetic explanation would have the meaning that the mythological representations have been generated not with the intent to *assert* or *teach* something [XI 12] but rather only in order to satisfy a (of course, at first incomprehensible) poetic drive for invention. Thus, the explanation would bring along with itself the exclusion of every doctrinal meaning. Now, the following would have to be brought against it as an objection.

All poesy requires some sort of basis independent of it, a ground from which it springs forth. Nothing can simply be poetically invented [*erdichtet*], simply be plucked from the air. The freest poesy, which invents wholly from out of itself and excludes every reference to true events, has therefore its presupposition no less in the actual and ordinary incidents of human life. Every individual occurrence must be similar to those that are otherwise attested or accepted as true (ἐτύμοισίν ὁμοῖα), like Odysseus boasts[a] of his stories, even if the entire plot touches on the unbelievable. The so-called miraculousness of the Homeric epic poem is no objection against it. It has an actual foundation in the system of the gods, which from the standpoint of the poet is already *available* and *accepted* as true. The miraculous becomes the natural because gods, who intervene in human affairs, belong to the actual world of that time and are appropriate to the order of things once the latter is believed in and taken up into the ideas of that time. If, however, Homeric poetry [*Poesie*] has as its background the full totality of the belief in gods, how could one again make poetry the background for this totality. Obviously nothing preceded the full totality that was only possible after it and was mediated by it itself—just like free poesy [*Dichtung*].

In consequence of these remarks the poetic explanation would more precisely determine itself to this effect: there is indeed a truth in mythology, but not one that is placed in it *intentionally* and thus also not one that could be established and be expressed as such. All elements of reality are in it, but in the way in which they also would be in a fairy tale of the type of which Goethe has left behind for us a brilliant example—namely, where the actual lure rests in this, that it mirrors a meaning for us [XI 13] or points to it in the distance, but a meaning that itself perpetually withdraws from us, after which we would be compelled to hasten without ever being able to reach it. And, undoubtedly, he who would hold sway as master of this genre would understand most cleverly to deceive us in this way, to most often hold the spectator breathless and, as it were, make a fool of him. But this would in fact be the most proper description of mythology, which deceives us with the echo of a deeper meaning and entices us further without ever answering our question.

Or, who has ever succeeded in bringing these lost, directionless, wandering tones into a real harmony? They are to be compared to the tones of the Aeolian harp,[13] which excite in us a chaos of musical images [*Vorstellungen*] that, however, never unite themselves into a whole.

An interrelation, a system [*System*], would appear to show itself everywhere, but with this system it is like with *pure matter* according to the Neoplatonists, the pure matter of which they say: if one does not seek it, then it presents itself, but if one grasps for it or wants to transform it into knowledge, then it flees. And how many who have attempted to capture the fleeting appearance of mythology have not, like Ixion in the fable, embraced the cloud instead of Juno![14]

When only the intentionally imputed meaning is excluded from mythology, then also every *particular* meaning is of itself excluded; and if we will subsequently become familiar with a series of explanations, each of which deposits a different meaning into mythology, then the poetic explanation would be the one indifferent to every meaning, but for just this reason also an explanation excluding none, and certainly this would be no small advantage. The poetic view is able to allow for the idea that natural phenomena shine forth through the figures of the gods. It can believe to perceive in itself the first experiences concerning powers operating invisibly in human things—why not even religious shudders? Nothing that was able to shock the new man, who was not yet master of himself, will be foreign to the first emergence into being. All of this will mirror itself in those poesies and produce the magical semblance of a cohesion, indeed of a doctrine standing at a distance, a cohesion that we gladly admit as *semblance* and only [XI 14] reject if a low and unrefined mind [*Verstand*] wants to transform it into reality. Yet *every* meaning in mythology is merely potential, like in chaos, but without therefore allowing itself to be limited and particularized. As soon as one attempts this, the appearance is deformed, even destroyed. If one permits the meaning to be as it is in it, and rejoices to himself about this infinity of possible relationships, then one has the proper attunement to grasp mythology.

In this way it appears that the idea, which in the beginning could appear as almost too comical to find a place in a scientific development, would have attained a certain stability. And we hope thereby to have spoken in agreement with the sense of some others, even though they did not find it proper to give their view precisely as an explanation. And who, in the end, would not like to stick to this view, if other considerations allowed for it? Would it not completely be in agreement with a well-known and popular way of thinking to presuppose for the later, serious times of our human species an epoch [*Weltalter*] of a clear and serene poesy, a condition that was still free from religious terror and all those uncanny feelings by which later humanity was harried, the time of a happy and guiltless atheism, where just these ideas that later—under peoples that had become barbaric—darkened into exclusively religious ones still had a purely poetic meaning, a condition perhaps like the one the ingenious *Baco*[15] imagined when he called the Greek myths the breath of better times, which have fallen to the pan flute of the Greeks.[b] Who would not like to imagine a human race—if not one now on faraway islands, then one found in the primordial time—for whom a spiritual Fata Morgana would have raised all actuality into the realm of fables? In any event, the view contains an idea through which everyone passes, even if none tarry with it. However, we rather fear one would allow it to be poetically invented than to withstand a historical test. For whatever more precise determination one wanted to give to it, it would always [XI 15] have to be explained at the same time how humanity, or a primordial people, or people at all, were in their earliest times equally seized upon by an irresistible inner drive and how they would have produced a poetry whose content was the gods and the history of the gods.

Whoever is endowed with a natural sense was able to have the experience, with complex problems, that often the first interpretations of things are the correct ones. But they are only correct to the extent that they designate the goal for which thought should strive, but not such that they would already have reached the goal itself. The poetic view is also one such first interpretation. It undoubtedly contains what is correct, to the extent that it excludes no meaning and indeed permits mythology to be taken properly. And so we will be careful not to say that it is false; on the contrary, it shows what is to be reached. Only the means to an explanation are missing. Thus this interpretation itself compels us to take leave of it and continue on to other inquiries.

The explanation would indeed gain very much in certainty if one, instead of only in general seeing poesy [*Poesie*] in the history of the gods, descended to the actual, individual poets and made them into creators—perhaps according to the instructions of the famed and much discussed passage by Herodotus, where indeed he does not speak of poets [*Dichtern*] in general, but does say of Hesiod and Homer: these are they who have formulated theogony for the Hellenic people.[c]

It lies in the plan of this preliminary discussion to search out everything that is still somehow able to cast a historical light on the emergence of mythology. It will also be desired on this occasion to impart what can be historically known about the earliest relationship of poetry to mythology. For this reason, we will consider the passage by the historian as worthy of a more precise examination in the present context. For, even if linguistic usage allowed it,[d] the context [XI 16] would not permit understanding the words merely by the contingent and outward relationship, that is, that the history of the gods was only first sung by both in *poems*. Something more essential must be meant. And something historical is also undoubtedly to be gained from the passage; for Herodotus himself presents his statement as the result of expressly conducted investigations and urgent inquiries.

If only Hesiod were named, then theogony could be understood as the poem. But because it is equally said of both poets that they are the ones who have formulated theogony for the Hellenic people, it is apparent that only the thing, the history of the gods itself, can be meant.

Now, however, the gods cannot be invented by both of them, after all. The historian cannot be understood as though Greece only first knew of the gods starting with the times of Homer and Hesiod. This is already impossible on account of Homer. For he is familiar with temples, priests, sacrifices, and alters of the gods, not as something that emerged recently but rather as something actually ancient. Indeed, one was often able to hear that with Homer the gods are now purely poetic beings. Correct!—if one thereby wants to say that he is no longer thinking of their solemn, darkly religious meaning. But one cannot say they have in general only a poetic meaning for him. For the people whom he represents, they have a very real value; and he found, not invented, the gods as beings of a religious and therefore doctrinal meaning. Meanwhile, for all that, Herodotus does not in fact speak of the gods on the whole but rather of the history of the gods, and thus explains himself more precisely: from where each god hails, or if all have been since time immemorial, this is first known, so to say, since yesterday or before yesterday, namely, since both poets, who lived no more than four hundred years before him. These are they who produced the history of the gods for the Hellenic people, gave the gods their names, allotted honors and functions among them, and decided on a form for each.

Therefore the primary importance is to be placed on the word *theogony*. This whole, Herodotus wants to say—in which is determined for every god his natural [XI 17] and historical condition [*Verhältnis*], in which to each is ascribed his own name and particular position, and in which his form is given—this system of the gods, which is the *history* of the gods, the Hellenics owe to Hesiod and Homer.

However, understood simply as such, how could this statement be justified? For where do we actually see Homer occupied with the genesis[16] of the gods? Most seldom, and even then does he involve himself in an elaboration of the natural and historical relationships of the gods only occasionally and in passing. To him they are no longer beings in the process of becoming, but rather ones that are already there. No one asks about their foundations and first origins, just as little as the epic poet, when he describes the life of the hero, makes mention of the natural processes through which the hero was formed. His poem, hurrying ahead, also takes no time to assign names, positions, and ranks to them; all of this is treated as a given and mentioned as something present since time immemorial.— Hesiod? Now, admittedly, he lauds in song the genesis of the gods, and in light of the expounding and didactic character of his poem it could be said that theogony was made by him. But on the other hand, however, only the unfolding of the history of the gods could move him to make it an object of an epic presentation.

Now, to be sure—we can add this as an objection—the history of the gods did not emerge into being through their poems, or only as a consequence of them. But considered precisely Herodotus does not say this either. For he does not say that these natural and historical differences between gods *were not* everywhere *there* beforehand. He only says they *were not known* (οὐχ ἠπιστέατο). Thus he only credits to the poets that the gods were known. This does not prevent, but rather necessitates—judging by the matter—assuming that it was thematically present prior to both poets, only in a dark consciousness, chaotically, like in Hesiod especially (πρώτιστα). Here, accordingly, a double emergence into being shows itself—once according to the material and in envelopment, then in the unfolding and exposition. It thus becomes clear that the history of the gods [XI 18] was not immediately present in the poetic form in which we find it. The implicit history could *basically* well be poetic, but not *actually*; thus it did not emerge into being poetically. The dark foundry, the first forging place of mythology, lies beyond all poesy [*Poesie*]. The foundation of the history of the gods is not laid by poesy. This is the clear result of the words of the historian, if they are considered in their full context.

Now, but even if Herodotus simply wants to say that the two poets have first articulated the previously implicit history of the gods, it is not yet thereby clear how he at the same time thought of their particular relationship. So here we must draw attention to a moment in the passage: Ἕλλησι— he says; they have fashioned the history of the gods for the Hellenics. This is not there for nothing. In the whole passage Herodotus is only concerned with emphasizing that of which the investigations, to which he refers, have convinced him. But what these investigations have taught him is only the *newness* of the history of the gods as such, that it is completely and utterly Hellenic; that is, that it first emerged into being with the Hellenics as such. Herodotus places the Pelasgians[17] prior to the Hellenics. For him they have—it cannot now be said through which crisis—but for him they have *become* the Hellenics through a crisis. Now, in another passage standing in close relation with the present one, he knows the following about the Pelasgians: namely, that they sacrificed everything to the gods, but *without differentiating them through title or name*. So here we still have the time of that mute, still enveloped history of the gods. Let us think ourselves back into this state where consciousness still grapples chaotically with the representations of the gods, yet without being able to draw them out of themselves or make them objective, and for just that reason without being able to separate them and explain them—where consciousness therefore is, on the whole, not in a *free* relation to them. In this ardent and intense state poesy also was *completely* impossible. Hence, without regard to the content of their poems [*Dichtungen*], the two oldest poets, as *poets*, would designate the end of that unfree condition, of the still Pelasgian consciousness. The liberation [XI 19] that became the lot of consciousness through the cision of the representation of the gods first gave poets to the Hellenics, and conversely only the age that gave them the poets also brought along with itself the completely unfolded history of the gods. Poesy did not take the lead, at least not actual poesy; and, properly speaking, poesy also did not produce the articulated history of the gods. Neither precedes the other. Rather, both are *the mutual and simultaneous ending of an earlier state*, a state of envelopment and silence.

We have now drawn ourselves significantly nearer to the historian's meaning. He says: Hesiod and Homer; we would say: the epoch of both poets produced the history of the gods for the Hellenics. Herodotus can express himself as he has, for Homer is not an individual like later poets, such as Alkaios, Tyrtaios,[18] or others. He designates an entire age, is the dominating power, the principle of an epoch. With the two poets it is not meant any differently than it is meant when Herodotus recounts of Zeus, with almost those same words, that after the end of the struggle against the Titans he was asked by the gods to take over leadership and meted out honors and rank to the immortals.[e] It is only with Zeus as head that the properly Hellenic history of the gods exists; and it is simply the same turning point, the beginning of the properly Hellenic life [XI 20], which the poet designates *mythologically* through the name of Zeus, and the historian *historically* through the name of both poets.

But now we are going still one step farther when we ask: who, out of everyone who especially knows how to read Homer carefully, would not in fact see the gods *emerge into being* in the poems of Homer. Certainly the gods arise from a past unfathomable for him, but one at least feels that they arise. In Homeric poetry almost everything sparkles with newness; this historical world of the gods is here still in its initial vigor and youth. The divinity of the gods alone is that which is primordially ancient, but also only that which appears from out of the dark background. The historical, the part of the gods that is freely mobile, is the new, that which is just in the process of emerging. The crisis through which the world of the gods unfolds itself into the history of the gods is not external to the poets. It takes place in the poets themselves, forms their poems, and thus Herodotus can truly say: the two poets, in his decisive and well-founded opinion the earliest of the Hellenics, made the history of the gods for these people. And, as he must admittedly express himself, it is not them as persons who create the history of the gods but rather the crisis of the mythological consciousness within them. They form the history of the gods in an entirely different sense than that in which one tends to say that two swallows do not yet a summer make. For the summer would also happen without any swallows. But the history of the gods comes about in the poets *themselves*; it comes into being in them, it succeeds in unfolding in them, it is first there and explicit in them.

And so we would have justified the historian to the letter, a historian whose extraordinary discernment, especially in the oldest relationships, no matter the object, continually holds good even in the deepest investigations. He views himself still close enough to the genesis of the history of the gods to attribute to himself a historically grounded judgment about it. We may also cite his opinion as such a judgment and assert it as proof that poetry [*Poesie*] could indeed be the natural end and even the necessarily immediate product of mythology [XI 21]; however, as actual poetry (and to what end would it serve to speak of a poetry *in potentia?*) it could not be the generative ground, the source of the representations of the gods.

This is what shows itself in the most lawful development of the Hellenics, in the development of the preeminently poetic people, the Hellenic people.

If we go back further, in order to cover everything still historically knowable about this relation, then initially the *Indians* join ranks. To be sure, if everything that one or several people happen to claim were immediately to become dogma, then we would have expressed no small historical heresy when we situate the Indians immediately prior the Greeks. In fact, however, the Indians are the only people who have in common with the Greeks a free art of poetry [*Dichtkunst*] that is developed in all forms and likewise arose from mythology. Entirely apart from everything else, this richly unfolded poetry alone would already assign this status to the Indians. But there is in particular something else that by itself would be no less decisive: the language, which does not merely belong to the same formation as the Greek language but is also most closely related to it in grammatical form. He who is made aware of this would have to have lost all sense for a lawful course of every development—thus also especially for historical phenomena—if he could still assent to the opinion that elevates the Indians to a primordial people [*Urvolk*] and historically projects them beyond all peoples, although the first emergence of this opinion can be explained if necessary and to some extent excused. For the first knowledge of the language in which the most exquisite monuments of Indian literature are written could not have been obtained without significant effort and a great talent for languages. And who would not like to render recognition to the men who, in part already in years in which the acquisition of languages in general no longer happens so easily, not only learned Sanskrit itself, even if at a great distance, but also have simplified and smoothed away the prickly path to knowledge of it for those who follow? Now, it is fair to expect significant success from great effort [XI 22]; and if the initial forerunners could consider the acquisition and conquest of Sanskrit as their highest reward, then followers and students, the kind that can always be found when it comes to the extension of human knowledge, must have desired to in another way recoup the pains taken—even if through careless exaggerations and hypotheses that subverted the previously accepted order and sequence of the peoples and turned what is highest into what is lowest. In fact, this elevation of the Indians in their effect might not be judged much differently than the geological hypothesis of uplift has been judged by Goethe,[19] who states that it proceeds from an idea in which one can no longer speak of something that is *certain* and *lawful* but rather only of *contingent* and *disconnected events*[f]; a judgment with which one can indeed agree—at least as far as it concerns the uplift hypothesis in its form up to now—without thereby mistaking the importance of the facts on which it relies, or finding the previously accepted modes of emergence more believable, or even wanting to defend them.

It should not surprise you if I speak out decisively against such arbitrariness in the very beginning of this investigation. For if one were allowed to proceed at all in the manner in which one has attempted to do it with the utilization of the Indian, I would prefer to immediately give up the nascent investigation, because an immanent development, a development *of the matter itself*, would no longer be possible, and, on the contrary, everything would be brought into a merely external and contingent relationship [*Zusammenhang*]. In this way one could use that which is youngest and most distant from the origin as the measure of that which is first and originary, and cite what is latest as proof and evidence for a shallow and unfounded view of that which is oldest. Even, for example, in investigations about the genesis [*Genesis*], the general name *mythology* must serve as the pretext for such a pressing and urgent involvement of the Indian in everything, an involvement with which the true experts of the Indian [XI 23] are certainly least in agreement. For under this title [of the genesis of mythology] those things which are most isolated, entirely separate domains, often opposite ends, are treated as fully identical. Nevertheless, there are large and considerable differences in mythology itself, and as little as we can admit that the individual gods differentiated through names and rank are compared with each other in every which way, that it is attempted to annul their differences, just as little will we allow that the true—indeed, immanent and thereby lawful—succession of the great moments of mythological development are effaced and completely annulled. And this is all the less so because, in the case that this were allowed, every scientific investigation of higher antiquity would have to be abandoned, for which precisely mythology offers the only sure guide.[g]

Were mythology on the whole really a poetic invention, then that of the Indians would also have to be one. Now, the Indian poetry, insofar as it is known as of now, has met with the most obliging recognition, and as a new phenomenon has been, perhaps in part, excessively appraised. To the contrary, one was, very generally, unable to find the Indian gods particularly poetic. *Goethe's* pronouncements about their lack of form are well known and powerful enough, but not to be called unjust precisely, even if one perhaps wanted to perceive therein an addition of displeasure, in which the strikingly real and doctrinal character [XI 24] of the Indian gods and the all-too-marked impossibility of applying to them the merely ideal explanations, with which one could reassure oneself in the case of the Greeks, might have some part. For one cannot leave the Indian gods unexplained; they are not to be swept away with a mere judgment of taste. Odious or not, they happen to be there, and because they are there they must be explained. However, one can, so it appears, just as little establish a different explanation for the Indian gods and a different explanation for the Greek gods. If one wanted to draw a conclusion from the comparison of both, then it would have to be this: that the doctrinal element, the properly religious element, of the mythological representations was fully overcome only gradually, and for the first time in the ultimate decision [*Entscheidung*].[20]

The crisis that gave the Hellenics their gods has, manifestly, at the same time given them freedom vis-à-vis these gods. On the other hand, the Indian has remained still more deeply and internally dependent on his gods. The formless epic poems of India, like the artful dramatic poems, carry in themselves a far more dogmatic character than any Greek work of the same type. In comparison with the Indian gods, what is poetically transfigured in the Greek gods is not something ultimately original but rather is only the fruit of the deeper, indeed the complete, overcoming of a power that still exercises its dominion over the Indian poesy [*Poesie*]. Without a *real* principle at their foundation, the famed ideality of the Greek gods could itself be only a stale one.

Creative poesy, a poetic art moving freely in all forms, is found outside of the Greeks only with the Indians. That is to say, it is to be found precisely in the peoples who are the last or first in the mythological development. But again, the relation between the Indian and the Greeks shows that the doctrinal appears dominant with the Indians and is by far more visible than with the Greeks.

Going back further, we initially encounter the Egyptians. The Egyptian system of the gods is petrified in massive works of architecture and colossal images. But a fluid poesy, holding sway along with the gods as an independent entity free of its origin, seems fully foreign to them [XI 25]. Except for a single lugubrious song and ancestral music, to which, as Hesiod explicitly says,[h] no new ones were added, there is no trace of poetry with them. Neither does Herodotus make mention of a poet similar to one of the Greeks—whom he, so inclined to comparisons, certainly would not have failed to specify; nor has one of the numerous inscriptions on obelisks and temple walls as yet proved itself to be a poem. And yet the Egyptian mythology is one so developed that Herodotus—certainly not "persuaded by Egyptian priests"—recognizes the Greek deities in the Egyptian.

Still further back we find a system of the gods—one not so extensively but still considerably advanced—with the Phoenicians, and the first elements of the same with the Babylonians. One could, at the most, ascribe to both peoples a doctrinal, psalmlike poetry similar to the old Hebraic one; yet we know nothing of a Babylonian poetry, and just as little of a Phoenician poetry.

Poesy never shows itself as something first, original, like it is presupposed in so many explanations; it also had an earlier condition to overcome and appears all the more fluid, all the more as poesy, the more it has subdued this past.

Accordingly, all of this might incite concern about the unconditional validity of the purely poetic view and explanation, which shows us that we are not concluding with it and that an indefinite breadth of other types of investigations and elucidations still lies before us.

Lecture Two

[XI 26] If we reluctantly distance ourselves from the poetic view, this is mainly because it imposes no restriction on us, because it leaves to us complete freedom vis-à-vis mythology, because it leaves the latter itself untouched in its universality; but especially because it permits us to come to focus and dwell on the *proper and authentic*[1] meaning, although it cannot do otherwise, as it moreover at the same time excludes a properly doctrinal meaning. Thus, this may well be its limit. Therefore there will come a different viewpoint which admits of truth and a doctrinal meaning, which maintains that truth was at least originally meant in it. Now, however, as it is mostly wont to proceed, this view will sacrifice the other—that which is proper and authentic[2] in the matter—in order to make room for the view admitting truth and a doctrinal meaning, and instead of the proper and authentic will introduce the improper and inauthentic sense. Truth is in mythology, but not in mythology as such; especially since it is the doctrine [*Lehre*] and history of the *gods*, and thus seems to have a religious meaning. Thus mythology says or seems to say something different than is meant, and the interpretations appropriate to the articulated viewpoint are generally, and taken in the broadest sense of the word, *allegorical*.[a]

The various possible gradations will be the following.

There are personalities meant here, but not gods, not superhuman beings belonging to a higher order; rather, human-historical beings and also actual events are meant, but events of the human or civil history. The gods [XI 27] are only heroes, kings, legislators exalted to divinities; or, when, as in today, finance and trade are major considerations, seafarers, discoverers of new routes of trade, founders of colonies, etc. Whoever would feel the inclination to see what a mythology explained in this sense looks like, one could refer him to Clericus's remarks on Hesiod's *Theogony* or to Mosheim's remarks on Cudworth's *Systema intellectuale*,[3] and to Hüllman's *Beginnings of Greek History*.

The historical method of explanation is called the *eumeretic*, after Eumeros—an Epicurean of the Alexandrine period—who appears to have been its most ardent defender, although not the oldest. As is well known, Epicurus assumed *real, actual* gods, but fully idle ones unconcerned with human affairs. Contingency, alone in force according to his teaching, admitted of no providence or influence of higher beings on the world of human things. Against such a teaching, the popular belief of gods actively intervening in human events and actions was an interpolation that had to be done away with. This occurred when it was said of them that they are not actual gods but only men represented and imagined as gods. You see that this explanation presupposes real, proper gods, whose representation—as is well known—Epicurus derived from an opinion *preceding every teaching*, from an opinion embedded in human nature, an opinion which for this reason is supposed to be common to all men.[b] "Because this opinion is not introduced through an organization or through custom or law, but rather is met with in advance in all humans, gods must exist": thusly concluded Epicurus,[c] more prudent herein than some who come later [XI 28].

This also highlights how unfitting it is when some, in Christian times, indeed in our times, who do not believe in actual gods but perhaps believe in quite a few other things, at least in part purport to be able to apply the eumeritic explanation.

A second gradation would then be to say that no gods are meant in mythology at all; neither proper and real nor improper and unreal, no personalities, but rather impersonal objects that are only represented poetically as persons. Personification is the principle of this method of explanation; either ethically customary or natural properties and phenomena are personified.

Because the gods are ethical beings, and in each of them some sort of spiritual character trait or trait of temperament is in evidence to the exclusion of another, thereby giving them a status above that of human life, they can be employed as symbols of ethical concepts, as has occurred since time immemorial. Use is made of what already is there, but the use does not explain the emergence into being. The poet, when he has need of a deity that demands moderation and self-control, will call upon the contemplative Athena rather than the wrathfully disposed Hera. But this goddess is not the personified wisdom for that reason merely, neither for the poet himself, nor for mythology. In his little book *De Sapientia Veterum*, Baco,[4] living in an age of great political factionalization, used mythology as the dressing for political ideas. To present mythology as an artfully clothed moral philosophy—as the demon says in Calderón's *Wonderful Magus*,[5]

> they are only fairy tails wherein the profane writers/ presumptuously through the name of the gods/ artfully enclosed moral philosophy—

was not so much a scholarly as it was a pedagogical invention of the Jesuits, who, competing with the schools of Protestants, also suggested the ancient poets to their followers (although usually in a very reductive way), and with this end in view also explained mythology [XI 29]. As far as the physical interpretations are concerned, their material possibility is not to be denied; but the explanation is not thereby justified that one would have to then first isolate nature itself, disavow its connection with a higher and universal world, which perhaps reflects itself in mythology just as much as in nature. That such explanations are possible only testifies to the universality of mythology, which is of a type, in fact, that—once given the allegorical explanations—it is almost more difficult to say what it does not mean that what it does. Attempts of the type—when they do not even think of the *formal* explanation that shows how mythology in such a sense has emerged—are for this reason at most empty dalliances worthy only of idle minds.

Whoever, without a sense for the universal, allows himself to be settled through mere contingent impressions can even lower himself to *specific* physical interpretations, as has frequently happened. At the time of thriving alchemy, adepts were able to see the so-called philosophical process in the struggle for Troy. The interpretation itself was supported by etymologies that are not inferior in probability to some of the usual ones of today. For *Helen*, the source of the struggle, is *Selene*, the Moon (the alchemical sign of silver); but *Ilium* [Ilios], the sacred city, is just as clearly *Helios*, the Sun (which in alchemy indicates gold). When the antiphlogistic chemistry aroused general attention, one could believe to recognize in the masculine and feminine Greek gods the substances of this chemistry—for example, in the all-mediating Aphrodite, the oxygen initiating every natural process. Today, natural scientists are concerned mainly with electromagnetism and chemistry: why should the latter two not also be found in mythology? It would be futile to want to refute such an interpreter, for whom the discovery affords the immeasurable happiness to view his own most modern face in the mirror of such high antiquity; whereby he finds it superfluous to show, on the one hand, how those who are supposed to have invented the myths have come to the beautiful physical knowledge that he presupposes [XI 30], and, on the other, what has motivated them to cover and hide this knowledge in such a surprising way.[d]

Still higher than these specific interpretations would be the explanations that believe they recognize the history of nature in mythology. Indeed, to some it is simply an allegory of that which repeats itself yearly, of the seeming movement of the sun through the signs of the zodiac;[e] to others it is the poetically presented, actual history of nature, the series of changes and upheavals that have preceded the present, quieted condition of this same nature—a view to which the antagonistic relations of the successive races of the gods, especially the Titans' struggle against the last of the former, gives the proximate cause. One can proceed still further to a natural *theory of the emergence of the world* (cosmogony), which is supposed to be contained in mythology. After some before him, this latter has been chiefly attempted[f] by *Heyne*, who at the same time was the first one to deem it necessary to also make the genesis comprehensible in this sense.[6] He was not reluctant to consider philosophers as creators; more or less connected philosophemes about the formation of the world are to him the original content of mythology. Zeus has robbed father Kronos of the throne, and according to some accounts, of manhood; this means (perhaps I do not precisely avail myself of his words): creative nature for a long time produced merely the wild, the monstrous (say, the inorganic); whereupon a point of time entered where the production of mere quantities [XI 31] of stuff stopped, and the formed organic was produced instead of the unformed and formless. The cessation of this unformed production is the emasculation of Kronos; Zeus is the already self-formed force of nature and the force of nature bringing forth and producing that which is formed—the force of nature through which that production that is first and wild is blocked, restricted, and inhibited from further reproducing. This is certainly a meaning that is worth considering, and such explanations may always function as preparatory exercises; in an earlier time they served at least to preserve the notion of a real content in mythology. Now, if one asks how the philosophers have come to dress their valuable insights in this form, then at least Heyne seeks to remove this artificial dress as much as possible. They have not freely chosen the presentation, but rather were urged toward it and nearly forced; in part, the oldest language was missing scientific expressions for general principles or causes. The poverty of language has obliged it to express abstract concepts as persons, logical or real relations through the image of reproduction. In part, however, they have been so seized by the objects themselves that they strived to also place them before the spectators' eyes, so to speak, dramatically, as acting*f* persons.*g*

They themselves—the supposed philosophers—*knew* that they did not speak of real people. Now, however, how did the personalities created by them become real ones, and thereby become gods? Through a very natural misunderstanding, one should think, a misunderstanding that was unavoidable as soon as the representations came to those for whom the secret of the emergence of these personalities was not known. Yet Heyne conceives [XI 32] of the transition differently. The personifications at one point just happen to be there, well understood by all who know the meaning. There the poets notice that, taken as *real persons*, they would provide material for all sorts of delightful fairy tales and stories, with which one could hope to be well received by a people made joyful by amusement. Heyne is not even averse to ascribing even to Homer just this transformation of philosophically meaningful myths into entirely base stories. The philosophical meaning is, supposedly, well-known to him, as one can learn from some intimations that escape him. Only he acts as though he knows nothing. Heyne contends that he understands his advantage as a poet too well to allow the meaning to more than at most shine through; for philosophical ideas are not well loved by the people, and meaningless stories appeal to them much more, as long as there is a certain noticeable variation of objects and events. Thus, in this manner the mythological personalities have supposedly achieved the independence from their scientific meaning—in which they present themselves with the poets—and have arrived at the senselessness in which only popular belief still knows them.

It appears to be a fact worthy of notice that the origin of mythology was no more understandable to the Greeks—to whom it was much closer—than to us; like the Greek natural scientist stood no nearer to nature than one today. For, partially at least, already in Plato's times entirely similar interpretations of mythological traditions were attempted; in the *Phaedrus* Socrates says of these interpretations: to do them and to bring them to completion, it takes a man making immense efforts, and who is therefore not particularly happy and enviable; for—with this sort of coarse understanding (ἄγροιχος σοφία)—in order to get an exact or at least an approximate result much time is necessary, which not everyone who could concern himself with things that are more serious and important has available to himself.[h]

In Cicero, the academic expresses similar opinions about the difficulty of these interpretations [XI 33] with reference to the Stoics.[i] For it is striking that the only two remaining systems of philosophy ultimately left on the stage of philosophy in Greece and Rome, the *Epicurean* and the *Stoic*, split themselves into the two explanations, the *historic* or *eumeritic* and the *natural-scientific*. The Stoics did in fact, on account of great deeds, admit of deified men where this origin seemed to be clear, as with Hercules, Castor and Pollux, Aesclepius, etc. But everything deeper in the history of the gods—like the emasculation of Uranus, Saturn's overwhelming defeat by Jupiter—they explained through purely physical relations.[j] Ultimately both were supplanted by the *Neoplatonists*, who finally saw an actual metaphysics in mythology, and who were obliged to this end mainly in order to give the spiritual content of Christianity a counterweight to the one analogical to paganism.[k] Meanwhile, because—in view of the endeavors to in part set their own speculative ideas in harmony with the traditions of the old religions, and in part, alternatively, to support the former through the latter—they are so far removed from thinking of a natural origin of mythology, which they on the contrary presuppose as an unconditioned authority, they are unable to find a position among the actual explainers of mythology.

Heyne had taken precautions against one calling allegorical his explanation or the cloaked form of wording of his philosophers themselves; namely, because the latter have not chosen it with the intent to disguise their teachings or opinions [XI 34]. As if it were a matter of that! In short, they speak of gods where they are only thinking of natural forces; thus they mean something different than they say, and express something about which they are not actually thinking. Now once one has come so far as to accept the *content* as scientific, would it not be desired also to find the *expression* entirely properly and scientifically [*wissenschaftlich*], and thereby to at least arrive wholly and purely at the side opposed to the poetic view, to which end Heyne stopped halfway? He was really not at all the man to completely carry out a conclusion or even by way of thought experiment to think it through to its ultimate point. Perhaps it was a blissful frivolousness that prevented him from bringing the philosophical explanation to the ultimate test, a test which a more formal spirit, *Gottfried Hermann*,[8] Heyne's famed successor in philological research, had it undergo, namely the Gottfried Hermann who established the thoroughly proper sense of the matter in the way that he—if we disregard a superficial personifying tinge to the expression—sees even in the names only scientific nomenclature of the *objects* themselves; in this way, to him Dionysus, for example, does not signify the god of wine, but rather, strictly etymologically, the wine itself, while Phoebus[9] does not signify the god of light, but rather, likewise, light itself; this is an explanation that, as a revolt against the allegorizing interpretations alone, is already well worth the attention and a detailed presentation.

If one investigates—which is the way the most worthy grammatician constructs[1] his theory—the supposed names of the gods, then in general all at first appear *meaningful*. If one investigates the meaning more closely, then it is found second—owing to an etymology that is sometimes self-evident and sometimes knowable only through deeper analysis—that it contains *in toto* only predicates of forms, forces, phenomena, or activities of nature. Investigating further the connection and interrelation in which they are set, one can only conclude that the names also are supposed to be merely nomenclatures of natural objects [XI 35]. For if one takes them as the names of the gods, then quickly every perceptible interrelation is lost; and if one takes them for purely scientific nomenclatures of the objects themselves, which contain the characteristic predicate of them (the predicate which in the usual random nomenclatures is either generally unexpressed or no longer perceptible), and if one grants still additionally to the presentation the entirely natural means to express the dependence of one phenomena on the other via the image of *reproduction*—just like we also, without even considering that this is spoken metaphorically, have warmth be *produced* by light, or have a principle or even a concept *descend* from another—then a detailed whole reveals itself, a whole whose parts represent among themselves a completely intelligible and scientific interrelation. This interrelation cannot be something contingent; the whole must for this reason also have emerged on the basis of purely scientific purposes, and if one places, at the foundation, Hesiod's *Theogony* as the purest attestation of the first emergence into being, then one will not be able to consider the origin of this whole in any other way than the following:

There once lived—but no, in this way Hermann's theory itself would begin like a myth, and indeed in the most commonplace form—so we will say: there must (that is, sometime and somewhere), perhaps in Thrace, where the Greek legend places Thamyras,[10] Orpheus and Linus, or in Lycia, where it placed the first bard, Olen[11]; later, of course, it is revealed that we must go back to the Far East; enough—there must have once lived men, among an otherwise ignorant people, who elevated themselves above the common whole, and who were distinguished by means of special intellectual gifts, who perceived and recognized forces, phenomena, and even laws of nature, and who therefore could think to be in a position to draw up a formal theory of the origin and interrelation of things. In this they followed the method that alone makes[m] possible determinate, sure, and clear knowledge, as it seeks out the differentiating predicate of every object [XI 36] to assure itself in this way of its *concept*. For whoever designates snow as snow, for example, represents the object to himself but does not properly think it. They who followed the method, however, are concerned with the concept, and this concept is supposed to be captured by the nomenclature. So they want, for example, to express the three forms of bad weather, snow, rain and hail. It is found of hail that it *crashes down*; thus they could say "he who crashes down," but in this way only a predicate, and not an object, would be expressed. Thus they name it the crasher—the Greek χόττος (from χόπτω), which is, as is well-known, the name of one of Hesiod's hundred-armed giants. Of rain it can be said that it digs furrows into the field (admittedly, more often still it might flood them); thus it is named the *furrow-maker*—the Greek γύγης, the name of Hesiod's second giant. It is found of snow that it is encumbering and heavy; thus they name it the *heavy-man* [*Schweremann*], βριάρεως, but do not thereby think of a man, and still less of a giant, but rather only of snow.[12] The object itself is not personified, as with Heyne, but rather, if one will, only the expression, and this merely *grammatical* personification is of no more consequence here than in expressions as they appear in every language, as when a type of sword is named "the *pricker*," or when the tool with which one lifts wine out of a cask is named "the *lifter*," or when the country peasants name the fire in the grain "the *burner*," or name "the *glutton*" the mites by which the trees are smited. To represent the objects themselves as *persons*, as when in a popular joke a strongly passing wind is called St. Blasius, was entirely against the intent of the founders or founder (for Hermann himself ultimately only speaks of one).[n] Relishing in personifying presentation in Heyne's sense was no longer possible for an era marked by a scientific seriousness that was necessary to produce a whole like Hermann sees in Hesiod's *Theogony*, in which so much thorough knowledge, such a consistent contextual relationship [XI 37], such a cohesive order is found (these are his own words) that he does not hesitate to pronounce the teaching lying at the foundation of the *Theogony* as the most astonishing masterpiece of antiquity. He does not see in the myths some superficial collection of hypotheses but rather theories grounded in *long experience*, careful *observation* and even precise *calculation*, and in the whole edifice of mythology not only thorough *science* but deep wisdom.[o]

We must put aside the question of which part in these indeed somewhat hyperbolic panegyrics would be had by either the natural predisposition for the objects of our own (true or presumed) discoveries, or by a not all too precise concept of the worth and validity of such predicates—which still would not appear too trifingly, if the subject were Laplace's *Systèm du Monde*—or also what part by both causes at the same time.[13] Indisputably, among these results of a thoroughgoing and solid science, teachings such as the following are not counted: that the seed ($περσεφόνη$) has to be hidden in the earth (carried off by the god of the underworld)[14] in order to bear fruit; that the wine ($διονυσος$) comes from the grapevine (the Semele)[15]; that the ocean waves are constant but their direction mutable; and similar teachings, which every man who enters this world receives as a gift, gratuitously as it were. In order to convince oneself of the philosophical spirit of the *Theogony*, what must be taken into account is not the singular subject—although one cannot avoid running across well-known philosophical statements—but rather the whole, in particular the beginning, to whose explanation according to Hermann we will happily dedicate a few moments.

Thus that ancient philosopher, from whom the first foundation—which had already become inscrutable to Hesiod himself—is derived, wanted, with the explanation of the world, to begin at the beginning; that is, from where there was still nothing. With this in view, he says: before everything there was *Chaos*; etymologically this means the *expanse* (from $χάω$ $χαίνω$), that which still stands open to everything [XI 38], that which was unfilled, thus the *space empty* of all matter. Of course, nothing can follow this apart from what fills it, namely *matter*; however, the latter itself is to be thought as still formless— etymologically ($γάω$, $γέγαα$) *that from out of which everything becomes*, thus not the earth but rather the primordial substance of all becoming, the as yet unformed foundation of everything that will emerge into being in the future. Now, after that *in* which and that *out* of which everything emerges into being is posited, only that third is missing, *through* which everything becomes. This third is the band that links everything, the uniter, *Eros* (from $εἴρω$)—which here has *only* this scientific meaning, not that of the later *god*.[16] And after he has posited these three elements, the philosopher can proceed to explain the creation of the things themselves.

The first three products of space,[17] considered as the first element, are: 1) *Erebus*, the concealer; with this name is evidenced darkness, which concealed the matter before something was formed out of it. 2) *Nyx*, but not meaning night, rather one must also follow the original and primordial meaning here; the name is from $νύειν$ ($νεύειν$), *nutare, vergere*, to incline downward. For the next stage (thus generation) of space is movement, but the first and simplest movement is the one downwards, falling. These two generate now, together, the *Aether* and the *Hemere*, clearness and brightness; for when the darkness, which the poet of cosmogony envisages as something corporeal and as fine mist, unites with Nyx—that is, precipitates out—it becomes clear and bright above.[18]

Now follow the products of the second element, of the still formless matter.[19] This element generates initially for itself,[20] and without consort,

Uranus, that is, the higher one. The meaning of this is: that finer part of matter *elevates and exalts itself*, and, as Heaven, was separated from the coarser part, which remained as the actual and proper earthly body. This coarser part is alluded to through the great *mountains* and the *Pontus* mentioned here,[21] the latter not meaning the sea—as Hesiod already misunderstood—but rather as Doctor Hermann now much better understands, the abyss in general: from the verb πιτνεῖν, with which the Latin *fundus* [XI 39] is also related. Thus now only after the extrusion of that which is higher does Gaia have the meaning of the *Earth*; by entering into reciprocal action with *what is higher*, its first product is *Oceanus*, the cosmic ocean [*Okeanos*], not the world-sea [*Weltmeer*] but rather—etymologically from ὠχυς—the swift runner, the water that spreads over everything and fills every abyss.[22] An enormous confusion of the elements accompanies this effusion of the primordial water, such that they shoot about in confusion, hither and thither, upward and downward, until they finally attain a mutually restrictive calm. This tumult is designated by the children of Gaia and Uranus, who come after the primordial water and are the *Titans* grouped in pairs—that is, the strivers (from τείνω, τιταίνω), for they are the forces of the still wildly striving, unpacified nature. Each of the two, according to their names, expresses one of the antitheses that one has to presuppose in the still tense nature, a nature in disunity with itself. Namely: 1) Krius and Koeus, the *Cisioner* (from χρίνω) and the *Admixer*; 2) *Hyperion* and *Iapetus*, the *Ascender* and the *Descender*; 3) *Theia* and *Rhea*: the common concept of both is that of *being driven away*, the difference, however, is that some thereby retain their substance (Theia), and some others lose it (Rhea, from ῥέω, to flow); 4) *Themis* and *Mnemosyne*, which in this context cannot keep the customary meaning; the one is that which brings what is fluid to a stop or to settling, and the other, to the contrary, is that power which excites and moves the rigid; 5) *Phoebe* and *Tethys*, that which purifies and sweeps away the superfluous, and the force that attracts the advantageous; ultimately, the last of all is *Kronos*, the completer, from the verb χραίνω: for Chronos, which means Time, first received its name from Kronos, because it also brings everything to completion.[23]

Hermann assures and affirms that here there is not only a thoroughgoing scientific coherence but also even *true* philosophy; which, namely, keeps itself free of everything extra-physical,[24] and, on the contrary, only seeks to explain everything naturally. Of gods, if one does not want to impute them arbitrarily, there is no trace. The whole is proof of a way of thinking that one would have to be inclined to hold as more atheistic than theistic [XI 40]. And if one sees how all the way back to the first beginnings and up to the final appearances only the natural interrelationship is given prominence, then one cannot refrain from judging that the author of this interrelationship does not merely want to know nothing of gods, but rather that his *intent* is even *polemical*, directed against already present representations of the gods.[p]

Herewith we have arrived at the pinnacle of Hermann's theory, through which, as *you* see, Heyne's attempt—weak on the whole—to excise from mythology every originally religious meaning is far outdone.

At the same time, however, it becomes apparent that Hermann himself restricts his explanation merely to the properly mythological gods. He does not want to explain the origin as such of the belief in gods. On the contrary, in his assumptions he already presupposes a people who were supposed to be freed by the philosophers from an already present religious superstition, philosophers who, in their attempt, moreover, give rise only to a new and different belief in gods.

Of course, it cannot also be thought that this people, among which in Hermann's opinion such a discerning philosopher was able to elevate himself, was on the same footing as those tribes [*Völkerschaften*] in whom till now no trace of the representations of gods has been found. A people whose language was so richly articulated and sufficiently flexible to designate scientific concepts with thoroughly particular terms will not have expressed itself through mere clicking sounds, like the African bushmen. The people to whom the presumed philosophers belong cannot be thought of on the same level as that of those savages in South America; to whom—and as Don Felix Azara[25] recounts, even Concilien virtually denied humanity—the Catholic clergy had refused to impart the sacraments and who finally were able to be pronounced human only via a decree of the pope, and in continual opposition from clergy [XI 41] in that land.[q] For up until now only the human races of the type mentioned have been encountered without any religious representations.

Even independently of the presumed polemical intent, we will have to concede representations of gods (admittedly of the first and, as he says, for this reason, coarsest sort) to the people presupposed by Hermann. In all probability its religion consisted in a crudely physical superstition that rested on the idea of invisible beings standing in connection with natural phenomena. Moreover, the *matured intellectual capacity* of a few takes notice that the putative gods are nothing other than nature and its forces; here, then, emerges that purely physical knowledge, free of every religious element, which the creators impart with the intent to make the people free for all time from all representations of the gods. Hereby it is explained, in a surprising way, why mythology remained ungraspable up to this point; for one wanted, contrariwise, to have mythology emerge into being from out of the representations of the gods. Here, however, that which is wholly new and astonishing is uncovered: that it was invented in *order to bring all religious representations to an end*, and precisely by those who knew best that nothing like gods exist.[r]

If the noble aim that Hermann ascribed to the inventor of *Theogony* were attained, then a philanthropic man of our time could rejoice to find in antiquity a species free of all religion instead of superstitious polytheists,[26] a free race that grasps everything in only a natural way, and is free and independent of every super-natural madness. Meanwhile, however, the intentions failed, as the inventors indeed present their teachings to the people, but inexplicably neglect—vis-à-vis a people already full of ideas about invisible beings standing behind natural phenomena—to offer beforehand an explanation of the merely grammatically intended personifications: so that in the end the people are left to their own devices to find the true meaning [XI 42]; or, misunderstanding it, only *to deceive themselves*. How, then, the people take the forces of nature (only named as persons) for *actual persons*, "of which nothing more is to be thought"[8]: this can, to some degree, be understood, although it is not easy. But, now, however, how the people does not merely misunderstand the teaching but rather *adopts*—to which end it is obliged by nothing—that which is misunderstood, and how in place of the invisible beings—which for the people stand in connection with natural phenomena and thereby had meaning—the completely misunderstood persons (or, rather, only the senseless names of them) can be put: this so exceeds all plausibility that we gladly refrain from following the esteemed author in the further course of his explanation. We have only regarded his hypothesis as in general worthy of consideration because: first, because it is the last possible in the indicated direction, because it has the advantage that it is no longer to be surpassed with a scientific content of mythology; second, because, in any case, something in it is important for us, the philological foundation and the indisputable truth of the observation from which it proceeds. For we can in no way assent that *nothing at all* true or correct lies at the base of the view of *such* a man, a view that he moreover has executed not as a joke—as some want to assume in a way that is truly insulting for him—but rather with all the seriousness perceptible in each of his other works, which he has done so most diligently.

Accordingly, we cannot find it other than creditable that in general the attention has been steered again to the product of antiquity that is as remarkable as it is enigmatic, to Hesiod's poem, and especially to the seldom noticed scientific side of it. This *scientific* meaning of the names, which Hermann was not the first to notice but the first to remove all doubt from its significance, is also a *fact* that no theory making a claim to completeness [XI 43] will be allowed to leave unheeded or unexplained; and precisely what some of the associates in his specialty thought allowed laughter at the expense of this famed man—the use of one's knowledge of language for a higher goal—is what the true researcher has to thankfully and profitably recognize.

But especially in the main observation, from which all of this proceeded, we cannot help but to completely acknowledge his correctness in the noticing, namely, of the *philosophical* consciousness, which particularly in the beginning of the *Theogony* steps forth so definitely and unmistakably. The deception begins only when Hermann is immediately prepared to confer this scientific consciousness to the imaginary primordial writer of the poem (who, as said, we ultimately would have to find in the Far East) instead of ascribing it to the actual writer of the poem in its originally existent form—even if it has fallen apart here or there, or been distorted through insertions and later additions—: namely, to Hesiod himself. Only this too hastily conceived opinion could have led him to overlook so much that is conspicuous and not at all in accord with his theory; namely, that precisely the beginning has so much that is abstract, impersonal, and for this reason entirely unmythological: like when Gaia engendered by herself the great mountains (οὔρεα μαχρά) without assistance from Uranus, which mountains do not yet become personalities just because the words are written with capitalized first letters. For in Greece, as with us, outstanding mountains (Olympus, Pindus, Helikon, etc.) were, through their names, individuals but not persons. If the *Theogony* itself is penned by a philosopher who makes it his rule to designate things not with their common names, but rather with scientifically formed ones, why do the mountains not receive a *general* name derived from their quality of reaching into the heights, like later the name *Titans* is also one common to more than one?

The neuter form of *Erebus* gives rise to another observation. Through his translation (*opertanus*), Hermann furtively makes it into a masculine, but it remains what it is. Homer also knows it only as genderless; to him, it never means anything [XI 44] other than the *place* of darkness under the earth. This impersonal form does not hinder the poet from having the [*das*] Erebus (for we must call it so) wed Nyx in love and produce children with her—

Ὅς τέχε χυσσαμένη Ἐρέβει φιλότητι μιγεῖσα.[27]

As with the great mountains, where proper is mixed with improper and the common nomenclature with that which is presumably personifying, so here a concept that has remained abstract is nevertheless artificially mythologized. Whoever does this is certainly not the inventor of mythology; rather, he obviously has it already as a model.

The children of Erebus and Nyx are Aether and Hemere. Certainly the aether is a purely physical concept, which not only the originator of the poem did not consider as a divine personality, but also no one else had ever considered a divine personality, or a personality at all: he would have to enter in the appeal that Aristophanes had Socrates say:

Ὠ δέσποτ᾽ ἄναξ, ἀμέτρητ᾽ ἀήρ, ὅς ἔχεις τὴν γῆν μετέωρον Λαμπρός τ᾽ ΑΙΘΗΡ.— — —

(O' King and Master, immeasurable air, which carries around the floating Earth, and illuminating Aether). But just this appeal is proof that the aether is not considered as a mythological personality, for the comedian's intent is that Socrates appeals to *nothing* of the sort.[t]

Among the grandchildren of pernicious Nyx even the deceptive words (ψευδέες λόγοι), the equivalent and ambiguous words (ἀμφιλογίαι), are entirely unpersonified. Indeed, here Hermann must resort to an interpolation. However, when he designates with Obelus the entire progeny of Nyx,[28] in order to express that such concepts cannot *originally* be derived from the *Theogony*, then he would already justly have had to remind himself of this prior sign of repudiation, and initially with Eros, in the chorus of birds in Aristophanes, where Eros is the subject of philosophical reflections in entirely [XI 45] the same manner as here. But above all he would have had to immediately apply it[29] right away to the *first verse* of the *Theogony*: See, initially there was chaos. For it is truly to be deplored how the principle of grammatical personification suffers shipwreck right in the first verse, for where would chaos ever have been considered in effect as a god or as a personality? Who would ever have spoken *that* of chaos?[30]

Fully foreign to Homer, and audaciously placed at the beginning, this concept of chaos—which in Aristophanes already has become the battle-cry of a philosophy directed *against* the gods and striving to overcome popular belief—most definitely announces the first stirring of an abstract way of thinking that withdraws from the mythological, the first stirring of a free philosophy. Chaos and aether, which is also found amongst Hesiod's first concepts, are the earliest demonstrable seeds of that purely physical wisdom whose components are summed up in the oath of Socrates—

Μά τὴν Ἀναπνοην, μὰ τὸ ΧΑΟΞ μὰ Ἀέρα—

by Aristophanes, who with basic and good old-fashioned sensibility does not tire of making fun of this funny philosophy.

Thus Hermann correctly saw the philosophical in the beginning of the *Theogony*, but the explanation lies precisely at the opposite end from that where he seeks it. As he assures, Hesiod does not suspect that he has something scientific before himself and naively and guilelessly takes the nomenclatures expressing the philosophical concepts for names of actual gods, which, as indicated with some, he was even unable to do, like with chaos and aether. If no one ever thought them to be gods, then certainly Hesiod, least of all, was able to take them in this way. Chaos, which only those who come later first explain as empty space or even as a coarse mixture of material elements, is a *purely speculative* concept, but it is not the product of a philosophy that precedes mythology, but rather of one that *follows* mythology, a philosophy that strives to grasp it, and for this reason proceeds through it and beyond it. Only the mythology that has arrived [XI 46] at its *end* and, from there, is *looking back* into the *beginning*, seeking from there to conceptualize and grasp itself, was able to place chaos at the beginning. Just as little as poetry [*Poesie*] did philosophy precede mythology; but indeed the first movements of a philosophy are recognizable in Hesiod's poem, a philosophy that extricates itself from mythology in order to later direct itself against it. How? What if the poem deserved that significant place, which Herodotus assigns to the poet alongside Homer, indeed even prior to him, and if it designated an essential moment of the development of mythology precisely because it would be the first product of a mythology *striving to become conscious of itself* and *to represent itself*? What if, entirely in accord with the lawfulness that we perceive in the Hellenic culture, the two poets, Homer and Hesiod, so very different from each other (and between whom very old stories and sayings already know of a struggle and thus of a certain opposition), designated the *two* equally possible—not *beginnings* but—*exits* from mythology? If Homer showed how it ended in poetry, Hesiod in philosophy?

I append but a single observation. Whatever one may find unbelievable in Hermann's explanation, the most incomprehensible seems to me that his critical feeling could allow him to let every name, without distinction—those names, whose origin is manifestly lost in the night of the past, like Kronos, Poseidon, Gaia, Zeus, and those whose comparatively new origin is self-evident, like Pluto, Horai, Charites, Eunomie, Dike, and so many that are similar—to let every name emerge into being, *all together* and *all at once, from out* of the head of an individual.

Lecture Three

[XI 47] The purely poetic viewpoint, as we have named the first one, and the philosophical, as we will moreover name the second viewpoint—not that we held it for particularly philosophical, that is, worthy of a philosopher, but rather because it gives a philosophical content to mythology—these two viewpoints, to which we were at first led in a natural and unsought way, we have initially investigated and have had each express itself in its *particular* presupposition; this happened to give us the advantage that some factualities were discussed in advance, factualities to which we do not need to again return, which now can be presupposed as something already ascertained. But for precisely this reason that *which is common to both* is not yet thrown into relief, and still less has it been judged.[1] Now, the particular presuppositions of each one could be found to be untenable and yet could remain common to them and be considered as a possible foundation of a new attempt. In order to finish completely with the two main views it will be necessary, accordingly, to bring into focus just that in which both agree, and also submit that to judgment.

Now, at the very least, it is not difficult to recognize the first presupposition shared by both: this is, that mythology in general is an *invention*. However, it must be decided if this generality is also to be abandoned, or if the error perhaps lies merely in this: that the one view sees only poetic invention in mythology, the other, only a philosophical one. Above all, however, it is to be noticed [XI 48] that in themselves neither of the two really excludes the other entirely. The purely poetic view actually acknowledges a doctrinal content, albeit one merely accidental and unintended; the philosophical view cannot be without that which is poetic, but to *the philosophical* the poetic is now rather that which is more or less artificial, and thus simply accidental in another way.

Now, the former, the mere accidentalness of every doctrinal content, which doctrinal content the purely poetic explanation solely leaves as a remainder, is already contradicted by the systematicity in the sequencing of the lineage of the gods, the sepulchral seriousness itself, which characterizes some parts of the history of the gods. For we do not at all want to think hastily that mythology really governed as the *doctrine* of the gods [*Götterlehre*], that it imperiously determined the entire behavior and the entire life of the peoples,

37

which in any case would have to be explained. However, still more than this accidentalness in the one explanation, it is the coarse deliberateness—which the other explanation places in the first emergence—that repels us. How happily in particular one would like to save the philosophers assumed by Heyne the double occupation of first procuring the content and then especially having to seek the form or wording again. How right it might then seem to ask if—by retaining the general presupposition that mythology is in general an invention—those two elements may not be brought nearer to each other, if both explanations might be elevated to a higher place by drawing them into one, and if the opposition which we feel vis-à-vis each particular explanation may be overcome through a blending of both. After all, it can even be asked in general if poetry [*Poesie*] and philosophy are as separate from each other as they are assumed to be in both explanations, if there does not occur a *natural* affinity, an almost necessary, mutual force of attraction between both. One must know, after all, that no less a *general validity* and *necessity* is required of *truly* poetic forms than is from philosophical concepts. Admittedly, in having the present era before one's eyes, only a few exceptional masters have succeeded in instilling a universal and eternal meaning in the figures—whose material they were only able to take from accidental and transient life [XI 49]—and in investing them with a form of mythological authority. Yet these few are also the true poets, and the others are in reality only so in name. On the other hand, philosophical concepts are not supposed to be merely general categories; they should be actual, determinate essentialities.[2] And the more they are, the more they are endowed by the philosopher with actual and individual life, then the more they appear to approach poetic figures, even if the philosopher scorns every poetic wording: here the poetic idea is included in philosophical thought and does not need to come to it from outside.

Now, however, one could still ask in particular if in mythology's era of emergence *poetry* and *philosophy* as such—that is, in their formal opposition—could really have been present at all; because we have seen, on the contrary, how as soon as a mythology is present and has completely filled consciousness, both initially depart from each other in different directions, from out of mythology as from a mutually held middle-point, albeit even then they separate themselves very slowly. For if the first trace of philosophy's separation from mythology is already in Hesiod, then it takes the whole time from Hesiod up to Aristotle before philosophy separated itself from everything mythical and, therefore, also from everything poetic. The way is not far—not from the realism of the Pythagoreans to Aristotle's nominalism, for the principles (ἀρχαί) to the one are just as much essentialities to the other, just as indeed also their inner identity is perceptible. But it is far from the almost mythical expression of the first to the other's purely conceptual form of representation. Now, however, would not precisely this common stepping forth from out of mythology be a proof that precisely in it both were still unified, whereby then admittedly neither of the two was able to be active for itself and as *such*, and still less could the one or the other precede mythology and itself have been a factor of it.

Linguists and philologists least of all should [XI 50] have confidence in the conclusion that poetry and philosophy, because they are found in mythology, have contributed toward its emergence into being. In the formation of the oldest languages a wealth of philosophy can be discovered. However, was it therefore actual philosophy by virtue of which these languages had the ability, in the nomenclatures of often even the most abstract concepts, to preserve their original meaning that had become foreign to the later consciousness? What is more abstract than the meaning of the copula in a judgment? What is more abstract than the concept of the pure subject, which appears to be nothing; for *what* it is we only experience via the statement, and yet even without the attribute it cannot be nothing: for what is it then? When we articulate it, we say of it: it is this or that—for example a person is healthy or sick, a body dark or light; but what then is it, before we express this? Evidently, only that this—for example, healthy or sick—is that which is a capacity to be. Thus the general concept of the subject is to be pure *capacity* to be. Now, how strange that in Arabic the word "*is*" is expressed by a word that is not merely homonymous with our word "*can*," "*is able to*," but rather is inarguably identical in that, contrary to the analogue to all other languages, it is not followed by the nominative of the predicate, but rather by the accusative, like "can," "to have the capacity for," "to be able to" in German (for example: "to have the ability" for a language), or *posse* in Latin (not to mention the others).[a 3] Was it philosophy that spun a web of scientific concepts into the various and, at first glance, most heterogenous meanings of this same verb, a web whose context and coherence philosophy has trouble finding again? Arabic in particular has verbs rich in completely disparate meanings. What one customarily says, that originally separate words—which the later pronunciation no longer differentiated—are here coalesced, may be believable in some cases; but it would only be acceptable when all means of uncovering an internal interrelationship were applied without success. But it indeed occurs [XI 51] that other investigations unexpectedly put us in a position where between apparently irreconcilable meanings, in this ostensible confusion, a philosophical coherence and interrelationship, a true system of concepts, reveals itself: concepts whose sound coherence and interconnection lie not on the surface but rather disclose themselves only to deeper scientific interventions.

The roots of the Semitic languages are verbs, and are regularly double-syllabic ones, consisting of three radicals (with the words, too, that have become monosyllabic with respect to pronunciation the original typology is restored in individual forms). In accordance with this structure of language, one cannot avoid tracing the word that means *father* in Hebrew back to a verb that expresses *desiring* and *longing*, and thus at the same time contains the concept of neediness, a concept that is also visible in an adjective derived from the verb. Accordingly, one could say that the philosophical concept here expressed is that the patriarchal, as what is preceding and beginning, is that which is in need of something that follows it. Against this view it will be objected with full justification: the Hebrews will not have first derived their expression for father from a verb, and so completely philosophically—the Hebrews will not have known the abstract concept "desire" prior to having known the concept of father, which belongs to the naturally first concepts. But that is not at all the point; the question is whether or not—indeed not the Hebrew individual, but rather—the spirit which created the Hebrew language, by naming the father thusly, also thought that verb, just as creative nature, by forming the skull, has also already the nerve in mind that is supposed to take its way through it. The language is not piecemeal or atomistic; in all its parts it is on par with the whole and, accordingly, has emerged into being organically. The aforementioned connection and interrelationship is one objectively inherent in the language itself and for precisely this reason is certainly not one contrived by the intent of men.

Leibniz says of the German language: *Philosopiae nata videtur*; and if, in all cases, it can only be the spirit that creates the tool appropriate to itself, then here a philosophy that was not yet really [XI 52] philosophy has made ready a tool of which it shall subsequently first make use.

Because not only no philosophical consciousness, but rather also no human consciousness at all, is thinkable without language, the ground of language could not be laid consciously; and yet, the deeper we inquire into language, the more definitely it becomes known that its depths exceed by far that of the most conscious product.

It is with language as it is with the organic beings; we believe we see them blindly emerge into being and cannot deny the inscrutable intentionality of their formation, right up to the smallest detail.

However, can *poetry* perhaps already be recognized in the mere material formation of language? I am not speaking of the expressions of spiritual concepts that one is customarily given to call metaphorical, although in their origin they were scarcely considered unreal. But how many treasures of poetry lie hidden in language itself, treasures that the poet has not placed in it, that he only puts into relief so to speak, or retrieves out of it as from a treasure house, or that he merely induces the language to reveal. Is not, however, every name-giving already a personification; and if all languages conceive as sexually differentiated those things that admit of an *antithesis*, or expressly designate them in this way—when German says: the masculine [*der*] sky, the feminine [*die*] earth; the masculine [*der*] space, the feminine [*die*] time— then how far is it really from there to the expression of spiritual concepts through masculine and feminine deities.

One is almost tempted to say: language itself is only faded mythology; what mythology still preserves in living and concrete differences is preserved in language only in abstract and formal differences.

After all of these considerations one could now feel inclined to say: a philosophy that has to first seek the figures in poetry could not be active[4] in mythology, but rather this philosophy was itself and essentially at the same time poesy [*Poesie*]; likewise vice-versa: the poesy that created the mythological figures did not stand in the service [XI 53] of a philosophy separate from it; rather it was itself and essentially also knowledge-producing activity, philosophy. The latter point would bring about that truth would be in the mythological representations, and not simply contingently, but rather with a type of necessity. The former point would bring about that the poetic in mythology would not be something appended externally but rather something itself immanent, essential and given with thought itself. If one calls the philosophical or doctrinal the content, and the poetic the form, then the content would never have been for itself; it would only have emerged into being in this form and for this reason would be inseparably and indissolubly bound up with it. Then indeed mythology would not in general be only a *natural* product, but rather an organic one; this is certainly a meaningful step in comparison to the merely mechanistic type of explanation. But it would also be an organic product in the following respect. Poetry and philosophy each for itself, is for us a principle of free, intentional invention, but because they are bound to one another neither, properly speaking, can freely be active: mythology would thus be a product of in themselves free activities, but here, however, of unfreely causally effective activities, just as the organic is a birth of freely necessary emergence; and to the extent that the word invention is still applicable, mythology is here a product of an unintentional-intentional, instinctive invention, which on the one hand would hold at a distance from itself everything merely fabricated and artificial, but on the other hand would at the same time allow that the deepest meaning and the soundest relations inherent in mythology be seen as not merely contingent.

This would thus be that which is higher, which may be reached from out of both explanations through a synthesis of them, a synthesis of which, unmistakably, one had to think in consequence of a direction given to thought through later philosophy; whereas the concepts of the Kantian school could lead almost exclusively to an explanation like Hermann's. And certainly, vis-à-vis the explanations like the one just mentioned, the organic interpretation could already fancy itself to be something. But let us witness precisely what would be gained for an actual *explanation* through such a synthesis.

[XI 54] Should the opinion somehow be that, in its *effect* [*Wirkung*], the *principle* producing mythology amounts to the unifiedly causally-active philosophy and poetry—*without the principle itself having something of each in themselves*—then this could be admitted as right and proper without there being thereby given the scantest knowledge of the actual nature of that principle, in that this principle could be in itself something *entirely different from both*, and which would have nothing in common with them both. Or if the opinion is that both philosophy and poetry are to be maintained as *causally active*—only not separated, but rather perhaps operative together like the masculine and feminine in procreation—then here will also be valid what makes itself felt in general where two somehow counterposed principles unite themselves in an effect: that is, because both cannot dominate, only one is actually what is causally effective, the other resigning itself more to a passive and instrumental function. Now we would again have also simply either a philosophical poetry or a poetic philosophy, which would again comport themselves to each other in the same manner as poetry and philosophy alone would comport themselves. Everything that one would have obtained with this elevation would be a formal improvement of both explanations: this certainly would be something, but only if those explanations were themselves something.

Or—to show the same thing in a different way—the ostensible synthesis still *speaks* of poetry [*Poesie*] and philosophy, activities well known to us, but precisely because both as *such* are not supposed to be causally effective, they also do not *explain* anymore. What is explanatory does not lie in them but rather in that which submits both to itself, in what does not allow them to operate actively but rather merely allows them—as we could say—to interact. *This* would be the essence, the real principle or that which we are seeking. The poetic [*Dichterische*] and the philosophically scientific [*Wissenschaftliche*] would only be found in the product; it would be that which necessarily emerges into being concomitantly, but precisely as such it would be only something appended and contingent.[5] Instead of only one, either the doctrinal or the poetic, having to appear as contingent, as was the case in the first two views, here both would be diminished to the contingent; what is essential, however, what is properly explanatory in the matter, would be something independent of both [XI 55], what lies above and outside of both, which is still now a fully unknown quantity, and from which it may only be perceived that—as what subordinates philosophy and poetry to itself—it can have nothing in common with free invention and would have to come from somewhere entirely different. But from where? Because no path from the two principles alone known to us—that of philosophy and poetry—leads to their causally active and real unity, for the present merely conjecture would remain. Indeed, someone could recommend the oft-used—and laid claim to by so many—*clairvoyance* with which certainly much could be explained if only one were first to see more clearly about this clairvoyance itself. A *dream state* would perhaps also not be found unpleasant, just as Epicurus is able to have conceived of transitory appearances—through which he has the gods be attestable—only as dream appearances. For, after all, in the dream state the poetry and philosophy natural to man can also interact.[6] Even *madness*, as a state that excludes every free invention, although not every influence of reason and imagination, would by no means have to be utterly dismissed. But what would be gained with all these sorts of explanations? Not the slightest; for every state that one would assume, in order to explain thereby the products of mythological ideas [*Vorstellungen*], would have to itself be explained—that is, at the same time, be historically motivated. The substantiation of this state of affairs would have to consist in this: that it would be shown through which natural or divine providence such a state was at some point imposed on the human species or a part thereof: for mythology is above all a *historical* phenomenon.[7]

This observation shows us that no more headway is to be made with the abstract presuppositions of the two explanations with which we have so far been occupied—as then these explanations themselves could not help but connect with their abstract presupposition a historical one. As we prepare ourselves to consider the latter, our investigation is now also shifted from the realm of abstract discussions to the historical basis.

[XI 56] We are returning to the opinion that mythology in general is an *invention*. Once this is presumed, then the next, *external* presupposition will be that it is invented by individuals. This presumption is unavoidable for the philosophical explanation. The poetic explanation will at first resist it but in the end will also hit upon the individual poet, if it does not want to dispense with every historical construction or melt entirely into the indeterminate. Now however, considered precisely, this presumption of an individual as the creator of mythology is such a huge presupposition that one can only be exceedingly astonished at the unconsciousness with which it is so generally made—as if it could in no way be different. Indeed, in general no one finds it difficult to presuppose poets or philosophers, as one stands in need of them; with the vague representations of primordial time, which one justifiably supposes to view as an empty space into which everyone is free to interpolate anything that strikes his fancy or seems proper, almost everything is allowed. In addition to his poetic philosophers Heyne still has need of the poets proper, who, for him, transform the philosophemes into tales; moreover, he also probably still stands in need of power-hungry priests, who change them into superstition. Hermann's philosophers, who are likewise poets, albeit somewhat more even-tempered ones, appeal directly to the people. Only he neglected to explain one thing: how they also managed to get the people to listen to their self-devised wisdom, not to mention to impress this wisdom so deeply upon them that it was able to be confused by them for a system of the gods.

But, generally speaking, whoever knows what the mythology of a people is to them would, as easily as he has its mythology invented by individuals, regard it as possible that the language of a people has also emerged into being through the efforts of individuals among it. To introduce a mythology is not a matter that proceeds as easily as the introduction of school plans, textbooks, catechisms, and so on does for us. To create a mythology, to impart to it that authentication [*Beglaubigung*] and reality in the minds of men—which is necessary in order to reach the degree of popularity that it requires [XI 57] even in poetic usage—exceeds the ability of any individual person, and even that of a number of them who could unite themselves toward such a goal.

Nonetheless, granting all that, in this way a mythology would emerge for just one people—but mythology is not a matter of just one people, but rather of many peoples.

What felicitous time, where Heyne could be satisfied to have explained the *Greek* myths in his way and with his assumptions. Hermann is already less lucky; he knows that in the Greek myths there are too many similarities to the Oriental myths for both not to have had to have emerged in a similar way.[b] He senses that what explains *one* mythology must explain *each*. On the other hand he is too sharp sighted not to perceive that, according to his explanation, matters proceed miraculously enough with the emergence of mythology in just one people, and that it would fully exceed all belief to allow the same contingency—or, rather, the same sequence of contingencies, in which each succeeding one is more unbelievable than the preceding one—to repeat itself within a second, third, fourth people. His firmness in the matter is not thereby shaken; for it remains possible that the ideas that once initially emerged into being somewhere have propagated themselves in other peoples. And this possibility only raises the value of his discovery, in that it shows that the belief in gods—not only of Greece but also of Asia, Egypt, the whole world—itself derives contingently from that teaching or story about the genesis of things that was fortuitously invented in one people by a few individuals—and was still more contingently masked, and for this reason misunderstood, and nonetheless presumed as true and passed on in tradition—and whose original thoughts, miraculously saved, Hermann's etymological-grammatical interpretive skill has uncovered now in Hesiod's poem—in which the original Oriental names are simply replaced by synonymous, skillfully imitated Greek ones.[c]

[XI 58] Should we frankly but mildly say what we think about such a contingency, then we would say it reminds us of the explanation that the same scholar gives of the tale of *Io*. A granddaughter of Oceanus and daughter of Inachus, she is loved by Zeus and arouses the jealousy of Hera. In order to hide her from the goddess, Zeus transforms her into a cow, which distrustful Hera has guarded by a watchman, and so on. What else can the granddaughter of Oceanus (of the World-sea[8]) and the daughter of Inachus (Overflow, etymologically; that is, she is the daughter of an overflowing river or stream) be other than a *water* flowing forth, produced by the overstepping of the banks by a river or stream?[9] Actually, Io etymologically means only "what changes." Zeus's love for Io, what else can it be besides the rain that swells the water even more; what else Hera's jealousy of Io, other than the discontent that the *people* (Hera is translated here as *Populonia*) feel on account of the inundation; the *cow*, into which Zeus transforms Io, is the *crooked course* of the deluge gushing forth, for the cow has crooked horns, and crooked horns signify the crooked course of the water. The watchman is a *dam* erected against the water by the people; he is named Argus, the white, for the dam is made of white kaolin, and also the thousand-eyed, for the kaolin has many small reed-ducts or pores, which are filled by the water. Instead of the latter, the tale says: the watchman is lulled to sleep. The reed-pipe signifies the whispering of the waves; that the watchman is *killed* means: the dam is broken. Io's running, insane, to Egypt and marrying the Nile means: the water running forth mixes with the Nile. Io begetting Epaphus (*Occupus*) through the Nile means: via the water the Nile, *occupying* and *flooding* the *land*, emerges into being.[d]

So, would one like to say that such a quotidian event as the overflow of the river, and whatever empty and meaningless things further follow from it [XI 59], the oldest poetic art would have clothed in such expensive dress? That the tale of the insanity and straying of Io would have such a diluted beginning, the same madness whose description in Aeschylus fills us with wonder and terror? That the royal Nile lording over Egypt would have such a contingent origin? And, one might like to continue asking, that the living flow of the system and fable of the gods—a flow that from unfathomable sources would have deeply and powerfully gushed forth over the entire age of antiquity—would have no less an insipid origin from out of the both contingent and unproductive nexus of thoughts of an individual or a few individuals? That the millennia-long history of the aberration of peoples would have developed out of personifications and concepts of nature abstracted from random reflection and produced by a barren mind with meager knowledge—personifications and concepts of nature that, comparable at the most to the games of a childish wit, were hardly able for a moment to seriously engage their creators, even in comparison to the games of a childish joke—and that the dark and uncanny power of the belief in gods from a simultaneously weak and artificial beginning?

A contingency like the one just depicted, where namely the mythology of the Greeks, the Egyptians, the Indians, in short, of the whole world, is supposed to have its origin from an individual or a few individuals in a highly contingently devised, and then masked, and then ultimately misunderstood, and unthoughtfully believed cosmogony—such a contingency seems to be of the type wherein, all circumstances considered, even some of those who otherwise are of the opinion that the greatest and most powerful events of the world are brought forth by the most contingent and insignificant causes would not like to commit themselves to it.

Now, however, the higher interpretation, which has assumed a sort of instinctual invention, will also seek here to assume a superior position and will—when we present it as an absurdity to view mythology as an invention of an individual—on the other hand joyously answer us: indeed, mythology is not invented by individuals; it has proceeded from the *people* itself. The mythology of a people is bound up with its life and essence in such a way that it could only proceed from out of the people [XI 60]. Besides, everything instinctual works more effectively in the masses than in individuals, and just like in certain families of the animal kingdom a communal drive of ingenuity connects individuals independent of each other for the producing of a collective project, so a spiritual connection produces itself between various individuals belonging to the same people, and this of itself and through inner necessity—a spiritual connection that must manifest itself through a communal product like mythology. Indeed, this spiritual collaboration seems to have extended itself beyond the time of the first emergence of mythology. Wolf's investigations of Homer, understood somewhat more ingeniously than happened with his contemporaries, long ago offered a great and meaningful analogy. If the *Iliad*, and if the *Iliad* and the *Odyssey* are not the work of an individual, but rather of an entire race [*Geschlecht*] extending over more than one age, then one must at least acknowledge that this race poeticized like an individual.

With particular affection, one recognizes, in general but also as a natural product, a *popular* poetry [*Volkspoesie*] that is older than any poetic *art* and persists *alongside* it in fables, tales, and songs whose origins no one knows to name; likewise, one recognizes a natural world-wisdom, that, aroused through events of the communal life or through bright conviviality, constantly invents new aphorisms, riddles, and figures of speech. So, owing to an active cooperation of natural poetry and natural philosophy—not in a premeditated and intentional way, but rather without reflection, in life itself—the people create those higher figures that it requires in order to fill the emptiness of its spirit and of its fantasy, and through which it feels itself elevated into a higher plane, and that retroactively beautifies and makes noble its life, and that on the one hand are of as deep a natural meaning as they are on the other hand poetic.

And, indeed, if there were no choice other than between individuals and the people, who—especially today—would have protracted reservations for which he would speak out? But the more plausible the notion, the more closely [XI 61] one might watch if a tacit presupposition, which does not past the test, does not also creep in here. Assumptions of such a type are to the researcher what the coral reefs hidden under the water's surface are for the mariner; and the critical mind differentiates itself from the uncritical only in that the uncritical works with presuppositions of which it is not conscious; the critical, on the other hand, permits nothing hidden and unexplained, but rather, as much as is possible, brings everything into view.

It is true we breathe more freely, as it were, as soon as we hear that mythology did not proceed from individuals but rather from an entire people. But this people, by which is understood here only the whole, will still only be just one people. But mythology is not merely a matter of just one people, but of many peoples; and the agreement of the mythological representations between them is not merely a general one, but rather one that goes down to the smallest detail. Here, then, initially comes into prominence the great and irrefutable fact of the inner affinity[10] between the mythologies of the most varied and otherwise most dissimilar peoples. How can one be mindful of this fact? How does one explain mythology as a phenomenon that is *general* and on the whole everywhere the same? Yet not from causes and circumstances that can somehow be thought of as belonging to just *one* people? In this case, namely, when one had it initially emerge under just *one* people, there would obviously remain—in order to explain that agreement— no means other than to further assume that the mythological representations indeed did initially emerge under just one people, but then from it were passed down to a second, and constantly were transplanted into a succeeding people, although not without taking on modifications, but nonetheless in such a way that they remained, on the whole and according to their basis, congruent with the original representations. Not only Hermann explains the fact to himself in this way. Others also—without being obliged to this end by the specifics of their presuppositions—advance the explanation according to which mythology would only apparently be a universal phenomenon, and the material agreement of the various mythologies would just merely be an external [XI 62] and contingent one. It may seem convenient to explain this profound and not merely superficial affinity through such a merely external and secondary connection, but the type of agreement contradicts this assumption. Had the Greeks received Demeter only from the Egyptians, then Demeter, like Isis, would have to seek the slain consort; or Isis, like Demeter, would have to search for the stolen daughter.[11] The similarity, however, consists only in that both seek what is lost. However, because what is lost is different for each, the Greek representation cannot be a mere copy of the Egyptian nor be dependent on it; it must have emerged into being self-sufficiently and independent of the latter. The similarities are not like they tend to be between original and copy; they do not indicate a unilateral descent of the one mythology from the other but rather a common descent of all. It is not an externally explainable similarity; it is a similarity of consanguinity.

However, even if the affinity of different mythologies could be explained in that external, mechanical way, even if one would be able—despite this great fact about the mythological relation of Isis and Demeter, which one must esteem as a powerful developmental means of the true theory—to bear taking it so easily, then one thing would still remain presupposed: namely, that mythology is able to emerge in or among one people. However, whether it is indeed at all thinkable that mythology could *emerge* from or among one people—a question that has yet to shock someone—appears to me very much in need of investigation. For, first of all, what is a people, or what makes it into a *people*? Undoubtedly, not the mere spatial coexistence of a greater or lesser number of physically similar individuals, but rather the community of consciousness between them. This community has only its immediate expression in the common language. But in what are we supposed to find this community itself, or its ground, if not in a common world-view; and then this common world-view—in what can it have been originally contained and given to a people, if not in its mythology? [XI 63] For this reason it appears impossible that a mythology would be added to an already present people, whether it be through invention by individuals among it, or whether it be that it emerges by a collective, instinctual production. This state of affairs also appears impossible because it is unthinkable that a *people—would be* without mythology.

One would perhaps consider replying that a people is held together by the common industry of some sort of commerce—for example, agriculture, trade—or through common customary morés [*Sitten*], legislation, government, and so forth. Certainly, all of this belongs to the concept of a people, but it seems almost unnecessary to recall how with all peoples governmental authority, legislation, customary morés, and even occupations are immanently connected with the representation of the gods. The question is, then, if all of this, which is being presupposed, and which is certainly given *with* one people, could be conceived of without all the religious representations, which nowhere exist without mythology. One will object that there are still tribes [*Völkerschaften*], after all, in whom no trace of religious representations—and thus no trace of mythological representations—are to be encountered. Belonging therein, for example, are the aforementioned, merely externally humanlike races of South America. But precisely these also live, as Azara reports, *without any type of community among themselves*, fully like animals of the field, in that they acknowledge just as little a visible authority above themselves as an invisible one, and feel as foreign to each other as animals of the same species feel to each other. And they form a people just as little as the wolves or foxes form a people amongst themselves; indeed, they live more unsociably than some of the animals living and working in a community, such as the beavers, ants, or honey bees.[e] Every effort to make [XI 64] them into a people—that is, to produce amongst them a social connection—would be in vain. Introduced by violent fiat, such a connection would be their demise; it would be a proof that a people not born immediately as a people can come into being through neither divine power nor human power and that where the original unity and community of consciousness is missing, none can be produced.

Here language sets itself alongside mythology again. Right away it was perceived as absurd to assume its language would be able to emerge for a people through the efforts of *individuals* among them. But would it in any way be less absurd to consider it possible that it *emerges from out of or within the people* itself, almost as if a people could *be* without a common language, and not rather that a *people* would only be once it has a communal language?

The same thing would have to be said if one wanted to understand the opinion that in legislation not everything needs to happen through individual legislators and that the laws are produced by the people itself in the passage of its life, in such a way as though a people would be able from the very beginning to *impart* laws, and thus *exist* as a people without laws, since it is first a people, and indeed *this* people, through its laws. Rather, it has received the law of its life and its existence—the law from which all laws appearing in the course of its history can only be developments—with its concrete being *as a people*. But it can have obtained and preserved this primordial law [*Urgesetz*] itself only with the world-view innate to it as a people, and this world-view is contained in its mythology.

However one would explain the emergence of mythology from out of or within [XI 65] one people, one will always already presuppose the people itself, and thus for example assume that the Hellene was the Hellene, the Egyptian the Egyptian, before he got his mythological representations in one or another way. Now I ask you, however, if the Hellene is still the Hellene, the Egyptian still the Egyptian, if we take away his mythology. Thus he has neither adopted his mythology from others nor created it himself *after* he was a Hellene or Egyptian; he first became a Greek or Egyptian *with* this mythology, when this mythology became his. If its mythology obtains for a people in the course of its history, and this begins for every people as soon as the people is present; if it thus emerges for it especially through historical relations and contacts with other peoples, then it has history before it has mythology. The opposite of this is always assumed as a rule. Its mythology is not determined for it by its history, but rather, conversely, its history is determined for it through its mythology; or, rather, this mythology does not *determine*: it *is* itself the fate of history (like the character of a person is his fate), its lot, fallen to it from the very beginning. Or who would like to deny that with the mythologies [*Götterlehre*] of the Indians, Hellenics, and so on their entire history is given.

If it is impossible that the mythology of a people emerges into being from out of or within one that is already present, then nothing else remains except that it emerges with it simultaneously, as *its* individual popular consciousness, with which the people steps forth from out of the general consciousness of mankind and by virtue of which it is just this people and separated from every other no less than it is through its language.

As you see, however, herewith the explanations judged up to this point have totally had removed the basis on which they attempted to erect themselves: this basis was a historical one, that is, one presupposing the existence of peoples; meanwhile it has become evident here that the emergence of mythology occurs during the time in which the emergence of peoples took place. The origin of the mythology of every people goes back into a region where there is not time for invention—whether one has it proceed from individuals or from the people itself—and none for artificial wording and misunderstanding [XI 66]. Consequently, there is no longer time for the conditions that Heyne, Hermann, and the others assume. One can no longer go back, with the explanations that assume mythology in general as an invention, into the time where the peoples emerge, whether it be an invention of individuals who stand vis-à-vis a people, or whether it be as an invention of the entire people through a collective instinct. The mythological representations that emerge with the peoples themselves, and determine their first concrete being, *must* have also been meant as truth; and indeed as whole, full truth, and consequently as a doctrine of the gods [*Götterlehre*]—and we have to explain how they were able to emerge in this sense. We are *obliged* to find other points of contact for this investigation; for among everything that has presented itself until now there is nothing that went back into that region. We will not make the judgment, with respect to the now past explanations, that *nowhere do* they contain *anything* true. This would be too much; but they do not contain *the truth*. Thus the latter is still first to be found, but even now we will still not be able to reach this in a leap but rather only through a step-wise development passing over no possibility.— I happily recall the method of the investigation because I posit therein as its possible main gain that *you* learn how such a multiply intricate object, an object offering so many sides, can nonetheless be comprehended, mastered, and, ultimately, brought into full light through methodical proceeding.— Only this is preliminarily certain and the clear result of the most recent development: the true that we are seeking lies *outside* of the previous theories. In other words: the true lies in that which the explanations introduced and judged up to now exclude, and at least now it is not difficult to see what they all exclude univocally and in a similar way.

Lecture Four

[XI 67] If nothing is to be done either with the opinion that there was no truth at all originally in mythology or with the opinion that indeed concedes an original truth in it, but not in mythology as *such*—that is, especially so far as it is the doctrine of the gods [*Götterlehre*] and the history of the gods—then with the elimination of both these views the third is of itself grounded, and now already necessarily: mythology was thus, as it is, meant as truth; but this is already from itself the same as the claim that mythology is originally meant as the doctrine [*Götterlehre*] of the gods and history of the gods, that it originally has *religious* meaning. And just this latter is now also that which the earlier explanations exclude. For all sought to bring out that the religious meaning, which they had to grant to mythology insofar as it was undeniably in force as the *doctrine* of the gods [*Götterlehre*], has only later entered it and was foreign to its original emergence into being. Admittedly, the purely poetic explanation, insofar as it disavows only the intentionally imputed sense, is able to grant originally religious echoes, but for the same reason is immune to every religious *emergence into being*; and what is able to appear in mythology as something religious must count for it as something just as contingent and unintentional as every other seemingly doctrinal meaning. The matter is entirely different with the non-poetic, more philosophical explanations. Here the religious is not even admitted as something originally *contingent*. According to Heyne, the creators, on the contrary, are very well conscious that the personalities that they poetically invent [*erdichten*] are not actual beings and already thus [XI 68], for this reason, that they are not gods. For the least in the concept of the gods is that they are feared beings, but only actual ones or ones considered actual are feared. In the most consistent development, as is admittedly only found in Hermann, the religious meaning even has to become what is intentionally excluded.

Now, accordingly, if we wanted via a common name to call the previously judged theories as a whole the irreligious theories (as understood without any suspicious corollary meaning), then they would perhaps nevertheless reject the name because according to their opinion they in part at least *presuppose* of mythology actually religious ideas [*Vorstellungen*], and thus they do not *completely* exclude the religious. And, indeed, whoever for example concurred with Eumeros would have to imagine actual gods before the mythological gods, which for Eumeros are only inactual. Likewise, Hermann speaks of a preliminary level of mythology, of a coarsely physical superstition that, to be sure, conceived of actual beings believed to be in connection with phenomena of nature; and also Heyne, if one were able to question him about it, would not hesitate to accept this view. For he also, in order for his personalities—which are not actual gods—to be *taken* as gods, must presuppose actual ones. Thus, also these explanations want, according to their view, actual gods, and consequently what really is religious—at least as background. Thus it would appear that one would be unable to establish a category of irreligious views in general.

But, at least with reference to the views just mentioned, it would still first have to be decided if we will grant to the beings that the views presuppose to the properly and authentically mythological ones a claim to be beings of an *actually* religious meaning. For initially, indeed they are actual beings that man fancies to hide behind natural effects, whether it be on account of a lack of knowledge of the true causes, or from a merely animal and thoughtless fear, or in consequence of a positive proclivity—which one ascribes to man wherever he perceives an effect—to also presuppose will and freedom; or even if it were also simply because he only [XI 69] creates the concept of existence out of himself, the concept of existence under which he conceives things apart from himself, and only gradually generalizes and learns to separate from himself that which is bound up with this concept in human consciousness.[a] As ones that were overwhelming, superior in general to human force, these beings standing in connection with natural processes are feared (*primus in orbe Deos fecit timor*); and because according to their arbitrariness and moods they appear for human affairs at one minute as hindrance and at another as helpful, it is attempted to appease them by manifestations of subservience. Thus, one says, the belief in such things was the first religion.

In recent times this explanation was carried out especially by *David Hume*, although he derives the first representations of invisible beings less from reflections on natural phenomena. These, on account of their agreement and uniformity, he says, would have had to lead more likely to a single being [*Wesen*]: the view of many gods rather emerged from the observations and experiences of the contradictions and changes in human life. Because, however, the life of coarse man is itself only a natural life, and the change of his encounters depends chiefly on changes in nature, this difference is without meaning. According to D. Hume *this* first, actual polytheism only becomes mythological in that human individuals, who affected others in their time powerfully and beneficially, are included under those religiously venerated beings.

Joh. Heinrich Voss has followed a different path.[1] He also considers as still especially coarse the representations from which mythology is supposed later to emerge, and as having originated from a condition of half or complete animal dullness. He wants no doctrinal, especially originally religious meaning in mythology; he can also not consider it mere poetry. Thus, without appeal to the poetic, he must find a different antithesis to the doctrinal; and he finds it in the completely senseless. The more senseless the original representations, the better [XI 70], for thereby he has at the same time the root means against every effort to see sense in mythology and to transcend *his* treatment of it, a treatment that only will give heed to the dead, raw letter. Thus, in this first deep, dull condition, induced by natural occurrences, man has a presentiment[2] of beings in connection with these natural occurrences, beings similar to himself—that is, likewise coarse beings—which are his first gods. *Poets*, however, which Voss summons, must serve for the transition to mythology. For him, these poets are supposed to gradually work out the dark figures and indeterminate beings, supply them with more propitious human characteristics, and finally elevate them to ideal personalities. Ultimately these poets even invent a *history* of these beings through which the originally senseless is veiled in a pleasant and delightful manner. Thus did mythology emerge into being according to Voss's view.

Whoever has some sense for Hellenic mythology perceives in it something pregnant with meaning, rich in relationships, organic. It was only from that frightful ignorance about nature, which was prevalent in some circles of earlier philologists, that it was possible to think something organic would ever have been able to emerge from out of such wholly contingent and fully incoherent ideas [*Vorstellungen*] like those presumed. Incidentally, with this occasion it would lead us to question how in Germany one for a rather long time could have been so willing to have *poets* step forth directly from out of the coarsest condition, in which almost nothing remains of everything human. Was it due to passages from the ancients, such as, for example, where Orpheus is mentioned, as he cures the savagely living men of animal coarseness through the sweet sounds of his song, and leads them toward human life, like the passage from Horace?

> *Sylvestres homines sacer interpresque Deorum*
> *Caedibus et victu foedo deterruit Orpheus,*
> *Dictus ob hoc lenire tigres rabidosque leones.*[b]

These words, on the other hand, are related clearly enough to the particular orphic dogma that commands that one spare the life of the animals. [XI 71] However, this dogma has as little in common with the teaching of the gods, which calls for bloody sacrifice, as the orphic way of living does with the abundant diet of meat of the Homeric heroes. No ancient writer gives Orpheus a part in mythology. Voss, at least, certainly did not think of Orpheus. His view of pre-mythological poets probably can be traced back no farther than to the good old Göttingen era, where Heyne—of whom Voss is accustomed to speak as nothing other than of little value, but without, therefore, whatever concerns such questions, being able to deny his school—taught about the book of the Englishman Wood, *On the Original Genius of Homer*, that, for Homer,[c] one learns the most from travel descriptions of the mores [*Sitten*] of the savages, or—as he adds naively enough—those of *other peoples* who still live in an unformed society and civil constitution.[3] And, moreover, with respect to the good old Göttingen era, it was Heyne's students who compared Homer with Ossian and also with the old German bards, who were believed not only to inspire the sons of the Teutonic—still dressed in animal skins—to valor in battle, but also to have led them to a more human life generally speaking, although the image that the Homeric poems themselves draw of the joyful and refined sociability of their time does not allow us to conceive of the spectators of the time as anything less than savages or half-savages, as the words put into Orpheus's mouth already prove:

> Truly it is rapture to listen to the singer,
> to such as this one is—to the Immortals similar in voice!
> For I know of no pleasanter aim than when a fest of joy spreads within a people
> and 'round the hearths feasters hearken to the bard.
> Such seems to me in spirit the most blessed rapture of life.

Thus beings of the type described are supposed to have been the first gods, the actual gods proper, the gods that preceded the mythological gods, and it is therefore questionable if we can let these count for beings of an actually religious meaning [XI 72]. But we very much doubt whether representations [*Vorstellungen*] like those just mentioned are to be called religious. For, for example, the thoughtless dread before something uncanny and unseen in nature will not be foreign to the savages who roam about the wide plains of La Plata, a dread that we believe to perceive even in some animals. Even for them, dim visions [*Vorstellungen*] of ghostly beings stirring in the phenomena of nature will not be missing; and yet Azara assures that they are *without any religion*. Admittedly, one has made[d] objections against the assertion, but a man like Azara is not to be refuted with platitudes—among which one can also count the well-known one by Cicero, that no people will be met with so coarse and inhuman such that it would be without any representations of the gods. Indeed we can accept this proposition, for we have already observed that these disunified hordes are not to be called a people. One always finds it difficult to separate oneself from a long-cherished opinion. As is well known, the testimonials advanced by Robertson, testimonials that said exactly the same thing about some American tribes, already were exposed to similar objections. But the question of whether a number of persons that live before our own eyes and in front of us do and perform without dread everything according to their mores and nature, confer a type of cult to some sort of visible or invisible being, is of such nature that it is fit to be unequivocally decided through mere observation. Activities of adoration are visible activities. The spirited Azara cannot be placed in an equivalent status to that of other travelers. If it was the spirit of all encompassing natural research that guided our famed *Alexander von Humboldt* there, then it was the sense of the independent and unprejudiced thinker, of the philosopher, with which *Azara* entered those regions, from which he brought along tasks for the research of human and natural history, tasks that still await their resolution, and indeed for the most part—even in the scientific proficiency of our time, and in particular of our natural researches—await attention [XI 73]. He could not be mistaken about the fact that these savages exhibit through none of their activities a religious veneration for any object. The conclusion drawn from this, that they are without any religion, is likewise indubitable.[e]

If invisible beings mentioned in connection with natural processes were already *gods*, then the mountain and water spirits of the Celtic tribes, the goblins of the German tribes, the fairies of the East and the West would also have to be gods, for which they never counted. The Greek imagination also knows Oreads, Dryads, and Nymphs, which were in part venerated as servants of the deities but were never themselves considered deities.[4] The dread, which nonetheless is also felt before such beings, and even gifts, through which one seeks to attain their favor and to incline them to be favorable and friendly, are not yet proof of *divinely* venerated beings—that is, of beings of religious meaning. These attempts to elicit gods without God thus appear not to have attained the true power and force of the concept. Gods of this type would only improperly be named such. Hume himself admits this [XI 74] and articulates it. "Considering the matter precisely," so go his words, "this alleged religion is in fact only an *atheism* bound up with superstition. The objects of their veneration have not the slightest connection with our idea of the Divinity."[f] In another passage he declares: if one were to remove *God and the angels* from the old European belief (for these angels, as will-less tools of the Divinity, could not be thought without the latter), and retained only the fairies and the goblins, a belief similar to that alleged polytheism would be the result.[g]

Following this explanation by D. Hume, which admits of no disagreement, we are now also justified in condensing all of the previously arisen explanations under the general title of the "irreligious" explanations, and in this way to completely finish with them. And it is likewise clear that we are only now transitioning to the religious explanations as the object of a completely new development. The last development merely aimed at the question of which explanations could or could not be called religious. Common sense says: polytheism cannot be atheism; *actual* polytheism cannot be something in which there is nothing at all of theism. Gods proper can only be called those who take God as their basis—whether it be mediated through many intermediaries, or in whatever way so long as they take God as their basis in some way.— Herein nothing is thereby altered, when one decides to say that mythology is false religion. For false religion is not thereby irreligion, as error (at least what deserves to be called such) is not a complete lack of truth, but rather is itself simply the inverted truth.

However, as we herewith assert what we require of an actually religious view, the difficulty [XI 75] that the view encounters in its realization at once shows itself, and this difficulty now first shows which causes the earlier explicators had for stepping back so decisively from the religious meaning, and for instead leaving no stone unturned in allowing even the unbelievable to content them, rather than conceding something actually religious in mythology, or even allowing it in the ostensibly pre-mythological representations (of which Hume himself says that they contain nothing of God). For it lies in human nature to be frightened of difficulties that appear ineluctable, and to seek ways out; and only when one sees that all of these false means of alleviation grant no succor does one submit to the inevitable and undeniable.

With the actually religious meaning presupposed as the original one, the difficulty of how polytheism could originally take God as its basis must be explained. Also here *various* possibilities will present themselves, and their elaboration will be our next task. For in consequence of the fact that no other view remains for us outside the religious view, we will invest ourselves fully in the latter and see how it can be realized. And also here, again, we will be mindful to proceed from the first possible presupposition with which an originally religious meaning may be conceptualized.

The *first possible view* is, however, always the one that assumes the least; thus here undeniably the one that presupposes the least of an actual knowledge of God and presupposes, rather, only the potency [*Potenz*][5] or seed of such. For this, however, there is tendered the *Notitia Dei insita*—coming already from the ancients and, earlier, taught generally in the schools—with which, in fact, no other concept can be connected except that of a merely *potentially* present consciousness of God, which, however, would in itself have the necessity to transition to the *actus*, to raise itself to the actual consciousness of God.[6] Here might be the moment where the previously suggested, instinctual emergence could be able to attain to a determinate concept: it would be a *religious instinct* that produced mythology. For what else is one supposed to conceive under such a merely general and [XI 76] indefinite lore of God? Every instinct is bound up with a search for the object to which it relates itself. It appears that from such a grasping and tentative reaching for the vaguely demanded God a polytheism, which really is one, could be comprehended without great cost. For all that, there will not be a shortage of gradations here either.

The immediate object of human knowledge [*Erkennens*] remains nature, or the sensible world; God is only the dark, vague goal that is strived for and that is first sought in nature. The popular explanation through the *deification of nature* would first find its place here, because at the least an inborn, dark lore of God would always have to take the lead. Thus, earlier, this explanation was out of the question. Through the presupposition of a religious instinct it might be conceptualized how man believes to find the God that he seeks initially in the ubiquitous elements or in the stars that exert on him the most powerful or salubrious influence; and how he gradually, to bring God nearer to himself, visualizes him as descending to the earth, visualizes him even in inorganic forms, and fancies himself to be able to represent God, first in organic beings, for a time even among animal forms, and finally in purely human form. Thus, here would belong the interpretations that consider the mythological deities as deified natural beings; or in particular only one of these beings, the sun, which in its various positions in the course of a year would each time become a *different* deity—for example in the explanations of Volney,[h] Dupuis,[i] amongst others.[7]

The explanation proceeding from the *Notitia insita* would receive a more philosophical appearance if one let nature fall out of the picture, made the emergence into being entirely immanent and independent of the external world, by presupposing that that instinct has a law inherent to itself (the same through which the succession of gradations in nature also is determined); and also if one supposed that by virtue of this law it goes through the entire nature, possessing and losing again God on every level, up until [XI 77] it reaches the God towering above and transcending every moment, positing them as the past of itself and thereby as mere moments of *nature*, and accordingly, himself stands above nature. Because God is the goal (*terminus ad quem*) in this ascensive movement, God would be believed in at every level, and thus the last content of the hereby emerging polytheism would actually be God.

This explanation would be the first one to have mythology emerge into being through a purely immanent and simultaneously necessary movement that thereby would have freed itself from all external and merely contingent presuppositions. And, certainly, this explanation would have to be considered at least as the model of the highest to which we would have to advance. For it could not count for the ultimate or highest itself because it also has a presupposition not yet conceptualized: precisely that instinct, which, if it is powerful enough to hold humanity in this movement to the true God, must itself be something real, an actual potency whose explanation one could not hope to attain with the mere idea of God—for one would like to believe it has to do here with a mere logical trick, by which an impoverished philosophy might also perhaps happily come to the aid of this investigation, in order to first lower the poor, namely the idea of God to the meanest level, in order then to have it again artificially attain completion in thought. It is not a question of the interrelationship in which the material of mythology can certainly also be placed with the *mere idea* (mythology would tolerate this as nature also tolerates it). But as little as nature would be explained through such a deception, so little would mythology be explained through something similar. But the question is precisely one of explanation, not with the mere ideal possibility, but rather with the real emergence of mythology. The presupposition of a religious instinct, no less real in its way than any other, could be the first step toward the realization that mythology is not explicable from a merely ideal relationship in which consciousness stands to some object.

In any case, it would be more difficult to have a [XI 78] formal doctrine, rather than a merely inborn lore of God, precede polytheism. Inimical in the presupposition of a doctrine is also the assumption of a distortion, a distortion that is bound up with a doctrine that is supposed to become polytheism. With successful thought David Hume challenges both the possibility of the emergence of such a doctrine and the possibility of the distortion of it. He never even considered the *Notitia insita*. In general, Hume belongs to those who want to know as little of an instinct as of inborn concepts. Because, as he maintains, no two peoples—indeed not two individuals—agree on the point of religion, he draws the conclusion that the religious feeling cannot rest on a natural *drive* like self-love or the mutual inclination of the sexes. And he wants to grant, at most, a proclivity, that we all have, to believe in an undefined way in the existence of *some sort* of invisible and intelligent power, a proclivity of which it still seems very doubtful to him as to whether it is based on an original instinct.[j]

Hume's intent is to dispute the actually religious meaning of mythology as one that is original; in this respect he would above all have had to dispute the *Notitia insita*, had he not already found it unnecessary due to the reason already indicated. For in his time that theory of an inborn lore was fully antiquated and had lost all validity. For this reason the only thing he believes necessary to challenge is the possibility of having a religious *doctrine* precede polytheism and mythology, a doctrine that would have distorted itself in both. Once one assumes a *doctrine*, then Hume knows of no other than one found scientifically, of no other than a theism (*Theisme raissonné*) resting on syllogisms, the terminus of reason. However, an explanation that would have presupposed such a theism has never really existed. Hume proposes this explanation merely (and because he knows nothing different) in order to refute it [XI 79], and thereby generally to disprove an originally theistic meaning. Then he has it very easy to show that such a theism—*raissonné*—was incapable of emerging in the periods before mythology, and if it was able to emerge, it was unable to distort itself into polytheism.

It is a curiosity that here in his natural history of religion Hume presupposes as possible what he is famously very disinclined to admit in his more general philosophical investigations: that it is possible for reason, through deductions and conclusions originating from the visible world, to attain the concept and certainty of an *intelligent creator of the world*, of a most perfect being, and so on—in short to attain to that which he understands under theism, and what is indeed something so devoid of content that it is far more credible to attribute it to a past time, or one in the process of expiring, than to one still fresh and powerful, and that Hume could reasonably have been able to spare himself his entire proof.

Whoever has in some degree observed the natural advances of our knowledge will be convinced that the ignorant masses would have initially been capable of only very coarse and erroneous representations. How then are they supposed to have elevated themselves to the concept of a most perfect being, from whom would stem the order and regularity in all parts of nature? Will one believe such a humanity will have conceived of the Divinity as a pure spirit, as an all-knowing, all-powerful, infinite being and not, rather, as a limited power, with passions, desires, and even with organs like our own? For then, one would just as easily consider it possible that there were palaces before huts were built or that geometry preceded agriculture.[k]

However, once men had convinced themselves through deductions and conclusions, based on the wonders of nature, of the existence of an ultimate being, then it was *impossible* for them to forsake this belief in order to fall into idolatry. The fundamental principles, through which this gleaming view had initially emerged among the people [*Menschen*], they had to preserve still more effortlessly [XI 80]. For it is infinitely more difficult to uncover and prove a truth than it is to maintain once it is uncovered and proven. It is very different with speculative insights obtained on the path of *Räsonnements* than with historical facts that are easily distorted. In views that are obtained through deductions the proofs are either clear enough and generally understandable enough to convince everyone—in this case they will suffice to everywhere preserve the views in their original purity, wherever they spread themselves—or the proofs are abstruse, exceeding the power of comprehension of normal men; therefore the doctrines which rest on them become known only to a small number of people [*Menschen*] and are buried in oblivion as soon as they cease to be occupied with them. Regardless if one assumes the one or the other, a preceding theism that would have degenerated into polytheism [*Vielgötterei*] will always be found impossible.[s] Easy deductions and conclusions would have prevented it from corrupting itself; difficult and abstract ones would have deprived it of the awareness of the great masses, under which alone fundamental principles and views are distorted.[l]

Thus, it must be noted in passing that for Hume theism proper—that is, what he calls by that name—cannot exist in humanity until the age of the already practiced and fully developed reason. Thus, such a theism is unthinkable in the time to which the origin of polytheism goes back, and what one may find in pre-historic time that resembles such theism *only appears so* and is simply explained in the following way: one of the idolatrous nations raises *one* of the believed-in, invisible beings to the highest status, either because it considers its land area under the being's special dominion, or because it has the opinion that under those beings it is as though under men, where one dominates the others as monarch. Now, once such an elevation has taken place, they will strive for this one being's favor in particular, pay court to it, increase its attributes [XI 81], as also happens with earthly monarchs, to whom one does not merely refer out of prescription as the all-superior and the most gracious, but rather as one can even hear be voluntarily called the *idolized*[9] *monarchs*, even among Christians. Once such a rivalry of flattery has begun, as one tries to outdo the other, then it cannot fail that it eventually reaches a limit through increasingly stranger and more pompous epithets, accompanied by continually increasing hyperboles, a limit where it goes no further: the one being is now called the *highest* being, the *infinite being*, the being without equal, which is *lord and preserver of the world*.[m] In this way there emerges the representation of a being that *externally* looks similar to the one we call God. For Hume himself, who in this way actually brings out the paradoxical and even bizarrely appearing thesis that polytheism has preceded theism, is too aware not to fully know that such a theism is actually only atheism.

Now, however, if we were to assume that it is for whatever reason always considered unavoidable to presuppose a doctrine before polytheism, then in part the content of the doctrine, and in part its emergence, would have to be determined. In the first, the material relationship, one could in no case be satisfied with one so empty and abstract, like the one taught in the present day schools, but rather only one rich in content, a systematic, richly unfolded doctrine could fit the purpose. For this reason, however, an invention would become still more unbelievable, and thus one would see himself, with reference to the formal side, pressed into assuming a religious doctrine that would have been in mankind *independent* of human invention: such a doctrine could only be one *divinely* revealed. Thus, an entirely new domain of explanation as such would have been entered, for a divine revelation is a real relation of God to human consciousness. The *actus* of the revelation itself is a real event. At the same time, herewith that opposite of all [XI 82] human invention would appear to be reached, an opposite that had already been demanded earlier, but had not been found; in any event, one would have a more solid presupposition in a divine revelation than in the ones earlier proposed, than in the dream state, clairvoyance, and so on. Hume was able to find it unnecessary vis-à-vis his time to even make mention of this possibility. Hermann, as he states, does not want to envy anyone for this pious opinion.[n] And yet perhaps he would have reason enough to speak of it with somewhat less contempt, partially because it agrees with his own theory in a major point, namely, the assumption of a *distortion*, and partially because—in the case that the dilemma he used, according to which no third term can be thought apart from self-invention and divine revelation, would have its correctness—he could happen to find himself assuming the pious opinion. Hermann's theory would indeed be wholly splendid had mythology existed nowhere other than on paper, or had it been a mere school exercise. However, what would it answer when one reminded it of the grotesque sacrifices that the peoples have brought to their mythological representations? Indeed, one could ask him, *tantum quod sumis potuit suadere malorem*? From out of that which you assume, from out of such innocent presuppositions, was so much wickedness able to emerge? "Admit it," one could call out, to all those who agree with him in the disputation of the originally religious meaning, that such consequences cannot be derived from such causes; "avow" that an imperative authority was needed just as much to demand those sacrifices as to perform them; for example, to burn alive one's most beloved children for some god! If only cosmogonial philosophers stood in the background and no memory of a real event that lent such representations an irresistible power over consciousness, then did not nature have to immediately enter into its rights again? Only a *supernatural fact* [XI 83], whose impression incessantly maintained itself in all the confusion, was able to impose silence on the natural feeling that was opposed to such monstrous demands.

Moreover, when one views mythology as a distortion of the revealed truth, then it is no longer sufficient to presuppose for it mere *theism*, for in this there simply lies that *God* is thought in general. But with revelation it is not merely God in general who reveals himself; it is the determinate God, the God that is, the true God, who reveals himself, and who also reveals himself as the true God. Thus, a determination must be added here: it is not theism, but rather *monotheism* that precedes polytheism. For through this determination, universally and everywhere, not merely religion in general, but rather the true religion, is designated. And this view (that monotheism preceded polytheism) was, then, in undisturbed possession of a complete and universal concurrence from Christian times up to the modern era, indeed up to the time of D. Hume. One considered it, so to speak, impossible that polytheism could have been able to emerge other than through the corruption of a purer religion, and that this purer religion descended from a divine revelation was a thought again inseparable, to some degree, from that assumption.

But the matter is not settled with the mere word monotheism. What is its content? Is it of a type that material for a later polytheism lies in it? Indeed, certainly not, if one has the content of monotheism consist in the mere concept of the singularity of God. For what does this singularity of God contain? It is just the pure negation of an other external to the one, just rejection of every multiplicity; now, how precisely is its opposite supposed to result from this singularity? Once articulated, what material, what possibility of a multiplicity does the abstract singularity leave over as a remainder? *Lessing* also sensed this difficulty, when he wrote in the *Education of Man*:[10] "Even if the first man was from the start endowed with the concept of a single, unique God, then this imparted and non-acquired concept nonetheless was unable to subsist in its purity for a long time. As soon as reason [XI 84], left to its own devices, began to process it, it dismantled the singular immeasurable God into many measurable ones, and gave a particular characteristic to each of these parts. Thus polytheism [*Vielgötterei*] and idolatry emerged into being in a natural way."[o] The words are valuable to us as proof that the fine man also once concerns himself with this question, even if only in passing: for, additionally, one may well assume that Lessing, in an essay of an aim much farther reaching, and where he was in general concerned to be brief, sought to get over the difficult point as quickly as possible.[p] Only what is true lies in his remark that a *non-acquired* concept, so long as it has not become an acquired one, is exposed to corruption. Additionally, polytheism is supposed to emerge into being in that the imparted concept (for the latter expression indeed explains the former: man is *endowed* with this concept) is processed by reason. Herewith, polytheism would be given a rational emergence: not it itself but rather the concept presupposed for it is independent of human reason. Presumably, Lessing found the means to the assumed dismantling of the one [God] in that the unity, however, was at the same time conceived as the embodiment of all relationships of God [XI 85] to nature and the world. The Divinity, as it were, turns a different countenance toward each side of these, without thereby itself becoming multiple. Of course, such that in each of these possible views the Divinity is designated with a different name; examples of such names, names expressing various relationships, are to be found even in the Old Testament. Subsequently these names—of which there easily can be an immense number—transition into just as many names of the particular deities. One forgets the unity in light of the multiplicity, and as this or that people, and even this or that tribe within that same people, or this or that individual under the same tribe, turns especially toward one of these sides according to needs or inclinations, polytheism [*Vielgötterei*] emerges into being. *Cudworth*, at least, conceived the transition this simply, this imperceptibly. This merely nominal diverging has, however, served as a prelude for a real one that subsequently was taken on.

Here it may behoove us to recall that mythological polytheism [*Polytheismus*] is not simply the system[11] of the gods [*Götterlehre*] but rather the history of the gods. Now, insofar as the revelation also sets the true God into a historical relation to humanity, it may be thought that just this divine history given with the revelation has turned into the material of polytheism, that its moments would have distorted themselves into the mythological ones. A development of mythology from out of the revelation taken in this sense would have been able to offer much worthy of consideration. Still, for all that we do not find such a development among the explanations actually advanced. In part, one might have run into too great of difficulties with the execution of this; in part one could have found it too daring, in another sense. Instead one took up the human side of the history of revelation and sought initially to use for eumeritic interpretations the merely *historical* content, chiefly from the Mosaic writings.[12] Thus the Greek Kronos, who committed an outrage against the father Uranus, is supposed to be the Ham worshiped by the heathens, the Ham who has committed an outrage against the father Noah.[13] The nations[14] [*Nationen*] of Ham are really preeminently worshipers of Kronos. In that time it was impossible to conceive of the reverse explanation [XI 86], that the myths of the gods [*Göttersagen*] of the other peoples were eumeritized [*euemerisirt*] in the Old Testament, were explained eumeritically as human events.

The primary originator of this eumeritic use of the Old Testament was *Gerhard Voss*, whose work *De Origine et progressu Idololatriae* has, in addition, for its time, the merit of a complete scholarliness, excluding nothing.[15] With an often unsuccessful wit, it was applied by Samuel Bochart, fully driven into the tasteless by the well-known French bishop Daniel Huet, in whose *Demonstratio Evangelica* one can read as proven demonstratively that the Phoenician Taaut, the Syrian Adonis, the Egyptian Osiris, the Persian Zoroaster, the Greek Cadmus and Danaus—in short, all of the divine and human personalities of the various mythologies—are only one individual: Moses.[16] These interpretations are ultimately to be mentioned as at most *sententiae dudum explosae*, in the case someone, as it happened recently with others, would remember to drag them out again.

In this way it was, in general, in the end, no longer the revelation itself, but rather it was the Old Testament *writings*, and within these chiefly only the historical [*historischen*] ones, in which one sought the explanation for the oldest myths. In the more *dogmatic* part of the Mosaic books, even if one could presuppose their content as already present earlier in the tradition, one was able to find all the less material for the emergence of the mythological representations the easier it was—even in the first pronouncements of *Genesis*, for example the creation story—to perceive clear consideration of *already present* doctrines of a false religion. In the way that the creation story has light emerge at God's command, and thereby first has the antithesis of light and dark emerge, in the way that God calls the light good without naming the darkness evil, in connection with the repeated assurance that all was good, it can appear to want to contradict the doctrines that view light and dark as two *principles*, which principles produce the world [XI 87] with one another in conflict and contradiction instead of being created as good and bad principle.[17] In that I express this as a possible opinion and interpretation, I refute all the more definitely the notion that these chapters themselves contain philosophemes and myths of non-Hebraic peoples. At the least one will not extend the conjecture to the Greek myths, and yet it would be so easy to show that, for example, the story of original sin has far more in common with the Persephone myths of the Hellenes than with anything else that one had the mind to put forward from Persian or Indian sources.

Thus the attempt to bring mythology in connection with revelation had remained within this limitation up until the end of the previous century. Since this time, however, because our knowledge of the various mythologies, and especially of the religious systems of the East, has so noticeably broadened, a freer view, and above all one more independent of the written documents of revelation, has been able to assert itself.

Through the correspondences that one finds among the Egyptian, Indian, and Greek mythology one was ultimately led, in the explanation of mythology, to a common whole of representations, in which the various systems of the gods have had their unity. This unity lying at the foundation of each system of the gods served, then, as the apex of a hypothesis. For such a unity can no longer be conceived in the consciousness of a single people (every people first becomes conscious of itself as such in the departure from this unity), not even of a primordial people. As is well known, the concept of a primordial people was put into circulation by *Bailly* through his *History of Astronomy* and his *Letters on the Origin of the Sciences*; but the concept, however, is actually a self-negating one.[18] For either one conceives of it with the differentiating qualities of an *actual people*, such that it can no longer contain the *unity* we are seeking, and such that it already presupposes other peoples besides itself; or one conceives of it without its own uniqueness and without any individual consciousness, such that it is not a people, but rather the original humanity itself, that is above the people. Thus, from the initial perception of those correspondences one has [XI 88], stepwise, finally reached the point of presupposing in pre-history—incited or imparted by *primordial revelation* that would not have been given to a single people, but rather to a whole human species—a system [*System*] far exceeding the literal content of the Mosaic writings, a system of which the teaching of Moses itself provides no completed concept but rather contains only a certain excerpt. Advanced in contradiction to and suppression of polytheism [*Polytheismus*], this teaching, with wise forethought, supposedly removed all elements from whose misunderstanding polytheism arose and confined itself only to the negative—to the repudiation of polytheism [*Vielgötterei*]. If one thus wanted to form a concept of that primordial system, then the Mosaic writings are insufficient for this goal. One would have to search out the missing components precisely in the foreign systems of the gods, in the fragments of the Eastern religions and the various mythologies.[q]

The first to be drawn to such conclusions by the correspondence of Oriental systems of the gods with, on the one hand, Greek representations, and, on the other, with the teachings of the Old Testament—although others were drawn to such conclusions by the correspondences even more—was the founder and first president of the Asiatic Society in Calcutta, *William Jones*,[19] who has made himself immortal in what he has done for the history of Eastern poetry and the study of Asian religions. If perhaps he might have been too spiritually carried away by the initial astonishment of the newly uncovered world, and have gone further in some matters than calculating understanding and the calm circumspection of a later time was able to sanction, then still the beauty and nobility of his spirit will constantly place him, with respect to the opinion of all those capable of seeing it, above and beyond the judgment [XI 89] of the common masses of coarse and merely mechanical scholars.

If the comparisons and conclusions by William Jones were all too often short of precise substantiation and execution, then, on the other hand, *Friedrich Creuzer*, through the power of a comprehensive and overwhelming induction, has raised the *originally* religious meaning of mythology to a historical fact no longer to be contradicted.[20] Yet the merit of his famous work[r] is not limited to this generality. The philosophical profundity with which the author discloses the most hidden relatedness between the various systems of the gods and the analogous representations of them has with particular spirit awakened the thought of an *original whole*, of a body of an unprethinkable human knowledge [*Wissenschaft*], which gradually declined or was struck by a sudden devastation, a knowledge that with its debris—which no single people but only all together completely possess—has covered the whole earth. And at the very least it is since then no longer possible to return to the prior explanations that atomistically form the content of mythology.[s]

Determined more precisely, Creuzer's whole view could be expressed in the following manner. Because the revelation itself is *not* immediately capable of alteration [XI 90], but rather only the result of it that has remained in consciousness, then certainly a teaching had to step in the midst here, but such a one in which God was presented not only theistically, simply *as* God, in his separation from the world, but rather at the same time as a unity comprehending nature and world; whether it be in a way that was analogous to *those* systems that, above all, a certain insipid theism designated *all* without difference as pantheism, or in the way that one conceives of that system more in the way of an ancient Oriental emanation theory, where the Divinity—in itself free of every multiplicity—descends itself into a multiplicity of finite figures, which are likewise only many manifestations or—to use a new favorite word—incarnations of its infinite essence. Thought in one way or the other the teaching would not be an abstract *monotheism* absolutely excluding multiplicity, but rather a *real* monotheism positing the multiplicity in itself.

As long as the multiplicity of elements is mastered and overwhelmed by the unity, the unity of God remains unsublated in consciousness. As soon as the teaching advances from people to people, indeed within the selfsame people in the course of time and tradition, it takes on an increasingly polytheistic [*polytheistische*] tint, as the elements withdraw from organic subordination under the dominating idea [*Idee*] and gradually develop themselves more independently, until the whole finally falls out of joint and the unity withdraws entirely, while the multiplicity steps forth. Thus W. Jones already found in the Indian Vedas—which we, following his view, would have to consider written a long time before the mission of Moses in the first periods after the great flood—a system far removed from the later Indian folk superstition, a system standing nearer to the primordial religion. The later polytheism [*Polytheismus*] of India does not derive from the oldest religion directly, but rather only through successive deformation of the better transmissions [*Überlieferungen*] still contained in the holy books. In general, a closer attentiveness clearly shows in the various systems of the gods a gradual and almost stepwise withdrawal of the unity. To the degree that the unity still has a greater power, the representations of the Indian and Egyptian [XI 91] system of the gods still appear with much more doctrinal content, but to the same extent also more uncanny, excessive, in part even monstrous. On the other hand, to the degree that the unity in the system of the gods is more renounced, Greek mythology actually exhibits less doctrinal content, but shows itself as all the more poetic. The error in it, has, so to say, purified itself from the truth, and to this extent actually ceases again to be error and becomes a truth of its own *peculiar type*, a poetic truth, a truth renouncing all reality that happens to lie in the unity; and if one still wanted to express its content as error, it would be at least a more delightful, more beautiful, and in comparison with the more concrete error in the Oriental religions, almost innocent error.

In this way mythology would be a *diverged monotheism*. This is thus the final height that the views on mythology have reached in steps. No one will deny this view being one that is superior to the earlier ones, and indeed precisely because of the fact that it does not proceed from the indeterminate multiplicity [*Vielheit*] of objects randomly raised from out of nature, but rather proceeds from the middle point of a unity dominating the multiplicity. It is not the isolated beings of a most highly contingent and ambiguous nature but rather the thought of the *necessary and universal being* (before which alone the human spirit humbles itself) that holds sway through mythology and raises it to a true system [*System*] of moments belonging together, a system that in its diverging presses its stamp even on every single representation, and for this reason cannot end in a mere indeterminate multiplicity [*Vielheit*] but rather only in polytheism [*Polytheismus*]—in a multiplicity of *gods* [*Götter*vielheit].[21]

Now, with this last elaboration—I ask *you* to well notice this, for in order to understand a lecture such as the present one in its whole meaning, one has especially to perceive the transitions—here it is no longer merely *philosophically* asserted that polytheism [*Polytheismus*], which it really is, presupposes monotheism; here monotheism has become a historical presupposition of mythology, while it itself is again derived from a *historical fact* (from a primordial revelation). Through these [XI 92] historical presuppositions the explanation becomes a hypothesis and thus at the same time becomes fit for a historical judgment.

Unquestionably the explanation has its most powerful historical support in that it offers the simplest means to explain the affinity of the representations in otherwise wholly different systems of the gods, and in this respect one could only be surprised that Creuzer pays less attention to this advantage and lays more weight on a historical connection of the peoples that is difficult to prove, indeed in the main cases unprovable, a connection from which he wants in part to derive those correspondences. But already our earlier developments have led us to determinations that make the present form of the monotheistic hypothesis, as we want to call it, appear as very indeterminate. Already earlier we were led to the statement that the mythology of every people can only emerge simultaneously with it. Thus the various mythologies also—and because mythology exists nowhere in *abstracto*, then polytheism in general—could only have emerged into being simultaneously with the peoples, and accordingly there would be no place to be found for the assumed monotheism other than in the time before the emergence of the peoples. Creuzer also appears to have thought something similar, in that he asserted that monotheism, which still maintained a preponderance in the oldest doctrines, was only able to exist as long as the tribes remained together and that with their cision polytheism had to emerge into being.[t]

True, we cannot determine what Creuzer understood under the cision of the *tribes*, but if we posit in its place the cision of the *peoples*, then there is shown that a double causal connection can be thought between this cision and the arising polytheism [*Polytheismus*]. That is to say, one could either say in agreement with Creuzer: after humanity had split itself into peoples monotheism was no longer able to exist, in that the doctrine that had been dominant up to that point grew dim in proportion to its distance from the origin and diverged more and more [XI 93]. Yet one could just as well say: the emerging polytheism was the cause of the separation of the peoples. And it must be decided between these two possibilities, if everything is not to remain in inconsistency and uncertainty.

The decision, however, will depend on the following question. If polytheism is only a consequence of the splitting of the peoples, then *another* cause, in virtue of which humanity split off into peoples, must be able to be found; and thus it is to be investigated whether there is such a cause. This means, however, it is to be investigated generally, and the question is to be answered that we have been pushed toward for a long time: what is the cause of this separation of humanity into peoples? The earlier explanations all already presupposed peoples. But how, then, did peoples emerge into being? Can one believe such a great and general phenomenon like that which mythology and polytheism are, or (for here is this expression first of all in its place) the pagan world is—does one believe, I say, such a powerful phenomenon can be understand outside of the general context of the great events by which mankind in general was affected? The question of how peoples have emerged into being is thus not one arbitrarily raised; it is one induced by our development, and for that reason is necessary and imperative. And with this question we may indeed rejoice in seeing ourselves transposed from the narrowness of the preceding investigations to a realm of research that is broader, more general and for this reason also one that promises more universal and higher conclusions.

Lecture Five

[XI 94] *How did peoples emerge into being?* Whoever perhaps wanted to declare this question superfluous would have to either advance the proposition that peoples *always* were, *since time immemorial*; or the other, that peoples emerge into being *of themselves*. One will not easily decide to make the first assertion. One could, however, attempt to assert that peoples emerge into being of themselves, and indeed that they emerge already in consequence of the incessant propagation of the sexes, by which is populated not only in general a larger space of the earth but rather by which the lines of descent also diverge more and more. However, this would only lead to tribes, not to peoples. One could say, however, that to the degree that powerfully growing tribes find it necessary to divide themselves and seek out dwelling places distant from one another, they become mutually alienated. But also not in this way to various *peoples*; for each piece of the splintered tribe would have to form itself into a people through other, additional moments. For tribes do not become peoples through mere external separation. The great distance between the eastern and western Arabs provides the most striking example. Separated by seas from their brothers, the Arabs in Africa are still today what their kindred in the Arabian desert are—setting aside a few small nuances of the common language and mores. Conversely, tribal unity does not hinder the diverging into various peoples. As proof: that a moment or event entirely separate and independent of the line of descent or lineage must be added so that a *people* emerges into being.

[XI 95] A merely spatial diverging would constantly yield only uniform elements, but never heterogeneous elements, like peoples—which, beginning from their genesis, in themselves are physically and spiritually heterogeneous. In the historical era we indeed see how one people crowds and drives out another, forces it to enclose itself in narrower borders or to entirely leave its original dwelling place; without thereby the defeated people, expelled or even driven into the greatest distance, in any way ceasing to maintain its character and be the same people. Even among the Arabian tribes, both among those who continue to live in the land of their birth and among the others that continue their nomadic life in inner Africa—naming and differentiating themselves according to the patriarchs of their tribe—there are mutual attacks and battles, without them thereby becoming peoples over and against each other or ceasing to be a homogenous mass: just like there is no lack of storms in the ocean, which cause powerful waves but which, after a short time, restore the old calm surface of the element, and, without leaving a trace, return to the same; or like the desert wind that sends the sands whirling upward into disastrous columns, which afterward quickly present the old, similar plains.

An *inner*—and for just that reason indissoluble and irreversible—separation like that existing between peoples cannot at all be effected *externally*; that is, it also cannot be effected by mere natural events, which one may initially like to consider. Volcanic eruptions, earthquakes, alterations in the sea level, land ruptures, in whatever extent one would assume them, would explain a separation into uniform elements but never into heterogeneous elements. Thus, in any event, there would have to be *inner* causes, causes emerging within the homogenous mankind itself, through which mankind was separated, through which it was destined to degenerate itself into heterogeneous and henceforth mutually excluding elements. For this reason these inner causes could still be natural ones. Still, more than *external* events, divergences of physical development that arise *internally* to humanity—and that began to externalize themselves in the human species according to some hidden law [XI 96], and through which in further consequence certain spiritual, moral, and psychological variations also arise—could be considered likely to be the causes through which humanity was destined to diverge into peoples.

In order to demonstrate the separating violence that physical divergences are able to exert, one could cite the consequences that, conversely, there have been each time great masses of human races [*Menschengeschlechter*], kept separate, as it were, through divine providence, contacted or even mixed with each other (for, as Horace already complains, in vain has the providential god separated ununifiable lands through Oceanos, if with a sacrilegious vehicle man nonetheless crosses over the forbidden, watery spaces). To this end one could recall the world-historical plagues that the crusades and that America—discovered or refound after thousands of years—have spread throughout the human species, or on the devastating sicknesses that periodically develop in consequence of the world wars through which peoples far distant from each other are brought together and become, as it were, one people for a moment. When the sudden unification of peoples cut off from each other by broad expanses of land, by rivers, bogs, mountains, deserts produces such pestilence and sickness; when (in order to posit a more modest example in addition to these grandiose ones) the small number of residents of the Shetland Islands—fully cut off from the world and social intercourse with the rest of mankind—every time a foreign ship, indeed every time the crew of the ship that delivers to them annually provisions and other necessities, sets foot on their bleak shore, are overcome by a convulsive cough that does not leave them prior to the departure of the foreigners; when something similar, indeed something more striking, occurs on the lonely Farro Islands, where the appearance of a visiting ship has for the residents, as a rule, a feverish cold as consequence, from which not seldom a comparatively speaking not inconsiderable portion of their weak population is carried off to death; when something similar was noticed on the islands of the south seas [XI 97], where indeed the arrival of some missionaries sufficed to induce fever, about which one did not previously know, and which lowered the population; thus when after an already arisen separation the momentarily reconstituted coexistence of a human race split apart from one another produces sicknesses, then likewise could the beginning divergences of the physical development and the thus aroused antipathies or even actually emerged sicknesses become cause of a mutual, perhaps instinctual elimination of human groups [*Gattungen*] that are no longer compatible.

Thus this hypothesis may be the one, among the merely physical ones, that agrees most with the lawfulness of all the original events. But, it partly explains only mutually incompatible groups [*Gattungen*]; it does not explain peoples. Partly, according to other experiences, it may rather be spiritual and moral differences that have as consequences a physical incompatibility of certain human races [*Geschlechter*]. Relevant here is the rapid extinction of all savages in contact with Europeans, before whom all nations [*Nationen*] appear destined to vanish if not protected by their countless numbers, like the Indians and Chinese, or through climate, like the Negroes. Since the settling of the English in Vandemiensland[1] the entire indigenous population has been extinguished. It is similar in New South Wales. It is as if the higher and freer development of the European nations becomes deadly for all other nations.

One cannot speak of physical differences of the human species [*Menschengeschlechts*] without immediately being reminded of the so-called races [*Racen*] of humans whose difference for some appeared great enough even to refute a common lineage of the human species.[2] Of course, as far as this opinion is concerned (for in an investigation like the present one it cannot be avoided to say something even about this question), the judgment viewing the racial difference as a decisive objection against the original unity of the human species would at any rate be termed a premature one; for it proves nothing that the assumption of a common line of descent is bound up with difficulties [XI 98]. We are far too much beginners in this investigation, and too many facts are still inadequately known, for us to be able to maintain that future research about this object could not give our views a totally different direction or expand them in ways that so far are not being considered. For even that which is tacitly presupposed with all the arguments is so far a merely assumed and unproven idea, that is, that the process by which the racial differences have emerged has supposedly only taken place in a part of mankind, in that which we now actually see degraded to races (for European mankind should not actually be called a race), whilst it can also be viewed as possible that this process has happened throughout the whole of mankind and that the nobler part of mankind is not that which remained entirely free of it but rather only that which conquered it and precisely thereby elevated itself to higher spirituality; and the actually existing races, on the other hand, are only the portion that have submitted to the process and in which one of those orientations of a deviating physical development has fixed itself and become a remaining characteristic. If we succeed in leading this great investigation to its end, then we hope to specify facts that might be suitable for allowing the thought of the universality of that process to emerge, and indeed such facts that are not merely derived from natural history—for example from the border between the various races, a border that has become more fluid, as it were, through new discoveries—but rather from entirely different places. For now it suffices to say that we have to adhere to the unity of the line of descent—which, moreover, is supported by the still not entirely refuted fact that the descendents also of individuals of various races are themselves again capable of reproduction—not merely for the benefit of tradition or in the interest of some moral feeling, but rather as a consequence of purely scientific consideration, as long as the impossibility is not proved to understand under this presupposition the natural and historical differences of the human species.

[XI 99] If now, in addition, the facts just placed in view also might even suffice as proof that the process of racializations [*Racenprocess*]—as we want to express it, to save time—has extended into the times of the emergence of peoples, then it is still to be noted, however, that the peoples were not separated by races, at least not through and through. To the contrary, there can indeed be shown that there are peoples among whom are found, between their various classes, differences that are at least almost equal to the racial differences: *Niebuhr*[3] has already mentioned the strikingly white skin and facial color of the Indian Brahmins, which becomes increasingly darker with the downward hierarchy of the other castes and disappears into a full ape-brown with pariahs who are not even considered castes.[a] One may trust of Niebuhr that he did not confuse an originary difference in facial color with the contingent one that the various ways of living produce, and that one generally perceives between the idle men mostly living in shadows and the man staying outdoors, the men exposed to the direct effect of sun and air. If the Indians are an example of a people within which a physical variation nearly approaching a racial difference resulted only in a division of castes, but has not negated the unity of the people itself, then the Egyptians are perhaps the example of a people in which the racial difference was overcome: or into what is that negroid race with curly-wooly hair and black skin supposed to have disappeared, that race that Herodotus still saw in Egypt, and which one there must[b] have pointed out to him as the oldest (because he founds conclusions about the descent of the Egyptians on this view), if one does not want to assume that he himself was never in Egypt or has merely told fictions.

Lecture 5

Through that which has been presented so far we will have adequately prepared ourselves for the question of whether it is the case that instead of being the causes, divergent directions of physical development were on the contrary themselves only an attendant appearance [XI 100] of the great spiritual movements that had to be conjoined with the first emergence and formation of peoples. For it is obvious to recall the experience that even in individual cases a complete spiritual rigidity also retards certain physical developments and, contrariwise, that a great spiritual movement also calls forth certain physical developments and anomalies, just like the number and complication of illnesses have increased with the manifold of spiritual developments, like—in accordance with the observation that in the life of the individual a defeated illness indicates not seldom the moment of a deep spiritual conversion—new sicknesses appearing in powerful forms appear as parallel symptoms of great spiritual emancipations.^c And if the peoples are separated not merely spatially and externally, and thus also not through mere natural differences; if they are masses that spiritually and internally exclude each other, but are thereby also, however, insurmountably held together in themselves; then neither can the original unity of the still undivided human species—to which we must ascribe some sort of duration—be thought without a spiritual power that kept mankind in this rigidity and did not even let come into effect what is contained within it, the seeds of physical developments diverging asunder. Nor is it to be assumed that mankind would have left that state—where there were no peoples, but rather mere differences among tribes—without a *spiritual* crisis that had to be of the deepest meaning and had to have occurred in the foundation of human consciousness itself if it was supposed to be powerful enough to enable or determine the heretofore united humanity such that it disintegrated itself.

And since this has now been said in general, that the cause had to be a *spiritual* one, we can only be surprised how something so obvious was not perceived immediately. For different peoples cannot really be conceived of without different languages [XI 101], and language is, after all, something *spiritual*. If through none of its external differences—to which language, from one of its sides, indeed belongs—the peoples are as internally divided as they are through language, and if only those peoples are really separated which speak different languages—then the emergence of languages is inseparable from the emergence of peoples. And if the differentiation of peoples is not something that has always been, but rather something that has emerged, then this must hold of the differentiations of languages. Were there a time in which there were no peoples, and thus also one in which there were no different languages, and if it is unavoidable to presuppose of the mankind cleaved into peoples one not so cleaved—then it is no less unavoidable to have a language common to all mankind preceding the languages separating the peoples. All of these are propositions that one does not usually consider, or that one forbids oneself from thinking by a brooding critique discouraging and atrophying the spirit (a critique, that, as it appears, is quite especially at home in some places of our fatherland). But they are propositions that, as soon as they are put forward, *must* be recognized as irrefutable; and no less undeniable is the consequence necessarily bound up with them: that a *spiritual* crisis in the *interior* of man had to precede the emergence of peoples, for the fact alone that the latter inevitably brought along with itself a dividing of languages. Here we encounter the oldest document [*Urkunde*] of the human species, the Mosaic writings, against which so many harbor disinclination only because they do not know how to deal with it, neither to understand it nor to use it.

Genesis[d] of course sets the emergence of peoples in connection with the emergence of the various languages, but in such a way that it determines the confusion of languages as the cause, the emergence of peoples as the effect. For the intent of the story is in no way to make understandable *only* the variation of languages, as those assert who pronounce it to be a mythical philosopheme [XI 102] fabricated for this purpose. Also, it is not at all a mere fabrication; on the contrary, this story is created from actual memory, which itself is in part also preserved by other peoples, a *reminiscence*—out of mythical time to be sure, but from a real event of the same.[e] For those who immediately take for poetry every story deriving from mythical time or mythical conditions do not at all seem to consider that that time and those conditions that we are used to denoting as mythical were nonetheless *actual* ones. Thus this myth, as one can indeed, in accordance with the subject matter as well as linguistically, name the story—irrespective of the incorrect meaning just mentioned—has the value of a real tradition, whereby it moreover goes without saying that we reserve for ourselves to be able to differentiate the *matter* and the *manner* as it appears to the storyteller from *his* standpoint. For to him, for example, the emergence of peoples is a misfortune, a calamity, even a punishment. Furthermore, we must also pardon it of him that he could present an event as though completed in one day, an event whose entrance apparently was a sudden one, but whose effects, however, extended over a whole period of time.

But in just this, that the emergence of peoples in general is an event for him, namely, something that does not come to pass of itself without a particular cause—in this lies the truth of the story, as well as the contradiction to the opinion that there is no explanation needed, that peoples emerge imperceptibly through the simple duration of time and by an entirely natural process. The event is a *sudden* one to him, and, to the humanity affected by it, even an incomprehensible one—in which case then it is also no wonder that it left behind that deep, lasting impression, whose memory itself continued into historical time. To the old storyteller the emergence of the people is a *tribunal*; thus, in reality, and as *we* have called it, a crisis.

[XI 103] But as immediate cause of the separation of peoples it names the *confusion* of the *language* that was common to the whole human species and united up until that point. Already in this way the emergence is articulated through a *spiritual* process.

For a confusion of language cannot be conceived of without an *internal* process, without a tremoring *of consciousness itself*. When we arrange the processes according to their natural sequence, then the most internal is necessarily an alteration of consciousness, the next, already more external, the spontaneous confusion of the language, and the most external the cision of the human species into henceforth not merely spatial, but rather internally and spiritually self-excluding masses—that is, into peoples. In this arrangement the middle term still has a causal relation, namely that of a *proximate* cause, to the most external term, which is mere effect. The story only denotes this proximate cause as the one that is most understandable, as the one *first* presenting itself to everyone who contemplates the separating differences of the peoples, because, indeed, the difference of the languages is *at the same time* an externally perceptible one.

But also *that* affection[4] of consciousness that initially results in a confusion of language could not be a merely superficial one; it had to shake consciousness in its *principle*, in its *foundation* [*Grund*], and—if the assumed result, confusion of the heretofore *common* language, is supposed to ensue—in precisely *that* which was common up till then and held humanity together. The *spiritual power* had to become unsteady, which until then had prevented every divergently striving development, the spiritual power that had kept humanity—despite the division into tribes, which in itself constitutes a merely external difference—at the level of a complete, absolute uniformity.

It was a *spiritual* power that effected this. For the remaining united, the non-divergence, of humanity requires for its explanation as much of a positive cause as the later divergence. *Whatever* duration we give to this period of homogenous humanity is entirely indifferent to the extent that this period in which nothing happens [XI 104] has in any event only the significance of a point of departure, of a pure *terminus ad quo*, starting with which time is counted, but in which itself there is not actual time—that is, not a series of different periods. Yet we must give *some* duration to this uniform time, and this duration cannot at all be conceived of without a power resisting every development that strives asunder. When we inquire, however, *which* spiritual power was alone strong enough to keep humanity in this rigidity, then it can immediately be seen that it had to be one *principle*, and indeed only *one* principle, by which the consciousness of man was exclusively seized and dominated. For as soon as two principles divided themselves in this domination, differences had to emerge in mankind, because this mankind inevitably divided itself between the two principles. But, further, such a principle—which gave space in consciousness to no other, permitted no other except itself—can only have been an infinite one, only a *God* which *entirely* filled consciousness, which was common to all mankind, a God that, as it were, pulled them into its own unity, denied to it every movement, every divergence, whether it be to the right or left, as the Old Testament says on several occasions. Only such a God was able to give a duration to that absolute rigidity, to that standstill of all development.

Now, however, just as humanity could not have been held together and kept in a rigid equanimity more decisively than through the absolute unity of God, by which it was dominated, on the other hand there cannot be conceived a more powerful and profound shock than what had to follow as soon as the heretofore rigid unity itself became mobile, and this was unavoidable as soon as another God or several other gods come into prominence or appeared in consciousness. This polytheism [*Polytheismus*], however it occurs (for a more accurate explanation is at this point not yet possible), rendered impossible a lasting unity of the human species. Thus polytheism is the means of cision that was hurled into the homogenous humanity. Various, diverging systems of the gods—which later in the process are even mutually exclusive [XI 105]—are the unfailing tool of the separation of the peoples. Even if other causes can be conceived that were able to effect a diverging of humanity, and although according to what has been dealt with so far we have every reason to doubt their existence, what *had* to cause—irresistibly and overpoweringly—the cision of and, finally, the complete separation of peoples was the decisive polytheism and the therewith inseparable variety of systems of the gods that were no longer compatible with one another. The same God that preserved the unity in unshakable self-equality now—itself having become mutable, non-identical to itself—had to disperse the human species, just as it had previously held it together; and just as in his identity he was the cause of the unity of the human species, in his multiplicity he had to become the cause of its separation.

This determination of the *innermost* process is admittedly not articulated in the Mosaic tradition, but even as it names simply the *proximate* cause (the confusion of languages), it has also at least hinted at the distant and final cause (the emergence of polytheism). For now, only one of these hints shall be mentioned, namely, that it names *Babel* as the scene of the confusion, the place of the future great city, which for the entire Old Testament counts as the beginning and first seat of the decisive and then incessantly spreading polytheism, as the place "where," as a prophet expresses, "the golden goblet was filled that made all the world drunken, and from whose wine the *peoples* have drunken."[5f] As we will subsequently convince ourselves, wholly independent historical research likewise leads to the conclusion that the transition to actual polytheism happened in Babylon. The concept of heathendom [*Heidenthums*], that is, actually the concept of peoplehood [*Völkerthums*] (for the Hebrew and Greek word, which in German is translated as heathen [*Heiden*], does not express any more than this), is so inextricably bound up with the name of Babel that right up to the last book of the New Testament Babylon functions as the symbol of everything heathenish and what is to be viewed as heathen. Such an indelible symbolic meaning [XI 106], like the one attached to the name Babel, only emerges in that it is derived from an unprethinkable impression.

It is true that in recent times people have indeed attempted to separate the name of the great city from the significant memory that the name preserves; they have attempted to find for it a different derivation than the ancient story gives it. Babel was supposed to be *Bâb-Bel* (portal, courtyard of the Bel, *Belus-Baal*); but for nothing! Already the derivation simply contradicts itself in that in this meaning *bab* is found only in the Arabic dialect. To the contrary, it is really *just as* the ancient story says: "*For this reason* its name is called Babel: because the Lord in just that place had confused the language of the whole world." Babel is actually only a contraction of *Balbel*, a word in which there manifestly lies something onomatopoetic. Oddly enough, the sound-imitation that is effaced in the pronunciation of Babel is still preserved in the later derivation of the same word (Balbel), a derivation belonging to an entirely different and much younger language. I mean the Greek βάρβαρος, Barbar, which so far one has known only to derive from the Chaldean *bar*, outside (*extra*), *barja*, foreigner (*extraneus*). Yet with the Greeks and Romans the word Barbar does not have this general meaning but rather defines those speaking incomprehensibly, as would already be illuminated by Ovid's famous verse:

Barbarus hic ego sum, quia non intelligor ulli.[g]

In addition, with the derivation of *bar* the iteration of the syllable, in which, above all, the sound-imitation lies, is not observed, just as precisely this alone would already prove that the word is related to the *language*, as Strabo has also already noticed. Thus the Greek Barbaros is [XI 107] only formed by virtue of the well-known, so often appearing transposition of the consonants R and L, in this case in the Eastern word *balbal*, which imitates the sound of the stuttering language that throws the sounds about, and which, with the meaning of a confused speaking, is also still preserved in the Arabic and Syrian language.[h]

Now, of course, here another question naturally is forced upon us: how can the emerging polytheism be thought as cause of a linguistic confusion; which connection and interrelationship is there between a crisis of the religious consciousness and the manifestations of the capacity for language?

We could simply answer: it *just is*, whether we perceive the connection or not. The merit of an investigation does not always merely consist in solving difficult questions; the greater service is perhaps to create new problems and to identify them for a future investigation, or to gain a new aspect of already existing questions (just like that concerning the foundation and interrelation of the languages). This new aspect may initially appear only to thrust us into a still deeper uncertainty, but precisely thereby it also prevents us all the more from trusting all-too simple and superficial solutions, and can become the means to answer the *primary question* more satisfactorily than heretofore—

in that it forces us to grasp this question from a perspective which has not yet been considered. But there is not a total absence of facts that testify to such an interrelationship and connection, even if those facts are for the present just as little explicable. There is much in Herodotus that is strange: what he says of the Attic people is among the most astonishing: "[B]ecause it is actually Pelasgian it has *also learned anew the language* with its conversion into the Hellenics."[i] The transformation [XI 108] of the Pelasgian being into the Hellenic, as was already indicated earlier in these lectures on the occasion of Herodotus's famous passage, was precisely the transition from the still unarticulated mythological consciousness to the developed, mythological consciousness.—In some cases, which I leave aside, some people claim to have observed affections of the capacity for language—and, indeed, not only of the external capacity but also of the internal one—that are related to religious states. But what could the *speaking in tongues* in the Corinthian religious community—a speaking in tongues that the apostle, moreover, allows no less than unconditionally and actually treats only with indulgence, but to which for precisely that reason he testifies as fact all the more surely)—be other than the consequence of a religious affection? We are simply too little used to recognizing as of universal meaning the principles by which the spontaneous religious movements of the human consciousness are determined—principles, which for that reason can, under certain circumstances, become causes of other, even physical effects. In the meantime, let us for the moment leave the connection and interrelationship unexplained; through careful, stepwise progressing much has become comprehensible to human research. The connection and interrelationship of religious affections with affections of the capacity for language, which is being questioned, is no more puzzling than how certain peculiarities of physical constitution were also bound up with a determinate mythology or form of religion. Organized differently by the Egyptians, differently by the Indians, still differently by the Hellenes, and if one investigates it more closely, each in a certain agreement with the nature of its system of the gods.

Yet we want to recall the phenomenon parallel to the confusion of language—more in order to justify the relationship to polytheism, a relationship we attribute to the old story, than to show yet another different example of the connection and interrelationship in which religious movements are with that language. In the entire sequence of religious history only one thing can be compared to the event of the *confusion of language*: the momentarily reestablished linguistic unity (ὁμογλωσσία) at Pentecost,[6] with which Christianity, destined to again link the whole [XI 109] human species to the unity through the knowledge of the *one* true God, begins its great path.[j]

May it not appear superfluous when I add that, likewise, only *one* event in all of history corresponds to the *separation of peoples*: the *wandering of the peoples*, which however is more similar to a gathering, a bringing together again, than to a dispersion. For it could only have been a force of the kind that is reserved for the highest points of change of world history, a force of attraction equal to the repelling and separating one of earlier, which led those peoples—reserved to that end—from out of the still unexhausted storehouse and onto the stage of world history such that they took up Christianity in themselves and formed it into that which it was supposed to become and which it was able to become through *them* alone.

In any case it is apparent that to the Old Testament way of thinking the emergence of peoples, the confusion of language, and polytheism are related concepts and connected phenomena. If we look back from here to what was found earlier, then every people is *first there* as such after it has defined and decided itself in view of its mythology. Thus this mythology cannot emerge for it in the time of the *already completed* division and after it had already become a people; because, moreover, it could equally less emerge for the people as long as the latter was, in the whole of humanity, still at the point of being like an until then invisible part of it, mythology's origin will occur precisely in the *transition*, because the people does not yet exist as a determinate one but precisely at this point is ready to extrude[7] and isolate itself as such.

[XI 110] Now, however, it must also hold good of the language of every people that it initially is determined only as they determine themselves as a people. Until then, and as long as it is still in the crisis, that is, in the process of becoming, its language is also fluid, mutable, not fully withdrawn from the others, such that to an extent, actually, various languages are spoken[k] promiscuously, just as the old story assumes only a *confusion*, not immediately a complete separation of the languages from each other. From this point, where the languages are not yet separated, but rather at the point of separation, the manifestly non-Greek, pre-historical deities may be derived from among the names of the Greek ones. Herodotus, whom we may presume to have a Greek feeling for language, and who would have sounded out[l] a Greek etymology—for example, from the name Poseidon—just as well as a grammatician of our time, says that almost all the *names* of the Gods have come to the Greeks from the barbarians, by which it is obviously not said that the *gods themselves* also came to them from barbarians, and also not exactly before the barbarians. From this point also are indeed explained individual material agreements between languages, which are otherwise formed according to wholly different principles. In comparisons of languages the following gradation generally takes place: some are only dialects of the same language, like the Arabic and Hebrew languages—here there is unity of tribe. Others belong to the same formation, like Sanskrit, Greek, Latin, German; still others neither to the same tribe [XI 111] nor the same formation, and yet there are agreements between the various languages, which are explained neither by historical relations—like Arabic words in Spanish and French[m]—nor from this—that the languages belong to the same tribe or to the same level of development (formation). The appearance of Semitic words in Sanskrit, in Greek, and, as it seems, also in old Egyptian, provides examples of this type; these are thus agreements that transcend all history. No language emerges for an already completed and present people; thus also its language does not emerge for a people outside of all connection and interrelation with the original linguistic unity, which still seeks to maintain itself even in the cision.

In spite of the great distance, as far as it is still perceivable through the mists of antiquity, the appearances and the conduct of the peoples points toward a unity whose power consists precisely in division.

Not an *external* impulse, but rather the impulse of inner agitation, the feeling not to be the entire humanity, but rather only a part of it; and no longer to belong to the *ultimate* One, but rather to have fallen prey to a particular god or particular gods: it is this feeling that drove them from land to land, from coast to coast, until each saw itself alone and separated from all the foreign peoples and had found the place proper and destined for *them*.[n] Or is mere contingency supposed to have governed in this also? Was it contingency that led the oldest Egyptian population—who announced through their dark skin simply the mysterious disposition of their own inner selves—into the narrow Nile valley[o]; or was it the feeling of only being able in such isolation to preserve [XI 112] what it was supposed to preserve in itself? For even after the dispersion the fear did not leave them; they felt the destruction of the original unity, a destruction that made room for a confusing multiplicity, and that seemed unable to end other than with the loss of all consciousness of unity and thus of everything human.

For this extreme condition too the evidence is preserved for us—just as monuments are certainly still preserved for everything that by itself knows or requires true and lawfully proceeding science, without consideration for the injuries of time. This is, as I have expressed often enough, the belief of the true researcher, which is not to be shamed. Here I again draw attention to that often mentioned, dispersed, and still only externally human population of South America. To see in them examples of the *first* condition, and, as one presumes, the one coarsest and most closely approximating animality, is entirely impossible; on the contrary, they refute most definitively the illusion of such a stupid primordial condition of the human species, in that they indicate that from out of such a condition no progress is possible. I feel myself just as little in the position to apply to these races [*Geschlechter*] the example of the former formation of peoples that have reverted into barbarism. The condition in which they find themselves is not a problem for minds that merely help themselves on with already used thoughts; the thorough thinker knew, until now, no place for them. If one cannot presuppose peoples as emerging from themselves, if one must recognize it as necessary to explain peoples, then also those masses who, although physically homogenous, amongst themselves have yet remained without any moral and spiritual unity. They seem to me to be only the tragic result of precisely that crisis from out of which the rest of mankind had saved the *ground* of all human consciousness, while this ground was fully lost for them. They are the still living testimony of the completed, utterly unrestrained dissolution; the entire curse of the dispersion has been realized in them—actually they are, properly, the flock that grazes without shepherd; and, without becoming a people, they were annihilated [XI 113] in just the crisis that gave the peoples determinate being. If there actually are—as I assume, independent of witnesses on whose trustworthiness I would not like to rely—some traces of culture in them, or, rather, some faint remainders of customs meaninglessly carried on, then those do not prove either that they are debris of a people destroyed and broken up through historical or natural catastrophes. For the pre-historical condition (in which they also had a part), that is, the condition preceding the emergence of peoples—this is, as arises sufficiently from our explanations, nothing less than a condition of complete un-culture and animal coarseness, from which a transition to social development would never have been possible. For at the least we have legitimately asserted the tribal division for that condition; however, where this is there are also already relations similar to marriage and family. Even tribes that have not yet become a people are familiar at least with movable property, and, insofar as property, undoubtedly contracts as well. But no possible political decay is able to reduce a whole—which was once a people and had the commensurate morals, laws, social institutions, and what is inevitably bound up with these, peculiar religious ideas and customs—to such a state of absolute lawlessness, and to such dehumanization (brutality), as is that in which those races are found that are without respect for any law, and any society, or any obligatory regulations, as well as without any religious ideas. Physical events can destroy a people materially but cannot rob it of its traditions, its memories, its whole past—as is the case with this type of human, which has as little a past as any species of animal. However, the condition of these people is indeed understood if they are the part of the original humanity in which all consciousness of unity has really perished. I have already remarked that the peoples are not to be explained through a mere diverging, that there is at the same time required a cohesive force: we see in them what the whole of humanity would have become, if it had saved nothing of the original unity.

[XI 114] Another consideration also attributes this position to them. These races [*Geschlechter*] in particular testify to the truth that lies in the old story of the confusion of the *languages*. The expression *confusion* has already been emphasized. Confusion only emerges where dissonant elements that cannot attain to unity are just as little able to diverge. In every language that is becoming, the original unity continues to be in force, as precisely the affinity of languages in part shows; the loss of all unity would be the loss of language itself, and with that of everything human. For man is only man to the extent that he is capable of a general consciousness transcending his own singularity; language too only has meaning as something communal. The languages of preeminently human and spiritually cohesive peoples spread and extend over great spaces, and there are only a few such languages. Thus, here a commonality of consciousness is still preserved in great masses. Moreover, these languages still preserve in themselves references to others, traces of an original unity, ciphers of common descent. I doubt any material agreement between the idioms of this American population and the languages of peoples proper, just as I must leave undecided to what extent the study that has been devoted to these idioms was able to fulfill the hope in which it was undertaken, namely, to arrive at real, namely *genetic* elements of them. It will have arrived at the last elements in them, but at elements of decay, not of composition and becoming. According to *Azara*, among these populations the Guarani language is still the only one that is understood in a broader sphere, and perhaps even this still requires closer investigation. For otherwise, as the same Azara remarks—and he did not pass through those lands, he lived and spent many years in them—otherwise the language changes from horde to horde, even from hut to hut, such that often only the members of the same family understand each other; and not merely this, but rather the capacity for language itself seems with them to be near termination and extinction. Their voice is never strong and sonorous; they only speak softly [XI 115], without ever crying out, even when one kills them. In speaking they hardly move the lips and do not accompany their speech with a look that demands attentiveness. Such a *disinclination* for speaking accompanies this indifference, that when they have business with someone who is a hundred paces before them, they never call, but rather run to fetch them. Thus, here language hovers at the final frontier, beyond which it ceases entirely, such that one may indeed ask if idioms whose sounds are mostly nasal and gargle tones, not chest and lip tones, and for the most part are not expressible through signs of our written language, deserve at all to be called language.[p]

Thus *this* fear, this horror before the loss of all consciousness of unity, held together those who remained united and drove them to maintain at least a partial unity, in order to persist, if not as humanity, then at least as a people. This fear before the total disappearance of the unity, and therewith of all truly human consciousness, provided them not only with the first institutions of a religious type but even the first civil institutions, whose goal was no other than to preserve what they had saved of the unity and to secure against further disintegration. Because, once the unity was lost, the individual ones also sought to isolate themselves and to insure their own possessions, they strained every nerve to hold tight the fleeing unity through (1) the formation of special communities, especially the strict separation of those in which the communal, the consciousness of unity, was supposed to continue living: the division of castes, whose foundation is as old as history and common to all peoples, whose constitution that is known to us stems from this time and that had no other intention than, in such isolation, to guard more securely that consciousness and mediately to preserve it for those others, in whom it unavoidably was lost more and more; (2) [XI 116] through strict priestly ordinances, codification of knowledge as *doctrine*, as appears to happen particularly in Egypt[q]: but externally they sought to hold themselves together (3) through those monuments manifestly belonging to a pre-historical time, monuments that are found in all parts of the known earth, and, through size and assembling, furnish proof of almost super-human power, and through which we are necessarily reminded of that portentous tower—which the oldest story mentions where the topic is the dispersion of the peoples. The builders say to each other: let us build a city and a tower, whose summit reaches to the heavens, that we may make a name for ourselves, *for we might perhaps be scattered across the whole earth*. They say this *before* language is confused; they intimate that which stands before them, the crisis which is announced to them.

They want to make a *name* for themselves, conventionally, make themselves famous. Only the mass speaking here cannot yet, as one can indeed translate it according to the linguistic usage, think of becoming famous before it has a name; that is, before it is a people, as also no man—as one normally says—could *make* a name *for himself* if he did not have one before. Thus, according to the nature of the matter, here the expression must be taken in its still immediate meaning, of which the other (becoming famous) is mere consequence. —Thus, according to their own words, they were up till then a nameless humanity. It is the name that differentiates and separates a people, just as an individual, from the others, but for just this reason at the same time holds them together. Accordingly, the words "that we make a name for ourselves" mean nothing other than "that we become a people,"[r] and as the reason for this they offer: so that they are not scattered into all lands. Thus, the *fear* of being dispersed, of no longer being a whole at all [XI 117], of rather being fully disbanded, motivates it to the undertaking. Stable residence is first considered when humanity is in danger of losing itself entirely and of disintegrating, but with the first stable abodes the separation begins, thus also the repulsion and exclusion, like the tower of Babel, which is supposed to prevent the entire dispersion, becomes the beginning and occasion of the separation of the peoples. Thus also those monuments of a pre-historic time belong to the time of just this transition, especially those so-called works purported by the Greeks to be Cyclopean, in Greece, on Mediterranean islands, and here and there even the Italian mainland; works Homer and Hesiod already saw,[s] walls and battlements, sometimes completed without cement from unhewn stones, sometimes assembled from irregular polygons, monuments of a race that had become mythic [*fabelhaft*] even for the late Greeks, a race that left behind no other traces of their existence, but is yet more of truly historic meaning than one thinks normally. For considering how Homer describes the life of the Cyclopes in the *Odyssey*, how they—each with wife and child—live without law and congress of the peoples, live for themselves and *have regard for none of the others*,[t] we must judge that a beginning toward those fully disbanded races is already in them, races that distinguish themselves precisely in that none show consideration for the others, in that they remain as foreign amongst themselves as animals do and are not bound through any consciousness to any sort of solidarity. In the modern world, this condition represented in Homer by the Cyclops is preserved, while the same race in Greece remains absorbed by the ever more powerfully pressing movement, and remains only in memory for the people that emerged in this way. In Homer they still live in natural but, as it appears, artificially expanded grottos [XI 118], just as the later legend also ascribed to them the underground structures, the grottos and labyrinths of Megara and Nauplia (*Napoli di Malvasia*), among others.[8] But this same race proceeds from these structures realized in the substance of the earth to those monuments raising themselves above the earth, which are executed with material independent and free of the earth. But with these monuments it immediately and at the same time disappears; for to these works is tied the transition to peoples, in which that transitional race [*Geschlecht*] passes away.

Lecture Six

[XI 119] According to the development advanced, of which one moreover easily sees that some more precise determinations are to be expected from further inquiry, it appears that one is no longer able to doubt that it will be this explanation with which we must remain, an explanation that presupposes a monotheism—not in general, but a historical one—to polytheism, namely, in the time before the separation of peoples. The only question that was in doubt between this explanation and ours—that is, if the separation of the peoples was prior to and had polytheism as the consequence, or vice-versa—is, we must judge, likewise settled. For from this we believe to have sufficiently convinced ourselves, through the preceding, that there is to be found no cause of the emergence of the peoples independent of polytheism, and the consequent conclusion, resulting from the development to this point, we consider the ground, on which we continue to advance:

If humanity separated into peoples, just as soon as various gods appeared in the previously unified consciousness, then the unity of the human species, which preceded the separation, a unity of human species that we can likewise just as little think without a positive cause, could have been preserved through nothing so decisively as *through the consciousness of* **One** *universal God common to all humanity.*

However, in this conclusion there is contained no decision at all about whether God (the universal God, the God common to the entire human species), because he was universal and common, also was necessarily the *One* in the sense of monotheism and indeed in the sense of a revealed monotheism [XI 120], that is, whether as such he had to be an *ultimately non-mythological* God, a God excluding from himself everything mythological.

To be sure, one will ask what this God, common to all humanity, could have been other than the truly One God and a still fully non-mythological God. And, now, the answer to this question is actually the main point: through it we hope to gain a basis on which can be built categorical conclusions, and no longer merely hypothetical ones, about the origin of mythology.

However, I will not be able to respond to this question without pressing more deeply into the nature of polytheism—which only with the religious explanation has become the main question for us—than has happened so far and until now indeed has not been necessary.

Here, then, we want to draw attention to a difference in polytheism itself, a difference that was passed over in all the explanations that have come forth up to now, a difference of which we took precisely for this reason no consideration but that *now must* be addressed.

Indeed, it can escape no one to whom it is pointed out that there is a great difference between the polytheism that emerges when indeed a greater or lesser number of gods is conceived, which are however *subordinated* to *one and the same god* as their highest and master, and that polytheism that emerges when *several* gods are assumed, but each of them is the *highest* and *dominating* in a certain time and for this reason can only *follow* one another. If we think to ourselves, say, that the Greek history of the gods had, instead of the *three* races of gods—which it has follow one upon the other—only one, say that of Zeus, then it would also only know of gods (all of which would be resolved into Zeus, as their common unity) coexisting and simultaneous with each other, it would know only of *simultaneous* polytheism. Now, however, it has *three* systems of gods, and in each one One god is the highest: in the first, Uranus; in the second, Kronos; in the third, Zeus. Thus, these three gods cannot be simultaneous ones but rather only *mutually excluding*, and for this reason ones *following one upon the other in time*. [XI 121] So long as Uranus dominates, Kronos cannot; and should Zeus attain dominance, Kronos must recede into the past. Thus we will name this polytheism the *successive* polytheism [*successiven Polytheismus*].

Now, however, the following is to be seen immediately. Only through the second type is the unity of God decisively raised—or, to express it entirely clearly, the singularity of God. Successive polytheism alone is the true one, the first *authentic* and *actual* one. For as far as the gods are concerned that are subjected in common to a highest [god], they are, if you will, indeed contemporaneous with this one, but not for this reason the same: they are *in* him, *he is external* to them; *he* is the god that comprehends them but is not comprehended by them; he does not rank among them and is, even if only considered as their emanative cause, prior to them, at least by *nature* and *essence*. The multiplicity of the others does not have an effect on *him*; he is always the *One*, *knowing not his equal*; for his difference from them is not a difference of mere individuality, like that between themselves, but rather a difference of an entire genus (*differentia totius generis*). Here there is no *real* polytheism [*Polytheismus*], for everything ultimately dissolves itself into unity again, or only perhaps a polytheism in such a way as the Jewish theology likewise names the angels Elohim (gods) without fearing that the singularity of God, of whom they are mere servants and tools, is thereby offended. Here, indeed, there is a *multiplicity of gods* [*Göttervielheit*]; but no *successive polytheism* [*Vielgötterei*].[1] The latter only emerges when *multiple highest*, and to this extent equal, gods follow one upon the other, which are unable to dissolve themselves again into a higher unity. Thus we must precisely keep in mind this difference between a multiplicity of gods and successive polytheism, in order, moreover, to transition now to the matter which is really at stake.

For *you* grasp at once and without reminding that both of these types of polytheism have a very different relation to every *explanation*. If one asks *which* of the two primarily demands explanation, then it is obviously the successive: *that one* is the puzzle, here lies the question, but for precisely this reason the explanation also. Certainly the simultaneous one is very easily and simply grasped through the simple diverging [XI 122] of an original unity; the successive is not as easily graspable in the same way, and at least hardly without artificial and forced corollary assumptions.

The successive polytheism also initially comes into consideration for the reason that it extends over and beyond every simultaneous one, and thus in the whole includes the simultaneous, while it [the successive] is itself what concretely exists freely and absolutely.

Now, we want to admit to ourselves straightforwardly that through everything that has come forth up to now, in this entire discussion, not the least has occurred for the explanation of *successive* polytheism [*succesiven Polytheismus*], and we are, as it were, in the position of beginning totally from the beginning when we ask: how is *successive polytheism* [*Vielgötterei*] to be understood?

But as soon as we merely take up the investigation it becomes clear to us that with this question we rest on an entirely different basis and sphere, that of reality, and that we approach a truth before which all mere hypotheses must disappear like fog before the sun.

According to the Greek theogony (at least it explains it in this way) there was thus once a time where Uranus alone ruled supreme. Now, is this supposed to be a mere *legend*, also something purely contrived and invented? Was there not perhaps actually a time where only the Lord of the Heavens was venerated, where they did not know of another, of Zeus, or even of Kronos, and is not in this way the completed history of the gods at the same time the historical record of its own emergence? In light of this record, will we still find believable that mythology has come into being all at once through the invention of a single person, or a few individuals, or (the other hypothesis) that it has emerged through the mere divergence of a unity— out of which, at best, could only emerge a simultaneous polytheism, a mere static juxtaposition, and in the final result only a distasteful exclusivity, not the living sequentiality of dynamic and multitoned (because richly segmented) mythology?

If we judge correctly, then the successive in mythology is just that in which lies that which is actual, what is actually historical, and thus also that which is real in it [XI 123], the truth of it in general; with this we find ourselves *on the historical ground*, at the basis of the actual course of events.

When one compares the mythologies of various peoples, it becomes fully incontestable that it is the actual history of its emergence that mythology has preserved in the sequentiality of its gods.[2] Here it is evident that the doctrines of the gods that have appeared only as *past* ones in the mythologies of the later peoples were the *actual* and contemporary ones of the earlier peoples; just as, vice-versa, the reigning gods of the earlier peoples are taken up in the mythologies of the later peoples only as moments of the past. Only thus is the oft-mentioned agreement correctly apprehended and explained. In the highest ranking, or we would more correctly say, in the exclusively reigning, god of the Phoenicians[3] the Greeks recognize with the most definite certainty the Kronos of their own history of the gods and name him thus also; it is easy to show the differences between the Phoenician and Greek god in order to thereby prove that the Phoenician god stands in no relation (affinity) with the Greek god, but all these differences are fully explained through the one difference that in Phoenician mythology Kronos is still the sole reigning god, whereas in Greek mythology he is displaced and already superseded by a later god, that Kronos in Phoenician mythology is the present god, but in Greek mythology only the past god. But how were the Greeks able to recognize *their* god in the Phoenician god, if they were not themselves conscious of their Kronos as from an actual past, not merely an imagined and fictitious past?

What unnatural explanations would have emerged had the earlier hypotheses not been satisfied to explain only polytheism [*Polytheismus*] *in general*, instead of primarily and first off the *historical* polytheism. Such a sequence of the gods *cannot* be merely imagined, and it cannot be invented; whoever *fashions* a god for himself or others at least makes a present one for himself and others. It violates nature that something be immediately posited as past; it can only *become* what is past [XI 124]; thus it must have initially been present. Whatever I am supposed to perceive as what is past, I must first have perceived as something present. What never had reality for us can never become for us a stage, a moment; the earlier god, however, must be really held firmly as a stage, a *moment*; otherwise no successive polytheism could emerge. At one time it must have dominated and even entirely captured consciousness; and when it has disappeared, it could not have disappeared without resistance and struggle, for otherwise it would not have been *retained*.

Even if we—in order to test the limit—presumed that an ancient philosopher explaining the world had made the observation that the world, as it is, is not explicable through a single cause, and could not have emerged without a certain sequencing of effective powers or potencies, in which the one as it were was taken as the basis of the other, and he accordingly had taken up into his cosmogony also a corresponding series of such causes that he imagines as personalities: then, whatever success we might otherwise attribute to his invention, that religious awe and reverence for gods merely *thought and imagined* as past would never have come into being—a religious awe and respect with which we find Kronos surrounded not only in Greek mythology but rather even in Greek poetry and art. These religious shudderings for an otherwise now impotent god are no mere poetic lie; they are ones actually felt and also for this reason alone something truly poetic. However, these shudderings could only have been felt if there remained for consciousness a memory of the god; if, in the course of constant and unbroken transmission from lineage to lineage there was also still impressed in it that this god had once actually reigned supreme—even if in an unthinkable prior time.

Certainly, mythology has no reality [*Realität*] *outside* of consciousness; but if it only takes its course in the determinations of consciousness, that is, in its representations, then nonetheless this *course of events, this succession of representations themselves* cannot again be such a one that is merely *imagined*; it must have *actually* taken place, must have actually occurred in consciousness [XI 125]. This succession is not fashioned by mythology, but rather—contrariwise—mythology is fashioned by it. For mythology is just precisely the whole of those doctrines of the gods that have actually succeeded each other, and thus it has come into being through this succession.

Precisely because the gods exist merely in representations the successive polytheism can only become real in that first a god is posited in consciousness, a god that is replaced by another one, which does not totally efface the first one (because consciousness would also cease to know of it) but that at least deposes it from the present back to the past as well as from the Godhead—not from the Godhead in general, but indeed from the exclusive one. Precisely herewith is the *pure fact* expressed—which one hears boasted of so often but seldom actually finds: the fact is not conjectured; it is present in the successive polytheism itself. We are not explaining *why* that first god is such a one that another follows it, nor according to which law this one follows it; all this remains to be seen. What simply is being advanced as fact is that it was such that mythology—as it itself indicates—has emerged *in this way*: not through invention, not through a divergence, but rather through a sequence that actually took place in consciousness.

Mythology is not merely a doctrine of the gods *imagined* as *successive*. A struggle between the gods succeeding each other, as happens in the *Theogony*, would not at all exist among the mythological representations if it had not *actually* taken place in the consciousness of *peoples* who know of it, and to that extent in the consciousness of humanity, of which every people is a part. Successive polytheism is only explicable if one assumes that the consciousness of humanity has *actually tarried*, by turn, in all of the moments of successive polytheism. The gods following one upon the other have actually successively taken possession of consciousness. Mythology as history of the gods, thus the actual mythology, was only able to be produced in life itself; it *had to* be something *lived* and *experienced*.

[XI 126] As I express these last words it redounds to my joy to notice that the same expressions have also been used by *Creuzer* in relation to mythology, at least in one of his incidental remarks. Apparently the natural impression has here gained victory over a preconceived assumption, and if we in part contradict the insightful man with respect to the formality of his explanation, we only bring to bear against him what he himself expressed in the most correct and truest feeling.

No one can fail to recognize that a succession of ideas, through which consciousness has actually passed, is the only natural explanation of mythological polytheism [*Polytheismus*].

Now, if with this insight we go back to the main question—on whose account this entire last discussion has taken place—to the question that demands to know if that God common to the entire human species had to be necessarily the *unconditioned One*, and for this reason the entirely unmythological One, then *you* see from yourselves that this is not a necessary result, and the effect—as far as both the holding together and the later separation are concerned—is, at the least, also entirely reached likewise even if this God is also just the first *element of a succession* of the gods—that is, of a successive polytheism, only an element not yet *as* such explained and perceived. If *you* think to yourself this God = A initially appearing in consciousness, then consciousness does not have a presentiment that a second = B awaits it, which will initially place itself beside—but then quickly above—the first. This one thus is up to now not only in general the One, but rather is so *in a sense* in which there can again be no follower. For to God B, God A has already preceded it in consciousness, and to God C (for it is assumed as cause that the second, which drives out the first, only makes way for a third), that is, to the third one, when it announces itself, A and B have already preceded it in consciousness. But God A is the one *before* which there was no other, and after which—that is how consciousness represents it to itself—none other will be; thus he is to consciousness not the merely contingent, but rather in fact the *ultimate and the unconditioned*[4] One. Yet, there is still no successive polytheism [XI 127] in the now defined meaning of the word. For this reason, if one understands under monotheism only the opposite of successive polytheism, then monotheism is still actually in consciousness. But it is easy to perceive that this [monotheism] is indeed an absolute one for the humanity included in it, but in itself and for us is merely a *relative* one. For the absolute [*absolut*] One God is the one that also does not admit the *possibility* of other gods outside itself, but the merely relative singular One is that one that only actually has no other before, next to, or after it. What Hermann insightfully noticed is here wholly applicable: a doctrine that merely contingently knows only *One* God, is, *accordingly*, true polytheism [*Polytheismus*] because it does not eliminate the possibility of other gods and only knows of *one* for the reason that it has not yet heard of others—or as we would initially say, has not yet heard of another.[a]—Thus we will say of our God A: he is for humanity, as long as it does not know of a second, a completely unmythological one—as in every series whose elements we designate A, B, C A is first a *member* of the series when B actually follows it. A mythological god is one that is a member of a history of gods; the assumed god is not yet actually such a member but is not for that reason an unmythological one by his nature, although he can appear as such as long as the other has not announced himself, the other who will depose him from his absoluteness [*Absolutheit*].

Even if we think of a system [*System*] of gods posited with the first god—but *subordinated* to him—then indeed thereby a multiplicity of gods, but never a successive polytheism, would be posited; and the gods of this system too could still be common to all of humanity. For they are not yet gods of *various types*—as, for example, the gods Uranus, Kronos, and Zeus are various in the Greek theogony: they are by all means gods *of one and the same type*. Every element that has nothing outside itself by which it is determined remains always and necessarily equal to itself. If the dominating god does not change himself then those subordinated [XI 128] to him are also unable to change, and because they remain constantly the same they also cannot be different and variegated for the various peoples, thus not cease to be common to all.

Now, that which has been presented up to now is already sufficient to prove that, in order to explain both the original unity and the consequent divergence of humanity, an absolute monotheism, a God that is the ultimate One—outside which none other can be—is at least not *necessary*; because, however, since only one of the two presuppositions can be the true one, it is impossible to stay with this result. We must decide between the two and therefore investigate if relative monotheism could perhaps even explain both (the unity and the divergence) better than absolute monotheism, or perhaps even alone *truly* explains it. Therewith we once again see ourselves led back to the genesis of peoples. The distinction, just found, of an absolute and relative monotheism—which, however, can for a certain time appear as absolute—indicates to us that an indeterminacy still lay in the first development; for in an investigation such as this one, one can in general only proceed in steps and always articulate everything only to the extent that it presents itself in this part of the development. This whole set of lectures is one constantly growing and progressing uniformly and in all its parts—the knowledge at which it aims not to be regarded as complete before the last stroke accomplished.

When the question,"How do peoples emerge into being?" initially spread from my lecture hall out into wider circles, it in part found a reception that clearly showed how new and unexpected it is to many; and since then I have had even more opportunities to see how little up to that point had been thought about the first elements of a *philosophical* ethnology, which presupposes a general ethno*gony*.[5] It was really just as I said in the last lecture: the explanation seemed superfluous to most; according to them, no particular cause is required, as peoples emerge into being *of themselves*. If with respect to the present standpoint—according to which the separation of peoples is perceived as a spiritual crisis—a thought is still bound up with this emergence-from-itself, then one would have to assume that the spiritual differences [XI 129], which became manifest afterward in virtue of the varieties of the peoples and the deviating systems of the gods, lay hidden and without effect in the original humanity, and only with the increasingly branching generations have they supposedly attained expression and development. Thus, the common lineage's ever-increasing distance from the middle point would be assumed and accepted here as the sole determining ground. If a certain point of this distance is reached, then those differences take effect. In this way, then, peoples indeed emerge into being through *mere time*. However, can there then still be talk of any sort of lawfulness? Or who dares to say in which generation—that is, at what point of distance from the common ancestor—the differences would have reached the strength necessary to separate the peoples. However, so that mere contingency does not govern over such a great event, so that the development takes place in an ordering comprehensible to the understanding, happens *non sine numine*, the duration that we must ascribe to the time of the complete homogeneity of the human species cannot be something merely contingent; it must be, as it were, secured by a *principle*, by a power that stays and restrains the higher developments that await humanity and subsequently will introduce within it differences other than those merely *natural*. Once in use, it is inadmissible to say of this power that it would lose its strength through the mere span of time: if it does lose this strength, then it requires for that *another*, an actual, second principle—one independent of it—that at first disturbs it and finally prevails over it entirely. The emergence of peoples is not something that of itself brings about a tranquil succession out of previously existing conditions; it is something through which an earlier order of things is interrupted and an entirely new one instituted. The transition from that homogenous concrete being to that which is higher and more developed—where peoples already exist, that is, the whole of spiritual differences—fashions itself of itself just as little as, *for example*, the transition from the inorganic to organic nature, with which that transition is indeed comparable. For if in the realm [XI 130] of the inorganic all bodies still repose in common heaviness, and even warmth, electricity, and everything similar is still *common* to them, then along with the organic beings emerge self-sufficient central points, entities existing *for themselves*, which possess all of this as their own and employ the heaviness itself—which they have received in their power—as free force of movement.

Accordingly, the principle that preserved humanity in its unity *could* not be an absolute one; it had to be one that another was able to follow and by which it was moved, transformed, ultimately even conquered.

Now, however, as soon as this second principle begins to manifest its effect on humanity, all the differences—differences possible by virtue of that condition in humanity, differences of which no trace was previously present—will, as with one blow, to be sure, be posited, but some as more nearly possible and others as more distantly possible. The reason for these differences lies initially in the fact that the heretofore immutable God [A], as soon as he is required to accept determinations from a second, cannot remain the same, and in the unavoidable conflict with this second God cannot avoid proceeding from figure to figure, cannot avoid taking on first one and then the other, according to the extent that the second God [B] gets power over it. It is indeed possible that even those gods of the Greek theogony, which we considered till now as an example of gods following one upon the other (Uranus, Kronos, Zeus), are only such various successively assumed forms of the *one* or of the first God, and that the second God—which compels him to proceed through these forms—is one standing entirely external to these forms, a God whose name has not yet been identified. But once the first form of God is posited, then those following are likewise posited—albeit as more distant possibilities. To the various forms of the God correspond equally various, materially differing systems of the gods, which likewise are all already potentially present with the appearance of the second principle, although they cannot all actually appear at the same time, but rather only to the degree that the God caught in continual overcoming, the God still holding humanity to himself [XI 131], submits to or allows. The various peoples correspond to the various systems of the gods; thus these peoples are also already potentially present with the occurrence of the second cause, even if they do not all enter into reality at once, but rather only in measured succession. Through that which is successive in polytheism the peoples are, at the same time, with regard to their appearance, their entrance into history, kept apart. Until the moment has come, the moment which it is supposed to represent, every people remains in a potential state as a part of the still undifferentiated [*unentschiedenen*] humanity, although a humanity destined for dissolution into peoples—like we have seen that the Pelasgians, before they became the Hellenes, remained in such an undifferentiated state. Because, however, the crisis that is the effect of the second cause is a universal one stretching out over all humanity, the people reserved for a later time and a later differentiation [*Entscheidung*] also passes through all moments, indeed not as an actual people, but as part of the still undifferentiated humanity. Only in this way is it possible that the moments distributed among various peoples unite themselves to form the completed mythology in the consciousness of the last people.

You see: the course of events of the genesis of both the different systems of the gods and the peoples paralleling them gains through this view of a movement proceeding from relative monotheism an entirely different and more determinate form than would be attainable through the mere divergence of an originary monotheism. See for yourself that our investigation is moving forward; we are no longer merely understanding peoples in general, like before, but rather also their successive appearance. However, we shall still need to take into consideration a possible objection. One could say: the differences or differentiating characteristics, which we first assume with the peoples, are already present in the tribes. For, if one keeps to the anciently derived division of Noah's three sons, Shem, Ham, and Japheth, a division that preserves itself still—then, for example, the Semites differentiate themselves from the Japhethites in that in the main they remained nearer to the primordial religion, but the Japhethites have distanced themselves further from it. Perhaps this already rests in the names [XI 132], very probably at least in that of the Japhethites, which perhaps presages as much the highest extension or unfolding of polytheism as the broadest geographical expansion.[6] This difference, which one would have to consider as one already given with the tribal diversity, would contradict the assumed complete homogeneity of the human species. To this it is to be answered: first, there had to be given in general the *possibility* of distancing itself from the primordial religion before that difference could somehow be present. This possibility only first *emerged* with the appearance of the second principle; *prior* to this appearance the assumed difference is not even in the position to express itself, and if one calls *possible* that which can express itself, then not even possible. The tribes only *receive* this *spiritual* meaning through the result, and, we have to say, in contradiction with the usual assumption: the tribes themselves are only first there with this meaning when the peoples are there; indeed, if the alleged meaning of the names is right, then the tribes only first received these names after they had become peoples.

Thus only relative monotheism explains the emergence of the peoples not merely in general, but rather—as we now have seen—also in their particular circumstances, namely, the succession in the appearance of the peoples. But something still remains, of which we had to admit earlier that it cannot be fully explained with the concepts attained at that time: namely, the emergence of various languages inseparably coupled with the emergence of the peoples—the confusion of the languages as consequence of a religious crisis. Now, should this connection and interrelationship, which appeared to us a problem still indefinitely far away from its solution, not also be at least somewhat more nearly moved to full understanding by means of the insight now acquired?

If there was a time in which, as the Old Testament states, the whole world had only one kind of tongue and language—and we realize as little how we are supposed to refrain from this assumption as from the other, that there was a time where there were no peoples—then we will also be able to grasp such a rigidity of language in no other way than [XI 133] that we think to ourselves that language was in that time dominated by *one* principle, which, *itself* rigid, held every alteration at a distance from *it* [*language*], thus held it firmly in the level of a *substantiality*,[7] as the first God A is pure substance [*Substanz*] and is first necessitated to assume accidental determinations through the second [God] B. Now, if it was a *principle*, and indisputably a spiritual one, through which language was held back on this level, then it is already in itself more easily understood how there was and even had to be a connection and interrelationship between this principle of language and the religious principle, the principle that in that time held and dominated not one part of consciousness but rather the whole. For the language could only resemble the God by which consciousness was filled. Now, however, a new principle comes about, by which that first—also as *what defines language*—is affected, transformed, ultimately made unrecognizable, and forced back into the depths. Now, if the language is determined by the two principles, not merely material variations of the language—variations that press forth in multitudes—are unavoidable, but rather, according as the effect of the second, transforming principle penetrates more deeply or superficially, thus as the language more or less loses its substantial character, there appear languages that are no longer merely *materially* mutually exclusive, but also *formally* mutually exclusive vis-à-vis the principles.

This much can be seen, without having brought into closer consideration the actual fundamental variations of language.

Now, however, I ask *you* to include the following. If our presuppositions are grounded, then humanity will proceed from relative monotheism or from having one God [*Eingötterei*] (here that word, completely inadmissible otherwise and as it was employed before, is fully appropriate), via having two gods [*Zweigötterei*] (di-theism), to the decisive successive polytheism (*successivem Polytheismus*). But the same progression is in the principles of the languages, which proceed from original monosyllabism, via di-syllabism, to an entirely unfettered polysyllabism.

Monosyllabism preserves the word in its pure substance, and there, where monosyllabsim itself appears as principle, we will be unable to refrain from presupposing an arresting principle [XI 134] refusing all contingent determinations. Yet—we hear the objection that there is no properly monosyllabic language. It is true: we know of only one linguistic system in which monosyllabism governs, Chinese, and the man (Abel Remusat[b]) who up till recently counted as the greatest expert of Chinese language and literature believed that he had to dispute the monosyllabic character in Chinese.[8] For all that, if we look more closely, then the scholarly man was moved to this, above all, only through the opinion that with that assumption a spot of barbarism would be attached to the people and the language to the knowledge of which he has contributed so much. Now, regarding this we feel confident to fully set him at ease; it is not our opinion that the condition in which consciousness was dominated only by *one* principle was a condition of barbarism; and whatever concerns the instances he adduced out of the language itself, he might require for himself perhaps only this appeasement, in order to become doubtful of their power of proof. The main point may be contained in the following: the designation unisyllabic supposedly has no meaning, for if one understands by this the *root, then all the world's languages are unisyllabic*; however, if one understands the words, then the languages that are usually considered unisyllabic are this no *more* than all the others, for the words in these are nothing other than an aggregate of syllables that only appear separate because in them there is involved the nature of the written sign. Now here is precisely false that which was mentioned first: that the roots of all languages in the world are unisyllabic. For the di-syllabism of the

Semitic roots[9] is nothing contingent; it is the principle proper to it, a principle with which an earlier barrier is broken through and a new development begins. True, in order not to be diverted from the comfortable path, where every explanation from *principles* is avoided and everything is derived as much as possible from contingencies, people have recently again (for the attempt is very old[c]) sought to trace the Semitic languages back to unisyllabic roots [XI 135], by asserting that many Hebrew verbs,[10] which agree only in two and at times only in one root [*Radikal*], nonetheless remain related according to their meaning; supposedly, the third consonant is in the main only an accretion, and this expansion of the word, they say, mostly shows only an expansion of the original meaning of the unisyllabic word. Thus, in Hebrew, *cham* (properly, chamam) means being warm, becoming warm, therefore, afterward *chamar*, being red, because red is a consequence of heat buildup. Thus *chamar* would not properly be a root, but rather *cham* (which, however, only appears unisyllabic in the pronunciation). But precisely this mentioned fact, if it could be fully confirmed, would, on the contrary, serve as proof that the monosyllabism was an actual *principle*, and therefore the Semitic languages were those that had to overcome it and for this reason alone still preserve what was overcome as a trace or as a moment. Now, however, for the Japhethite languages—thus, for example, the German language, Sanskrit, Greek, and so on—one should think that this principle already overcome in the Semitic languages could no longer have had any power or meaning. In contrast to this is the newest view, that precisely their roots are decisively monosyllabic, after which only a step is needed in order to declare the Semitic linguistic line, as it now is (with its di-syllabic roots), as younger, and Sanskrit as older, more authentic, more originary. Already earlier I have articulated in general my opinion about this reversal of every reasonable order; we do not intend here to dwell on the observation of how difficult it seems to uncover the roots in German and especially in Greek words—of which, when one robs them of their accidental (grammatical) determinations often only one *vowel* remains—while one, on the other hand, does not know how matters are to be handled with words that manifestly refer back to di-syllabic roots—words such as ἀγαπάω, which perhaps actually is connected with the corresponding Hebrew word. It will be simpler to uncover the reason for the deception. To wit, it might be the case that (a) Chinese is nothing but root, pure substance, (b) that in the Semitic languages [XI 136] the principle of monosyllabism was already overcome, and thus that (c) in the Japhethite languages the di-syllabism has likewise disappeared as *antithesis* and, accordingly, as *principle*. Now, whoever keeps in mind merely this latter point will thereby be led astray to again seek out monosyllabism; meanwhile, whoever recognized the true context and interrelation will not hesitate to say that these languages are polysyllabic in their *principle*, because in them monosyllabism and di-syllabism—both have lost their meaning as principle.

There will be opportunity in the Philosophy of Mythology itself to return to this relation, and thereby at the same time to counter misinterpretations, like the one that according to our opinion Chinese would have to be the originary language of the human species. But we will also, I hope, return convincingly, more thoroughly, to the parallelism of linguistic and religious development, with inclusion of new determinations that cannot be elaborated here.

Now, may the last remarks in general be regarded simply as *indirect* proofs for a merely relative monotheism in the consciousness of the original humanity! A *direct* deduction will now fully demonstrate the proof of just this presupposition and expose it as the only one possible.

If the successive polytheism is something that has actually occurred in humanity, *that is*, if as we have assumed—and here we want to recall that this is an irrefutable fact, as good as a historically attested one—humanity has actually passed through such a series of gods, then also at *some time* in humanity there had to be such a first God, as our God A is, who although only a first element of a future succession does not yet appear as such but rather is actually still the unconditioned *One* and for this reason spreads over the world the peace and calm of an undivided and uncontradicted dominion. But this peace was no longer able to endure as soon as the other God announced himself; for because with him, as indicated, confusion and division was posited unavoidably. For this reason, if we seek out the time in which there was still space for a first God [XI 137], then it makes sense that this space is not to be found in the time of the already completed separation and that he is no longer even to be found in the transitional time of the just *beginning* cision and thus that he is to be sought only in the purely and simply pre-historical time. Thus, either there was never such a first God as our God A—that is, there was never such an actual succession like we have to perceive in the actual polytheism [*Polytheismus*]—or such a God had reigned in the consciousness of the original, still fully unseparated humanity.

However, herewith the contrary is also produced: the one God, reigning over the placid, pre-historical time, was indeed the only one existing up to that point, but not in the sense that no second one *was able to* follow him; rather, only that another had not yet *actually* followed him. To this extent he was essentially (*potentia*) already a mythological god, although he only first became such actually (*actu*) when the second actually arrived and made himself into the master of the human consciousness.

If we compare this result with the assumption that has a pure doctrine (very closely related to the spiritual monotheism) preceding the emerging successive polytheism [*Vielgötterei*], then it is, as it must be and not to mention that the original unity of the human species was held together far more decisively through a blind power independent of human will and thought than through knowledge, considered bound up with a spiritual monotheism—but what is entirely independent of this is that the higher the pre-mythological consciousness is set through the assumption of a spiritual monotheism, the less is to be understood to which end it should vanish, because this alteration (as the defender of this view himself explains[d]) could lead only to the worse [XI 138]. However else one thinks of polytheism [*Polytheismus*], somehow it had to be mediation of a higher knowledge, transition to a greater freeing of human consciousness. This much on the reason for divergence.

Shortly the *how*, the manner of divergence, can come into consideration. To explain this manner Creuzer avails himself of a metaphor. If one will assume for the moment that it happens as tumultuously as with the formation of the universe, then how a planet scatters into many smaller ones can be explained, if need be, in more than one way; if one does not want to charge with this business a comet standing constantly at its disposal, then there are elastic fluids, which free themselves on the insides of the planets, metalloids that are able to explode with water; and with the occurrence of such an expansion or explosion a planet could indeed break up into pieces—in the most extreme case a high electrical charge would suffice for such an effect.

Here are positive causes of a rupturing or bursting; but in regard to that pre-mythological system merely unalloyed negative causes are introduced, the *eclipsing* and *gradual fading* of the original knowledge. Yet such a mere remission or slackening of an earlier insight would perhaps have as a consequence a cessation of the understanding of the doctrine and even a total forgetting of all religion, but would not necessarily result in polytheism [*Polytheismus*]. The mere eclipse of an earlier concept would not explain the fear that—by the indications already mentioned—humanity felt with the first appearance of polytheism. Once slackened, consciousness would easily, without struggle, and thus also without positive result [XI 139], have surrendered the unity. The *violence* by which polytheism emerges into being is as little explained through a mere *weakening* of the original knowledge, as, on the other side, the attachment to a simple *doctrine*—which, without this, already is assumed to be one that has become weaker—explains the opposed violence with which the unity holds its ground in consciousness and that prevents the full dissolution—which in the end would not even have left polytheism remaining.

Only a positive cause destroying the unity explains that horror of humanity at the first touch of successive polytheism [*Vielgötterei*]. From a standpoint in which we must also ultimately place ourselves, the effect of this cause will appear as one divinely ordained; it will appear as a judgment. Seen thus, the unity destroyed through a divine judgment could not have been the ultimately true unity. For a *judgment* is always promulgated only over the relatively true and the one-sided that is taken for comprehensive. The usual bemoaning of the decline of a pure knowledge and its splintering into successive polytheism is, for this reason, as little appropriate to the religious standpoint as to the philosophical one and to the true history. Polytheism was decreed over humanity not in order to destroy the true *One* but rather to destroy the one-sided *One*, a merely relative monotheism. Nonetheless, despite the appearance to the contrary, and as little as this can be made *comprehensible* in the present standpoint, polytheism was truly a transition to the better, to the liberation of mankind from a power in itself beneficent, but one that was stifling their freedom and repressing all development and thereby the highest knowledge. At the least one will admit that this is a more *comprehensible* and, as always, simultaneously more joyful view than that which has an originally *pure* knowledge destroy itself and pass away completely without purpose, and without that this process would have in any way appeared as a mediation of a higher result.

Up to now we have sought a departure point of the development, a departure point on which no longer merely hypothetical conclusions, but, rather, categorical conclusions [XI 140] about the emergence and the first origin of mythology can be built. But precisely here, as we believe ourselves assured of it, a powerful objection still threatens the result. So far we have judged the monotheistic hypothesis from only *one* side; let us not forget that through it not only a pure monotheism in general is asserted in the consciousness of the earliest humanity, but rather a *revealed* one. Now we have up till the moment taken into consideration only one side of it, the material one, and not also the formal side, the side of its emerging into being. However, the impartiality and equanimity that we have made into a law for ourselves with this entire investigation would already bid us to do justice to the other side, even if we did not have to expect precisely from this other side the most definite objection. Namely, one can object: what you presented would not be disputed if *there were no revelation*. In the merely natural process of human development such a one-sided monotheism would perhaps be the first. But the revelation—how will it be related to it? At the least that relative monotheism cannot be derived from it; the revelation cannot posit it; but if it cannot posit it, then it will forestall it, or at the least immediately confront and resist it and thereby sublate it. You see that this is thus a new instance that we cannot avoid, which must be overcome if we are to continue building with security on the foundation we have laid. We leave aside whether or not there is a revelation and ask only if, presupposing such a revelation, our assumption of a relative monotheism as the consciousness of original humanity could hold its ground.

Now, whatever thus concerns the forestalling that was asserted, it is of course known that not merely theologians, but even a certain class of philosophers of history, trace revelation back to the first man, and some would believe certainly to cause us no trifling embarrassment if they challenged us to explain if according to our opinion the religion of the first men [XI 141] was also already just that transient monotheism. We, however, simply want to remind them of their own assumption, that they themselves assume a double state of the first man, his state before the so-called fall and his state afterward; and there they would then have to explain above all—in order to go back with the revelation not merely to the first but rather also to the *original* man—how originally (that is, before the fall) the relation of man to God was also able to be one so mediated that they must consider it in the concept of revelation, if they do not want to rob the concept of all meaning by an unlimited expansion. To the best of our knowledge, revelation was formerly explained as God's compassion for the fallen species; according to the immutable concepts of ancient orthodoxy—and I confess that I far prefer these concepts, even if one may also call them *rigid*, to a newer extension of concept and word that dissolves everything and then indeed makes everything possible for the goals of a certain mawkish religiosity—thus according to these concepts revelation was consistently considered only as something mediated through earlier processes, never as something *immediate*, first, original. The *primordial* being of man is, even according to the assumed concepts—if it is sought in some measure to make them clear—to be thought only as one still extra-temporal and in essential eternity, which vis-à-vis time itself is only a timeless moment. And there is no room for a revelation, whose concept expresses an event, an occurrence in time; and there nothing could be between man and God through which man is separated from God and kept at a distance. And there has to be something of this type so that revelation is possible, for revelation is an actual[11] (resting on an *actus*) relation; there, however, only an essential relation can be conceived; there is *actus* only where there is resistance, where there is something that must be negated and sublated. Moreover, were the original man not *in itself* already consciousness of God, if a consciousness of God would first have to come to him through a special *actus*, then they who assume this would themselves have to assert an *original atheism of human consciousness* [XI 142], which of course would in the end certainly be against their own opinion; just as I have had opportunity to convince myself that—excepting those whose only concern is to knowingly or unknowingly give the principle of tradition the greatest possible extension—this derivation of all science and religion from a revelation happens with most only in the intention to thereby say something edifying and pleasing to delicate ears.

Thus, the concept of revelation cannot be extended up to that point, up to the primordial relation of man to God. Now, however, it is being further assumed that man was cast out of paradise by his own guilt—that is, was displaced from that primordial condition of a purely essential relation to God. But this relation cannot be thought without that, as man himself became another, *the God* also became an other to him; that is, it cannot be thought without an alteration of religious consciousness; and if one gives credence to the story of this event in *Genesis*, which must fill anyone who understands it with amazement, and, in whatever sense, certainly contains one of the deepest revelations (for in the different parts and passages of the Old Testament, despite the similarity on the whole, there are highly variable degrees of illumination that are not to be misapprehended)—if one thus gives credence to this belief, then that alteration was precisely of the type that corresponds to that which we have called relative monotheism. For God says: See, man has become like one of us, hence—how else can one understand the words?—he is no longer like the *whole Godhead*, but rather only like *one* of us, Elohim. But, as the Being of man, so also is his consciousness (and the relation which man has to God in consciousness rests precisely on the equivalence of his Being with the divine Being). Thus, without calling forth the axiom that the known is as the knower, there at the same time lies in the words that consciousness still has relation to only *One* of the Godhead, no longer to the whole. [XI 143] But what can this be other than what we have called relative monotheism?[e]

Thus, for this reason, to the asserted forestalling of a revelation—through which a relative monotheism in humanity would have been hindered—there is opposed the guileless and genuine narrative of a written work taken as revealed by the believers of revelation themselves, and thus therewith there is also opposed the revelation itself; and thus, instead of fearing from that side a checking of our development, we will, on the contrary, summon the revelation itself—that is, the writings viewed as revealed—as aid for our development, as we then in general, once the relation of mythology and revelation has been touched on, must not depart from this point without having cleared up this relation, insofar as it can be for the time present.

LECTURE SEVEN

[XI 144] Now, as we oppose those who trust only in conclusions provided by revelation, as far as the first state of the human species is concerned it is to be seen as good fortune for our investigation that our claims are as decisively confirmed by the Mosaic writings themselves as the first claim, that from the beginning of history—as *Kant* has with justification called the fall from grace into sin—the relative *One* has, within the consciousness of men, stepped into the position of the absolute *One*. And it will just as equally appear as one of the many false assumptions if one asserts in the usual way that in the consciousness of the first men the knowledge of God was still more pure and complete than those that followed. For, on the contrary, one would have to say that in the first man and his descendents the consciousness of the relative *One*—precisely because it did not appear as *such*—was still more powerful, pure, and unsullied than in those who followed, where the second God already approached consciousness. There, no doubt at all could arise to the effect that the relation to the relative *One* was not the *true* religion. For this God there was himself still the unconditioned God, and was this fully, *in place of* the absolute *One*, who was in him (and to that extent there after all). But for just this reason the absolute [*One*] was also not yet differentiated *as such*, and for this reason also not known as such. Thus it was not yet monotheism in the sense where it is knowledge of the true God *as such* and with distinction. For this distinction was first possible as the relative ceased [XI 145] to be the absolute and was explained as relative. And just this, that the very first human race in actuality knew nothing of the true God *as such*, is splendidly confirmed by *Genesis* itself. If this was not seen, then it is only because those oldest records had not yet met with the fortune of being considered and investigated wholly impartially and according to their own content—to which end adherents of the formally orthodox theology were as little suited as its opponents, and just as little those who have, more than with the content, busied themselves with the merely external composition of the writings. I belong neither to the one nor to the other of these categories. I have viewed these writings with the eyes neither of a theologian nor of an opponent of all theology nor also with those of a mere critic, but rather with the eyes of a philosopher—for whom the issue everywhere and primarily has to do with the *content* of the matter; and for this reason I have perhaps been able to notice a bit in those writings that has eluded others.

As long as the first human race simply and without doubt venerated the true God in the first God, there was no reason to distinguish the true as such. When that true God began to become doubtful through a following God, then the human race first sought to hold fast to the true God in him, and thereby learned to differentiate him. It has always been striking that the Hebrew people has *two* designations for its God: a universal one, Elohim, and then a particular one, Jehovah. But a complete induction may show that, in the Old Testament and most particularly in the Mosaic writings, the God who is the *immediate* content of consciousness is called Elohim, and the God who is *differentiated* as the true God is called Jehovah.[1] This difference is always observed. Already in the fourth chapter of *Genesis* there is a genealogy. It begins thus[a]: Adam (the first man) begat Seth, and Seth begat a son also, whom he called Enosh.[2] *From thence, thus from Enosh on*, they began to call to Jehovah. [XI 146] It is not said that they began to call to God in general, to Elohim. Seth and Adam had to know this [God] as well as Enosh did; it is only said of Jehovah. Because, however, Jehovah is otherwise also Elohim and Elohim Jehovah, the difference between the two *can* only be that Elohim is still the God *indistincte*, Jehovah the one differentiated as such. However, all the more decisive is precisely that only first with Enosh, thus only first in the third generation, have they supposedly called to Jehovah. Literally, it says that from then on they began to call to Jehovah by name. This is, however, really just the same as: he was differentiated, for whatever is called by a name is differentiated precisely thereby. From this it follows incontrovertibly: before Enosh, that is, prior to the human race[3] designated by this name, the true God was not differentiated as such; that is, until then there was also no monotheism in the sense of a knowledge of the true God as such. Of course, this was in too immediate a contradiction with the assumed concepts for one not to have sought to help through interpretation, as tends no less to happen in other cases. Thus, already Dr. Luther: at the same time they began to *preach* the name of the Lord; or others: to *name* themselves according to the name of Jehovah; others said the talk is only of a *public* cult; but there is nothing at all of this in the Hebrew, and to be linguistically appropriate the words can only be translated: Jehovah was called by name,[b] which then is of course as much as: he was called upon, for whoever, for example, is called by his name by another who is passing by is certainly also called upon. The most noticeable fact of all, however, is that this calling to Jehovah by name first begins with the second race. The first one (designated by Adam and Seth) knows nothing of it. To that race that knew only *one* principle no doubt could emerge about the truth, unity and eternity of the God by which it was filled; of simple heart (if I may express myself in such a way) it had venerated in him that which was ultimately eternal and singular [XI 147]. The necessity of differentiating this eternal and singular God as such, and of designating him with a special name, could emerge only when this God threatened to disappear through the appearance of a second, to become a relative God. Then it was necessary to call by name the truly eternal God, that is, the eternal one who is not transitory but who rather remains eternal, the one they venerated in that One God in himself—like we call one who threatens to leave us. This was the way to elevate oneself from the relative One to the absolute One *actually* venerated in him. The usual opinion, which ascribes to the first man full knowledge and veneration of the true God as *such*, we can thus consider all the more refuted—and indeed refuted through the Mosaic story itself—as precisely this story designates the second human race, beginning with Enosh, also in other respects as a different one and essentially distinguished from the first.

This occurs namely in the remarkable genealogy of the human race descending from Adam to Noah, a genealogy that is found in the fifth chapter of *Genesis*. This genealogy offers indeed still other things that are remarkable, namely, that it knows nothing of Cain and Abel, as also in the stories immediately following again nothing is mentioned of either (also *1. Chronicles* 1, 1 transitions immediately from Adam to Seth). But we cannot at the moment get involved with this, as it does not pertain to our goal. What does belong here is the following: that the genealogy mentioned marks itself as the one that is the most originary and authentic in part because it reaches back all the way to the creation of man, and in part through the particular superscription: *this is the book of the human race*—and that this genealogy says of Adam: he was 130 years old and begat a son *in his image*, and named him Seth. Seth, however, as is explained further, was 105 years old and begat Enosh. What is special here is first, that Enosh, according to the view of the genealogy, is *no longer* begat like Seth, in the image of the first man (for otherwise the addendum to Seth would contain an entirely unnecessary assurance). Seth still carries [XI 148] the image of the first man, Enosh no longer. Second, that the name, Enosh, of this grandson of the first man means nothing else than just again: man, like Adam, only with the corollary concept of the already weakened, sickened force. For the verb *anas*, with which the Greek word νόσος is connected, means to be sick. Thus, with Enosh there actually begins a *second* human race; a second because his first ancestor is again named man, and because it is no longer equal to the first descendent stemming directly from Adam. Now, one can raise the question of through what this second human race, represented by Enosh, distinguished itself from the first, the one descending immediately from Adam, from the man without corollary concept—that is, as it were, by what it was sick and weak in relationship to that first one. Now, if in answer to this question we add what has developed earlier from the other passage of *Genesis*, then the following will result of itself and without intervention. In Seth the human race was still strong and powerful, for it was driven by only *one* principle. In him the *one* and first God still lived. The second, however, is sick and weak, for the second God that weakens that first one had already approached him, breaking its power and might. For everything that is dominated by *one* principle is powerful and healthy; on the other hand, what is dominated by two is already weak and sick.

Thus, the result in toto is that according to the account of *Genesis* even the true God *as such* was only first known and familiar to a second human race, and, indeed, one in comparison to the first one already affected, and thus one subjugated by a potency foreign to the first race. This foreign potency can only be our second God (B), which we have come to know as the first, effective cause of polytheism. At the same time would thereby be explained that actual monotheism does not emerge without the danger of polytheism being present and that that simply relative *one* God is just as much the presupposition for the emergence of monotheism as of polytheism. Since we have in part relied on the meaning of the name (Enosh), we could at the same time advance further and find in this name [XI 149] the intimation of the God itself, by which the second human race is affected. For the most probable etymology of the name Dionysus, in and through which the second God was celebrated by the Greeks, is still that of an Arabic word (and among the Arabs, as we will see subsequently, the second God was first called by name), which means Lord in Arabic, and, like the Hebrew *baal* and like Enosh (man)—and indeed man with this corollary concept of the already sickened force—is combined with many other words. I could, I say, also make mention of this, if this combination could be further developed here; but the one observation may be sufficient enough, that in the great process of development, which we present, what is most distant—like the Old Testament and Hellenism, revelation and mythology—also lies far nearer than is thought by those who have grown accustomed to an entirely abstract manner of reflection—for example, of Greek mythology cut off from the general context.

We have had to acknowledge a first human race designated by Adam and Seth, and a second designated by Enosh. With the latter first come inclinations toward the second God, whose trace we now will follow further, and indeed in the history recorded by the revelation itself.

The next great turning point is the great flood; after this follows the confusion of the languages, the separation of the peoples, the *decisive* polytheism [*Polytheismus*]. Now, however, the great flood is introduced in the Mosaic account through the following story: As man began to multiply on the earth, the sons of *God* looked upon the beautiful daughters of *men*, and took them as wives, from whence emerged the giants[4] and the men of renown famed from time immemorial.[5] In this passage, which has for so long given the interpreters so much trouble, there is such a manifest reference to actual mythological relations that also this story can be nothing contrived, but rather only a reminiscence out of the real history of mythology—as indeed there is found a similar memory in the mythologies of the other peoples also [XI 150]. It is told how the sons of God (in Hebrew the article designates him as he who is *alone*), that is to say, how those—in whom the first, for his time, unconditioned God lived—look upon the daughters of *men*. But what can here be understood in contrast with sons of *God* among *men* other than adherents of the God through whom men properly first become men, and through whom they descend from that pristine force and power of the first time. That is, it is told how those in whom the powerful God of the primordial time still lives gravitate toward the daughters of men—that is, to the adherents of the second God—and unite themselves with them and produce that mediating race that we also find in the Greek mythology under the name of the Titans, where they likewise are in the middle between the god of the first time and the more human gods, the anthropomorphic polytheism of a later time, and are themselves opposed to the development into the human (for the god of the first time is superhuman in the sense meant here) and hold up the development. In just this way *Genesis* here lets that mediating race emerge, which, because it stands between two ages—and the continuation is incessant—cannot last but rather is consecrated to the demise that now happens through the universal flood. This fragment of such a wholly peculiar tone vouches through just that for the authenticity of its content, and that it is really derived from out of a pre-historical tradition. Something of the type could no longer be invented in later times. This highly mythological tone very much distinguishes the fragment from the subsequent story of the great flood, where everything is already represented more in accordance with the Mosaic standpoint. Yet this story also allows the true reason for the great flood to be perceived. What moves God to command the destructive flood over the earth is that the evil of men on earth was great. However, what are meant here are not evil thoughts in the usual (moral) sense; the particular expression, which God uses, shows this: that the disposition or composition[6] (*figmentum*) of the thoughts of their hearts is evil. The same figure of speech occurs elsewhere [XI 151], and always in a context that allows no doubt about its meaning. In the words to Moses, when his time to die has come, Jehovah speaks: "Thus, write now this song and teach it to the children of Israel, such that it is a witness among them, for I will bring them into the land that I have promised to their fathers — — — and when they eat, and become fat and satisfied, *they will turn to other gods*, and serve them and break my covenant — — for I know their thoughts (their disposition), that they are already forming, before I bring them to the land."[c] At the last royal assembly of King David he says to Solomon: "And you my son, *acknowledge the God of your father*, serve him with whole heart and with willing soul; for the Lord sees all hearts and understands the composition of all thoughts (*the disposition of all thoughts*); if you will seek him then you will find him, *but if you forsake him*, then he will reject you eternally."[d] King David, in his last prayer, after he set in order everything for the building of the temple, speaks likewise: "Lord, God of our fathers, preserve eternally such meaning and thought in the heart (such a *disposition of thoughts in the soul*) of your people, that it will serve you from a sincere heart."ᵉ According to linguistic usage these words have *religious* meaning. The ever more powerfully growing polytheistic inclinations are understood under the disposition of thoughts inclining ever more to the wicked.ᶠ

[XI 152] If Noah finds grace in the eyes of the true God, that is, when God reveals himself to him, then this is only precisely because he is a steadfast man and *blameless*, as Luther aptly translates—that is, he did not incline himself to the second God in his times.ᵍ Thus on account of those inclinations the great flood is spread across the earth. But what now is the result? Perhaps that they disappear and are extirpated? By no means. On the contrary, God sees in the end that the whole of the human heart is evil *from childhood*ʰ (a simple expression to articulate a natural and insurmountable propensity), and in that he states that he will for this reason (on account of these thoughts) not destroy any more the life on earth, he himself admits that the human race is no longer to be held back from the transition to polytheism. Thus also in the Mosaic presentation the great flood, in the end or according to its true result, is simply the boundary limit of the two ages, of the still superhumanly powerful race and of the race now entirely become human and devoted to the human, but for just this reason also the race resigning itself to polytheism.

Let us compare the Mosaic story with the same traditions of the other peoples! If one sees which divinities this story brings into connection with the destructive flood, then it is indeed *later* divinities. One of those traditions designates *Kronos*—who already in Greek mythology stepped into the position of the primordial God, Uranus—as the one in whose time the great flood occurs. However, in the Syrian Hierapolis, near the Euphrates, there was— according to Lukiano's well-known and detailed story—a temple where there was shown the chasm into which the waters of the flood had receded: this temple was consecratedⁱ to Derketo.⁷ This Syrian goddess, however, is just the *first female divinity* [XI 153], venerated under many names, through which (as we will see subsequently) *the transition from the first to the second God*, that is to the properly successive polytheism [*Vielgötterei*], is everywhere mediated. Thus, whoever ponders this and knows, moreover, what role the water has in all transitions from a *dominant* principle to a second, to which it yields, not merely in the history of the earth but rather also in mythology (also in Babylon, Oannes,⁸ who imparts the human law, arises from out of the Euphrates)—he will, if he is otherwise to a certain degree practiced in such investigations, and if he also in other respects concedes it as a physical event, actually just perceiveʲ in Noah's flood the natural sign of the great turning point of mythology. So perceived, this great turning point of mythology was later followed by the unceasing transition itself, the confusion of the languages, the successive polytheism along with the various systems of the gods, and the separation of humanity into peoples and states later, and to all of which the beginnings and seeds from out of the time before the flood had to be brought along, if in the first centuries after the flood the Near East is supposed to have been densely populated by people, and no longer merely by nomadic people, but rather ones united into states, and if there is supposed to have been already in Abraham's time a kingdom in Babylon, and on the coast of the Mediterranean the Phoenician traders, and in Egypt a monarchical state with all the institutions thereof, and if everywhere there are supposed to have emerged more or less developed mythologies.

Another indication of this meaning of the great flood, as transition to the overpoweringly emerging violence of the second God, is contained in a different feature of the Mosaic account, in that after the flood it has Noah become a man of the soil and plant the first vineyard.[k] What this means is elucidated through the following. The way of life of the oldest humans, before all successive polytheism, was nomadic [XI 154]. Not to sow seed, not to cultivate a vineyard, was also still religion to the very last remnants of this oldest race. This is shown by the example of the Recabites,[9] of whom the prophet Jeremiah speaks,[l] whom he holds up to his people as an example of the steadfastness and constancy in the religion of their forefathers, and to whom, according to his story, he served in one of the side rooms of the temple of Jerusalem bowls full of wine; to which they answer: "We do not drink wine. For our father Jonadab, the son of Recab, commanded us and said: You and your children shall never drink wine or build houses, sow no seeds, neither cultivate nor have vineyards, but rather shall live in shelters your whole lives, so that you live long in the land in which you wander."—You see: to build houses, that is, living in permanent residences, to sow seeds, to cultivate vineyards: here, a tribe that does not belong to the Israelites—but in the time when Nebuchadnezzar withdrew into the countryside, before the host of the Chaldeans and Syrians had drawn against Jerusalem and remained there—considered these activities forbidden for time immemorial. "We drink no wine, neither us nor our fathers, neither our sons nor daughters, and also build no houses in which to live, and have neither vineyards nor agricultural lands, but rather live in shelters"—and to refrain themselves from all that which Greek mythology preeminently celebrates as gifts and offerings of the second God was to them really *religion*. Thus the unbelievable lifespan of such tribes, for even in the times of Niebuhr there was, near Jerusalem, a tribe living nomadically that remained wholly true to this law—in the highest probability the descendents of those Recabites. What I have advanced about the Recabites—that they sow no seeds, cultivate no vineyards, do not reside in houses—Diodor of Sicily[10] similarly tells about the Kataters, an Arabian tribal people. Thus, when Noah becomes a man of the soil and cultivates the first vineyards after the flood, he is precisely thereby designated as the patriarch of a new human race, which no longer lives in shelters but rather establishes permanence residences, sows the soil [XI 155], becomes the nations [*Völkern*],[11] but for just this reason shall also fall prey to polytheism [*Polytheismus*] as an inevitable transition no longer to be checked.

If we draw the result of the facts developed thus far, then it is the following: only first with the second human race, designated by the name Enosh, is the true God—that is the abidingly *one* and *eternal* God—differentiated as such, differentiated from the primordial God, which vis-à-vis consciousness becomes the relative *one* and merely transitional *eternal* God. Meanwhile the fruit of polytheism becomes ripe, the human race is unable to remain bound to the first God, who is not the false, but yet also not the ultimately true God, the God in his truth—from which God the human race must thus be freed in order to arrive at the worship of God in his truth. But it can only be freed from him through a second God. Polytheism is to this extent unavoidable, and the crisis through which it is now admitted, and with which a new series of development begins, is precisely the great flood. From this point on there is also *found* the differentiation and veneration of the true God, which began with Enosh, and there is also found the revelation, which indeed can only be the revelation of the true God, *no longer* in humanity in general, for this as such has disappeared and is separated; just as little is it found (I ask indeed that this be noticed) with a people—for anything called a people has already fallen prey to polytheism; the knowledge of the true God is with one single race [*Geschlecht*], which has remained outside of the peoples. For humanity has not merely divided itself into peoples but rather into peoples and non-peoples, although, admittedly, the latter are by no means completely what the still homogenous humanity was—like when milk curdles, the noncurdling part is also no longer milk. Precisely this "not having partialized themselves" becomes for them a particularity, as the universal God to which they cling now indeed has become *their* god. Once individual peoples as such are formed, then the force of attraction of the merely natural, of the tribal relations, which here first receives its dividing force, is elevated for those remaining behind, while the consciousness of that power has, previously, on the contrary the meaning to preserve the *unity* of every race [XI 156] with the whole, with the collective humanity. The true religion, as well as the revelation, thus will be found neither in humanity nor in a people but rather in a lineage [*Geschlecht*] that has remained distant from the path of the peoples and believes itself still bound to the God of the primal time. This lineage is that of the Abrahamites, descended from Noah via Shem, which is in general contrasted with the peoples or nations [*Völker*],[12] with which the corollary concept of adherents of other gods has inseparably bound itself to it (with the concept of peoples or nations). This concept does indeed not adhere to the word; for where in our translations heathens is written, in Hebrew there are words that mean nothing other than peoples or nations—for even between the two words *ammim* and *gojim* there is no difference in this regard, like some imagine who know that the present-day Jews call all non-Jewish peoples *gojim*, and especially the Christians. The ancient Hebrew writers do not make this distinction; indeed, they at times likewise call their own people [*Volk*] (and Israel indeed later became a people) a *goi*. This connection of the two concepts polytheism and peoplehood or nationhood, which up until now has been touched upon by us only in passing, but which I now maintain as the ultimate and decisive confirmation of our *view* that polytheism has been the instrument of the separation of the peoples, has, from the first ages on, so deeply impressed itself on this species, that it, itself having long since become a people or nation, simply and without addition designates as peoples or nations the adherents of the false gods, a linguistic usage that continues into the New Testament, which also just calls the heathens the peoples ($\dot{\epsilon}\theta\nu\eta$). Among the kings whom Abraham attacks and defeats with his own, one—in addition to the others designated with the names of their land or peoples— is mentioned by his own name,[m] but only as a king of the peoples [*Völker*], that is, as a heathen king in general. Thus the Abrahamites considered themselves not to belong to the peoples or nations or to be non-peoples [*Nichtvolk*], and the name *Hebrews* [XI 157] also says just this. When[13] Abraham struggles with the kings of the peoples or nations, he is for the first time named *Haibri* (the *Ibri*) in contrast with these.[14] Also later, aside from perhaps in the poetic style, *Hebrew* is consistently given[n] to the Israelites only in contrast with the peoples or nations. Thus, it appears, the name would have to also express their difference from the peoples or nations. *Genesis* inserts an Eber[15] in the genealogical table itself, from whom it subsequently, in the sixth generation, has Abraham descend. Today we are convinced that this Eber, on the contrary, owes its origin as much to the Hebrews as the Dorus and the Ion in the Greek epic story owe theirs to the Dorians and Ionians.[16] After all, in this same genealogy names of lands are made into names of peoples or nations; it says, after all, for example: the children of Ham are Hus (Ethiopia), Mizraim (Egypt); and of Canaan: he begat Sidon (name of the well-known city), his first son.[17] A superstitious literalness would be out of place here. The name Hebrew cannot be traced back to the accidental existence of an Eber among their forefathers, for this line of descent expresses an antithesis to peoples or nations just as little as the "having come over the Euphrates." The name has the form of a name of the peoples or nations. For once peoples or nations are there, the Abrahamites also, as it were, that is to say in certain respects, become a people or nation, without being so for themselves. But a concept congruent to the constant usage of the name as a contradistinction with the peoples or nations only emerges when one derives it from the corresponding verb, which does not merely mean to cross over (over a river) but rather to travel through a place or region, to *pass by*[o] in general. Thus *Abraham the Ibri* means: Abraham, who belongs to those who pass through, to those bound to no permanent residence, those who live nomadically, like the patriarch also in Canaan is consistently called[p] the foreigner, for he who tarries nowhere is everywhere only a foreigner, a wanderer [XI 158].[q] The devotion to the *one* universal God is so absolutely brought into connection with this mode of living that it is said of Jacob, in contrast to Esau, who becomes a hunter and a man of the land, that he was a devout (actually, a whole, undivided) man (who remained with the One) and lived in huts;[r] and when Israel,[18] which had until then always had the God of its fathers for the sole shepherd and king, desired a king from Samuel, *as all peoples or nations have*[s] *one*, then God said to the prophet: "They are doing to you as they always have done, from the day when I led them out of Egypt and they forsook me and served other gods."[t]

It may appear peculiar, but the importance which this transition from mankind in general to peoples or nations has for our entire investigation may excuse it when I adduce an example of the contrast (of peoples or nations and non-peoples or non-nations) that I believe to have still found in a very late era. For at least I can consider the Alemanni—which in Caracalla's time appear on the Roman borders like a suddenly disturbed and ever-growing swarm, and invade Gaul and Italy—by all, even if scanty, descriptions[u] as only a part of a *Germanic* mankind, which part had not yet determined itself into a *people* or *nation*, and that for this reason also appears so late on the world stage.[19] The name accords in this, if one thinks herewith of *alamanas*, which in some fragments of the Gothic translation of the N.T. [XI 159] appears to mean simply man in general, without distinction—if one gives the *ala*[v] this basically negating meaning, then either Alemanni would be a nameless race [*Geschlecht*] (one not yet become a people or nation), and for just this reason a race not yet contained in definite borders (in this case the Marcomanni[20] would have to be thought of as counterexample), or one may simply recall *Almende*, a ground left fallow (uncultivated), and that is mostly used as meadow, and is not property of one person, but rather of all. A decisive aversion of the Alemanni to an existence as a people or nation is evidenced by the visible, and even later still deeply rooted, propensity of the Alemanni for the freely individual life, by their hatred of the cities, which they view as graves in which one imprisons[w] oneself alive, and by their destructive wrath directed against Roman settlements. Now, on the other hand, if the patronymic explanation of the name of the Germans as *Teut'scher* (descendents of the Teut) is in any case to be given up, and yet *Thiod* means people or nation, then the Deutschen (*Thiod'schen*) would be the Germans [*Germanen*] who have already particularized or separated themselves as a people or nation, like in the *theotiscus, theotisce*, commonly used since the seventeenth century, the relationship to people or nation still appears to stand out. It would be worth the effort to investigate also from the point of view of this contrast all the names under which are mentioned German peoples [*Völker*] or tribes [*Völkerschaften*]. No less perhaps could this distinction serve to compensate for the contradictions regarding the German system of the gods, for example between Julius Caesar and Tacitus.[21]

Thus now we have advanced until that point in the history of the religious development as it is recorded in the Mosaic records—on which alone everything rests that can be maintained of revelation—where the knowledge of the true God is preserved with only one lineage [*Geschlecht*], which has remained apart from the peoples or nations, indeed remained in opposition to them, and to this extent alone still represents the pure humanity [XI 160]. With just this lineage alone is there now also *revelation*, and just with the members of the lineage can the presuppositions of a revelation be clearly and definitely known, such that we—in order to direct the answer to the question, from which this last investigation has proceeded, to a complete result—cannot avoid turning our attention in particular to the Abrahamites. As everyone knows, the question proceeded from whether revelation has anticipated polytheism. In the way in which we began the investigation into mythology, revelation could not be excluded from mythology. Nothing more can be understood individually or in isolation; everything becomes understandable only in the large, general context, and this holds good of revelation itself as much as it does of mythology. Now, it is a consequence of what has been proven heretofore that the first human race worships the true God *implicite*: that is to say, in the relative *One*, but without differentiating him as such. But revelation is precisely manifestation of the true God as such, for which there was no receptivity in the first human race precisely because it did not require this differentiation. It is said of the second race that it called the true God by name; that is, it has differentiated him as such: thus here is the possibility of revelation, but it is not given before there was also the first impulse of polytheism. The most prominent figure was Noah, with whom the true God consorts; but even in his time polytheism too is no longer to be checked, and the great flood itself merely the transition from the age of the still restrained successive polytheism to that of the successive polytheism incessantly breaking forth and flowing over humankind. With the human race now following—within which monotheism in the proper sense (knowledge of the true God, and thereby revelation) is preserved—the conditions under which such a relation to the true God alone could consist most definitely have to be perceptible. You have followed the developments heretofore with so much interest that I promise this also for the conclusion, which will first lead to the satisfactory end.

[XI 161] Thus, now, as far as the monotheism and the relation to the true God are concerned, with whose glory the head of Abraham is surrounded, not only in the Old Testament but rather in the legends of the entire Orient (they[22] name him, unanimously, the friend of God)—and a later fiction was never able to produce this agreement of traditions—I thus want initially and above all to draw attention to the invariability with which *Genesis* says of Jehovah, but to my knowledge never of Elohim, that he *appeared*[x] to Abraham, Isaac, and Jacob. This already presupposes that he was not the immediate content of their consciousness, as those who advance revelation as the ultimately first principle of explanation think. No less remarkable is how in significant moments the patriarchs *call out*[y] Jehovah *by name* like you call out one who you want to seize or who is supposed to appear. If Jehovah is simply called and simply appears, then the immediate content of their consciousness can only be the God who is called Elohim in the Mosaic writings. Here is the place to explain about this name. A plural noun according to the grammatical form, it at times also has its verb in the plural—not, as some believe, merely on account of a rote accommodation to the form; for a closer investigation of the passages shows that the plural of the verb is used only in certain cases, and thus not at random; for, that is, as an example, when in the story of the Tower of Babel Jehovah speaks and says, "Let us go down and confuse their language," then the reason is clear, for God must multiply himself in order to separate humanity. Likewise in the creation story, where just Elohim alone speaks and says: "Let us make man, an image which is like unto *us*," for the ultimately *one* God as such is without image.[23] When Abraham says: the *Gods* have had[z] him go out of his Father's house, had him go astray [XI 162], that is, had him go into the desert, lead the nomadic life—then—because Elohim here is not written[aa] with the article, as opposed to in other passages—he can be understood to mean actual Gods (Abraham escaped the spreading idolatry in the house of his Father), and the other passages, where Jehovah commands[bb] his flight, would be no contradiction, because both can exist together. When, however, in a passage like the one just introduced the God expressly called Jehovah Elohim[24] says: "See, Adam has become like *one* of us," that is, *one* differentiated in himself and opposed to the other,[25] then indeed one must think of a plurality. The plural form of the name or the construction with the plural of the verb also cannot be explained as a remainder of an earlier polytheism, as some believe. But rather it can be explained by this: that the God as Jehovah is indeed always *One*, but as Elohim is that God who is still exposed to the solicitations of multiplicity, and moreover also the God who is a multiplicity—only one always suppressed—for the consciousness that in other respects holds firmly to the unity. It is not an older polytheism that intrudes here but rather a later one, from whose impulses also Abraham, for example, was not spared. Now, however, irrespective of this plural meaning that at times appears, it can no longer be doubted that Elohim, like many similar plurals, had a singular meaning, and is a plural not of multiplicity but rather of magnitude (*Pluralis magnitudinis, qui unam sed magnam rem indicat*),[cc] which often is used when something is to be expressed that, in its type, is great, powerful, or causing astonishment. However, the first claim to a name that expressed such astonishment belonged without doubt to that universal God [*Allgott*], the God outside of which there was no other in his time. Indeed, the name itself simply expresses astonishment, since it derives from a verb [XI 163] that in Arabic clearly has this meaning (*obstupuit, attonites fuit*). Without doubt, for this reason in Elohim is preserved for us the original Semitic name of the primordial God [*Urgott*], wherewith agrees that here, contrary to other cases, the singular (*Eloah*) was only formed out of the plural, as is shown in that this singular appears only in later books of the O.T., and mostly just in the poetic books. Because in *Genesis* and, in part, in the following books the names

Elohim and Jehovah alternate, people have sought to ground on this the hypothesis that *Genesis* in particular was put together out of two sources: the one was called the Elohim-source, the other the Jehovah-source.[26] Only one can easily convince oneself that in the stories the names do not change randomly but rather are employed with intentional differentiation, and the usage of the one or the other has its basis in the matter at hand and is not determined by a merely external or contingent circumstance. At times, especially in the story of the fall, both names are bound together, but only when the narrator speaks, and not when the female or the snake speaks; Adam, also, if he were introduced as speaking, would only say Elohim, because the first man knew nothing yet of Jehovah. Elohim is the God who also the peoples or nations, the heathens, still feared,[dd] who also comes[ee] in a dream to Abimelech, the king of Gerar, and to Laban the Syrian. The dream illuminates the natural mode of action of God, who already begins to become part of the past. Abraham prays to the natural, and for just this reason invariably present God, to Elohim, for the healing of Abimelech, the king of Gerar. That the actual word for prayer is used shows that the "calling out Jehovah by name" is not the same thing as "prayer."[ff] With respect to Abraham himself it is—and indeed as one clearly sees if one reads[gg] the passage in context—quite expressly Elohim [XI 164] who commands of him the *circumcision*, which was an ancient religious practice common also to a part of the peoples or nations and a tribute brought to the primordial God. It is Elohim, the universal God, by whom Abraham is tempted to slaughter his son as a sacrifice in the manner of the heathens, the appearing Jehovah, however, who holds him back from consummation. For because Jehovah only can *appear*, then, very often even in the later writings, instead of Jehovah the angel is referred to[hh]—that is, precisely the appearance of Jehovah.

In the relative *One* and *Eternal* the original mankind had *actually* meant the true, the essentially *One* and *Eternal*. Only the appearance of the second God brings consciousness to the point that it differentiates the essentially *Eternal*, who was the true, actual God in the merely contingently *Eternal*, and to the point that it distinguishes the essentially *Eternal* from that God that was the Eternal only for a time. Here one must assume that even those who had traversed the way of polytheism were still free to turn to the essentially *Eternal*—that is, to turn to the true God—which in the other God was the true God. Up to this point the path of humankind is the same; only at this point does it separate. Without the second God, without the solicitation to polytheism, there would also have been no proceeding to monotheism proper. The same potency that to the one part of humanity becomes the occasion for successive polytheism elevates a selected lineage to the true religion. After the God—the God who the first era, albeit unknowingly, also venerated in the relative *One*—appeared to Abraham, thus when he became manifest and differentiable, Abraham turned to him freely and consciously. To him, this God is not the originary God; he is the one that has become for him, appeared to him, but he had just as little invented him as he made him up. [XI 165] What he thereby does is only that he takes hold of what is seen (what has become revealed to him); but in that he holds fast to God, this God draws him to himself and enters into a special relation with him, through which he is fully removed from the peoples or nations. Because there is no knowledge of the true God without differentiation, the name is *therefore* so important. The worshipers of the true God are those who know his *name*; the heathens, who do not know his *name*—it is not the case that they do not know the true God at all (namely, not not in terms of substance), but rather they simply know his name not, or, that is, they do not know him in differentiation. But, so to say, Abraham cannot—after he has seen the true God—tear himself away from his presupposition. The immediate content of his consciousness remains for him the God of the primordial time, who has not *become* for him and thus also is not revealed, who—we must express ourselves this way—is his *natural* God. In order for the true God to appear to him, the ground of the appearance must remain the first God, in which alone that second God can become enduring to him. The true God is not merely temporarily mediated to him through the natural God, but is rather constantly mediated; he is to him never that which *has being*, but rather constantly only the one who *is becoming*, through which alone the name Jehovah would be explained, in which precisely the concept of becoming is particularly expressed. Thus Abraham's religion does not consist in him giving up that God of pre-historical time, becoming untrue to him; on the contrary, that is what the heathens do. The true God has become revealed to him only in that God, and for this reason is inseparable from it, inseparable from the God *who was from time immemorial*, from the *El Olam*, as he is called.

Customarily, one translates this expression as "the eternal God"; only one would be incorrect if one intended thereby to think of a metaphysical eternity. The word *olam* properly, in all actuality, designates the time prior to which mankind knew of none, the time in which it finds itself just as it finds itself, which has not *become* for humanity[27] and in this sense is indeed an eternity. The prophet calls the Chaldeans a people or nation *me olam*,[ii] a people or nation that exists *since* the time in which there were no peoples or nations. Accordingly, Luther [XI 166] translates it correctly: those who were the oldest people or nation; *olam* is the time where there were no peoples or nations. The earlier referenced fragment about the heroes and the men of renown of the pre-historical time says in the same sense that they are famed *me olam*, that is, since the time after which the peoples or nations emerged into being. Joshua says to the children of Israel: your fathers lived beyond the Euphrates *me olam*,[jj] that is, beginning from the time where there were still no peoples or nations, thus ever since there are peoples or nations.[28] The first historical time, the first time of which one knows, is found there. The *El olam* is thus the God who was not *since* that time, but rather was already in that time, where peoples or nations did not yet exist, the God before whom there was none, thus of whose emergence no one knows, the absolutely first, the *unprethinkable* God. The antithesis of the *El olam* are the *Elohim chadaschim*, the new gods, "those which have not emerged[kk] in the distant past," but rather recently. And thus to Abraham as well the true God is not eternal in the metaphysical sense, but rather as him about whose beginning one knows not.

As to him the true God is one and the same with the *El olam*, so also with the *God of heaven and earth*. For at one time the God common to the entire human kind was venerated as *such* a God. To him Jehovah is not materially *an other God* than this one; to him he is simply *the true* God of heaven and earth. When he has his oldest servant swear that he would take no wife from the children of the heathens,[ll] he says: "swear to me by Jehovah, by the God of heaven and earth." Thus this God is still for him in common with the entire older race of man. A figure that belongs to just this race is Melchizedek, who is king of Salem and priest of the God Most High, of El Eljon—who still appears under this name in the fragments of Sanchuniaton—of the God who, as was already said, *possesses* heaven and earth.[29] Everything about this figure, coming out from the darkness of pre-historical time, is strange—even the names, his own as well as the name of the land or place of which he is called king [XI 167]. The words *zedek*, *zaddik* in fact mean justice and just[30]; but the original sense, as is to be seen from the Arabic, is steadfastness, rigidity. Thus Melchizedek is the steadfast one, the one showing constancy; that is, he who remains[mm] steadfastly and firmly with the *One*. The same thing occurs with the name Salem, which is otherwise used when it is to be expressed that a man *entirely* is with or walks[nn] with Elohim—that is, is with or walks *fully* in unification with Elohim. It is the same word by which Islam and Moslem are formed. Islam means nothing other than the complete, that is, the whole, the undivided religion; a Moslem is he who is devoted entirely to the *One*. One comprehends the latter only when one has understood what is oldest. Those disputing the monotheism of Abraham or holding his entire story for fantastic have probably never thought about the successes of Islam, successes of such a ferocious type—proceeding from a part of mankind that had remained, by millennia, retrograde in development in comparison to that part of mankind that they conquered and subjugated—that they are only explicable by dint of the enormous violence of a past that, arising again, destructively and catastrophically breaks in upon that which has in the meantime come into existence and has been formed. Mohammed's teaching of unity could never bring forth this revolutionary[31] effect if it was not from time immemorial in those children of Hagar,[32] in whom the whole time from their ancestor up to Mohammed had passed by without trace. Yet with Christianity a religion had emerged that no longer simply excluded polytheism, like it was excluded by Judaism. Precisely there, at this point of the development where the rigid and one-sided unity was utterly overcome, the old primordial religion had to right itself again—blindly and fanatically, as it could appear no differently against the much more developed time. The reaction was not aimed merely at the idolatry that in Mohammed's time had partially spread even among the part of the Arabs that had not departed from nomadic life, but rather far more at the apparent [XI 168] successive polytheism of Christianity, against which Mohammed opposed the rigid, immutable God of the primordial time. Here everything is connected: Mohammed's law also forbade wine to his adherents, just like the Recabites reject it.

Thus Abraham subjects himself to this king of Salem and priest of the Most High God, for Jehovah himself is but an appearance mediated by him, the primordial God. Abraham subjects himself to him in that he gives to him a tenth of everything. A young but devout time always honors the older time as one that is, as it were, still closer to the origin. Melchizedek emerges from that race simply adhering without doubt and differentiation to the primordial God, a race unknowingly venerating in him the *true God*, against whom Abraham to a certain extent already finds himself less pure. For he did not remain free of the temptations that the peoples or nations had followed, although he surmounted them and rescued from them the true, known, and differentiated God as such. In exchange Melchizedek brings to Abraham *bread and wine*, the signs of the new time. For if Abraham did not become unfaithful to the old covenant with the primordial God, then he had at least to *distance* himself from him in order to differentiate the true God *as such*. As contrary to the oldest race, he has this distancing in common with the *peoples or nations*, which revolted against the covenant entirely and entered into a new one, as whose gifts or offerings they consider bread and wine.

To Abraham, Jehovah is simply the primordial God in his true, persisting essence. To that extent Jehovah is for him *also* the El Olam, *God of primordial time*, the *God of heaven and earth*;[oo] he is for him also the *El Schaddai*: this is his third attribute. The form already points to the highest antiquity; *schaddai* is an archaic plural and likewise a plural of magnitude. The fundamental concept of the word is strength, power, which, indeed, is no less the fundamental concept in the similarly old word *el* (distinct from Elohim and Eloah) [XI 169]. One could translate El Schaddai: the strong of the strong, but *schaddai* also stands alone and thus appears bound up with *el* merely through apposition, such that both in connection mean: the God who is the sublime power and strength over all.[33] Now, Jehovah says to Abraham: "*I am the El Schaddai.*"[pp] Here El Schaddai has the status of the explanatory predicate, and over against Jehovah the position of what is known in advance, and thus also of that which came before. Now, in the second Book of Moses[qq] there is a famed passage, of great historical importance, where—the other way around—Elohim says to Moses: "I am Jehovah," where Jehovah is thus presupposed as what is already better known, and "I have appeared to Abraham, Isaac and Jacob—*beel schaddai*," in the El Schaddai. Here we have express evidence that the El Schaddai—that is, the God of the pre-historical time—was the medium of revelation or appearance of the true God, of Jehovah. Our view of the first revelation could not have been more clearly articulated than it is here in its suggestion by Jehovah himself. Jehovah did not appear to Abraham without mediation; by virtue of the spirituality of his notion he cannot appear immediately; he appeared[rr] to him in the El Schaddai. Now, however, in the second part the words are: "And by or under my name Jehovah, I was not known to them [the patriarchs]."[34] It is primarily these words by which people wanted to conclude that the name Jehovah is, by Moses's own admission, not old, but rather was first taught by him. If one did not fully hold the Mosaic books to have been written by him, then one was able to descend with the name all the way to the time of David and Solomon. But the words mentioned at least cannot intend to say [XI 170] what they would like to find in them. The basic principle of Hebrew style is, as is well known, parallelism; that is, namely, parts that say the same thing with different words follow each other in pairs, generally in such a way that what is affirmed in the first part is expressed in the other through negation of the opposite—for example, I am the Lord and there is no other but me, or: the honor and praise is mine, and I will not surrender it to another. Now, when the first part here says: "I have appeared to the forefathers *in* the El Schaddai," then the second—"I was not known to them by my name Jehovah"—can only repeat the same thing in a negative way. It can only say: they knew nothing of me *immediately* (this just means: in my name Jehovah), without mediation of the El Schaddai. The *bischmi* (in my name) is just a paraphrase of: in myself. They have seen me in the El Schaddai; they have not seen me in myself. Thus the second part simply confirms the first; and, to be sure, a later and higher moment of consciousness, one that also knows Jehovah independently of El Schaddai—a consciousness, as we also must ascribe it to Moses for different reasons—is designated through the words. But a proof for the allegedly later origin of the name, whereby the central content of *Genesis* itself would fall away, is in any event not to be found in the passage.

Everything presented heretofore shows what type of monotheism had been the monotheism of Abraham, namely, that it was not an absolutely unmythological one, for it had as its presupposition the God that is just as well the presupposition of polytheism, and for Abraham the appearance of the true God is so much linked to this that the appearing Jehovah regards[ss] the obedience to the inspirations of this God as obedience to himself.[35] Abraham's monotheism is in general not an entirely unmythological one, I said finally; for it has as presupposition the relative *One* that itself is only the first potency of polytheism. It is therefore the *mode* of the appearance of the true God, because it cannot tear itself from its presupposition [XI 171]—even this is an entirely mythological mode, that is, such a mode with which the polytheistic always interferes. One wanted to find it sacrilegious to treat all the narratives, and especially those of *Genesis*, as myths, but they are at all events apparently mythical; they are indeed not myths in the sense that one normally takes the word: that is, fables. But they are real, albeit mythological, facts, which are told—that is, facts standing under the conditions of mythology.

This being bound to the relative One God is a limitation, which must also be perceived as such, and beyond which consciousness strives. But it cannot sublate the limitation for the present; therefore, it will overcome this limitation only to the extent that it, to be sure, knows the true God as the one merely appearing at the moment, but at the same time as the one who *will be* in the future. Seen from this perspective the religion of Abraham is monotheism pure and proper; but to him this is not the religion of the present; in this present his monotheism stands under the condition of mythology; but this monotheism is to him the religion of the future. The true God is the one who *will be*; that is his name. When Moses asks by what name he is supposed to proclaim the God who will lead the people out of Egypt, he answers: "I will be who I will be."ttt Thus, here, where God speaks in his own person, the name is translated from the third into the first person, and it would be entirely illegitimate to seek here also the expression of the metaphysical eternity or immutability of God. True, the actual pronunciation of the name Jehovah is unknown to us; but, grammatically, it cannot be other than an archaic future tense of *hawa*, or in the later form *haja* = being. The present pronunciation is in no case the correct one, because since an ancient time the vowels of a different word (Adonai) have been attributed to the name that should not be pronounced, a different word that means master, lord, from which also already in the Greek and all later translations *the Lord* is written instead of Jehovah [XI 172]. With the true vowels the name (likewise archaic) could be Jiweh; or analogously to other forms of proper names (like Jacob) Jahwo—the former in accordance with the Jewo in the fragments of Sanchuniaton, the latter in accordance with the Iao ('Ἰάω) in Diodor of Sicily and in the well-known fragment by Macrobius.[36]

We have previously explained the name of Jehovah as the name of the one who is becoming—perhaps this was its first meaning, but according to that explanation of Moses it is the name of he who is in the future, of he who now is only becoming, who *will* be in the future, and also all his promises are directed at the future. Everything that Abraham was privileged to receive are promises. To him who is not now a nation [*Volk*], it is promised that he shall become a great and powerful nation, indeed all nations of the earth shall be blessed by him, for in *him* lay the future of that monotheism through which in the future all presently dispersed and separated nations shall again be united."uuu It may be easy and conducive to mental laziness, which often puts on airs as reasonable explanation, to see in all these promises only fabrications of the later Jewish national pride. But where in the entire history of the Abrahamidic race is a point in time in which such a promise could have been fabricated in the presumed sense of political greatness? As Abraham must believe in this promised greatness of his nation, so he also believes in the future religion, which will sublate the principle under which he is caught, and this faith is reckoned[vv] to him as the complete religion. With respect to this future religion Abraham is right from the very beginning called a *prophet*,[ww] for *he* is still outside the law under which his descendents will be still more definitely confined and thus sees beyond this law, like the later so-called prophets saw[xx] beyond it.

[XI 173] If, indeed, the religion of the patriarchs is not free from the pre-supposition that permits the true God as such only to appear, not to be, then the law given by Moses is even more bound to this presupposition. The content of the Mosaic law is, certainly, the unity of God, but it is just as certain that this God shall only be a mediated one.

According to some passages—that are not to be understood very differently—an unmediated relation was vested in the lawgiver, who, as such, to a certain extent stands outside the people or nation. The Lord spoke with him face to face, like a man speaks[yy] with his friend; he saw the Lord *as he is*,[zz] and a prophet like him, with whom the Lord spoke as he did with him, will arise[aaa] no more; but the law is laid on the people or nation as a *yoke*. To the degree to which mythology progresses, the relative monotheism already in the struggle with the decisive polytheism, and already Kronos's dominion expanding over the peoples or nations, the relative God—in which the people or nation of the true God has to preserve the *ground* of the absolute God—must, to the people of the true God, become more severe, exclusive, jealous of his unity. This character of exclusivity, of the most severe, negative singularity, can only come from the relative *One*; for the *true*, the *absolute* God is not *One* in this exclusive manner, and as that which excludes nothing also threatened by nothing. The Mosaic religious law is nothing other than relative monotheism, as it alone, in a certain time, was able[bbb] to maintain itself in actuality, preserve itself, in contrast to the heathens encroaching from [XI 174] all sides. That principle, however, should not be preserved for its own sake, but rather just precisely as *ground*, and thus, then, the Mosaic religious law is also pregnant with the future, to which it points mutely—like a picture. The heathen, by which it appears thoroughly permeated, only has temporary meaning and will be dissolved simultaneously with heathendom itself. As it, however, obeying necessity, seeks chiefly to preserve the *ground* of the future, the actual and proper principle of the future is set in the realm of prophets, that other, completing side of the Hebraic religious constitution, and just as essential and actual to this latter. In the prophets, however, the expectation and hope of the future, liberating religion no longer breaks forth merely in isolated statements—it is the primary end and content of their speeches—and no longer is this the mere religion of Israel, but rather of all peoples or nations. The feeling of negation, under which they themselves suffer, gives them a similar feeling for the whole of mankind, and they begin to see the future in heathendom as well.

Thus, now, it is proved through the oldest documents, through the writings themselves taken for revealed, that mankind has not proceeded from pure or absolute but rather from relative monotheism. Now, I will add still some general remarks about this oldest condition of humankind, a state that is not meaningful for us merely as a religious one but rather also in a general context.

Lecture Eight

[XI 175] We may now articulate it as fact, and also the revelation has born witness to it, that a spiritual power, God, ruled over the time of the still *unified* and *undivided* human race, a God who restrained the free dispersal, a God who kept the development of the human race on the first level of Being that is divided by mere *natural* or tribal differences, but which otherwise is *completely uniform*—a condition that indeed alone would be correctly called the *state of nature*. And, certainly, just this time was also the much glorified *golden age*, of which, even in the farthest distance from it, the memory has remained for the human race, even for the one long divided into peoples or nations—where, namely, as the Platonic story that flowed from the same memory says, God himself was their guardian and head, and because he shepherded them, there were[a] no societal laws. For as the shepherd does not allow his flock to scatter, God, acting as a powerful force of attraction, held humanity, with gentle but irresistible power, enclosed in the sphere in which he deemed it appropriate to hold them. *Notice* indeed the Platonic expression that *God himself* was their head. Thus at that time God was not imparted to men through a *doctrine*, through a philosophy [*Wissenschaft*]; the relation was a *real* one and for that reason could only be a relation [XI 176] to God *in his actuality*, not to God in his essence, and thus also not to the *true* God. For the actual God is not immediately also the true God—like we even still attribute to him whom we look upon, in another respect, as a godless one, a relation to God in his actuality, but not to God in his truth, to whom on the contrary he is completely alienated. The God of pre-historical time is an actual, real God, and in him also the true God *Is*, but not known as *such*. Thus humanity worshipped *what it did not know*, to which it had no ideal (free) relation, but rather only a real relation. Christ says to the Samaritans (as is well known, these were seen by the Jews as heathens, so thus fundamentally he says of the heathens): "*You worship what you do not know, we*—the Jews, as monotheists, who have a relation to the true God as such—we worship what we *know*" (know at least as something to come). The true God, God as such, only *can* be in knowledge, and in complete contrast with a well-known word little reflected upon, but in agreement with the words of Christ, we must say: the God who would not be known would be no God. From the very beginning monotheism has existed only as a doctrine and knowledge [*Wissenschaft*], and never merely as a doctrine in general, but rather as one codified in script and preserved in holy books; and even those who presuppose of mythology a knowledge of the true God are obliged to think this monotheism as doctrine, even as system. Those who worship the true God—that is, God *in his truth*—can, as Christ says, only worship him conjointly *in spirit*, and *this* relation can only be a free one; as, however, that relation to God outside his truth, as it is accepted in polytheism and mythology, can only be an unfree one.

Once man has fallen out of the essential relation to God,[b] which also could only be a relation to God in his essence, that is, in his truth [XI 177], the way that humanity followed in mythology is not a contingent one, but rather a necessary one, when it was determined of humanity to attain the goal only through this way. The goal, however, is that intended by providence. Seen from this standpoint it was divine providence itself that had given to the human race that relative *One* as first head and guardian; humanity was dependent on this [*One*] and, as it were, set under his discipline. Even for the chosen people [*Geschlecht*] the God of the pre-historical time is only the bridle or restraint, through which it is held by the true God. Their knowledge of the true God is not a *natural* one, and for just this reason also not a static one, but rather is always only becoming because the true God himself is for consciousness not the existing one, but rather always he who is becoming, who precisely as such is called the living God, always only he who appears, who always must be called on and held on to like an appearance is held on to. The knowledge of the true God remains for this reason always a *demand*, a command, and also the later nation of Israel must be always called upon and admonished to love its God Jehovah—that is, to hold on with *whole* heart, with *full* soul and *all* its powers, because the true God is not the one who is natural to their consciousness, but rather must be held on to through a constant, expressive *actus*. Because God, to them, never becomes the one who is, the oldest state is the state of a devout submission and expectation, and Abraham is with justification called *the father of all believers*—not merely by the Jews, but also by others who come from the Near East—for he believes in the God who is not, but will be. All expect a future redemption. The patriarch Jacob, in the middle of the benediction with which he blesses his children, breaks out into the words: "Jehovah, I await your redemption." To understand this correctly one must go back to the meaning of the corresponding verb; this verb means to lead from the narrows[1] and into the expanse—thus, considered passively: to escape from the narrows, and therefore to be saved. All expect accordingly to be led out from these narrows, in which they have heretofore been held, and to become free of the presupposition (of the one-sided monotheism [XI 178]) that God himself cannot now remove, the presupposition within which they are enclosed along with the whole of the human race, enclosed as under *the law*, within necessity, up until the day of salvation, with which the true God ceases to be merely the appearing God, the merely self-revealing God, and thus with which the revelation itself ceases, as happened in Christ, for Christ is the *end* of the revelation.

We do not fear having accorded too much time to the great fact that the God of the earliest human race was also no longer the ultimate *One*, but rather only the relative *One*, even if not yet explained and known as such, and thus that the human race has proceeded from relative monotheism. To establish this fact from all sides had to appear to us of great importance, not merely vis-à-vis those who believe to be able to grasp mythology and polytheism only from out of a distorted revelation, but rather also vis-à-vis so-called philosophers of history, who, instead of from unity, have all religious development of mankind proceed from the *multiplicity* of thoroughly partial and indeed initially *localized* ideas, from so-called fetishism or shamanism, or from a deification of nature, which does not even deify *concepts* or *species*, but rather *individual* objects of nature—for example, this tree or this river. No, humanity has not proceeded from such misery; the majestic course of history has an entirely different beginning; the keynote² in the consciousness of humanity remained always that great *One*, who did not yet know his equal, who actually filled heaven and earth, that is—everything. Indeed, those who posit as the first matter of the human race the deification of nature, which they have found with the miserable hordes, deteriorated tribes, never with *peoples or nations*—compared with these historians or scholars, the others, who have monotheism precede mythology (monotheism in whatever sense, even if it were in that of one revealed), stand indefinably higher. In the meantime the relation between mythology and revelation has presented itself historically quite differently. We had to convince ourselves that revelation, that *the* monotheism, which can be historically proved a part of mankind [XI 179], is mediated through just that which also mediated polytheism—thus, that, far from us being able to presuppose the one to the other, the presupposition for both is a *common one*. And it seems to me that even the adherents of the hypothesis of revelation can, in the end, only be happy about this result.

Any revelation could only direct itself to an actual consciousness; but in the first actual consciousness we already find the relative *One*, which, as we saw, is the first potency of a successive polytheism and thus already the first potency of mythology itself. This mythology itself was unable to be posited through revelation; for this reason revelation must find it as a presupposition independent of itself; and does it not even require such an independent presupposition in order to be revelation? Revelation only occurs where some type of darkness is broken through; thus it presupposes a darkening, something that has stepped between consciousness and the God who is supposed to reveal himself.

Also the presumed *distortion* of the original content of a revelation would only be thinkable in the course of time and history; but the presupposition of mythology, the beginning of polytheism, is there as soon as mankind is there—so early that it is not explicable through a distortion.

If men such as the aforementioned Gerhard Voss explained individual myths as distorted events from the Old Testament, then it is indeed to be assumed that they were thereby concerned with an explanation of these individual myths and that they were far removed from the opinion to have thereby also uncovered the foundation of heathendom.

The use of the concept of revelation for every explanation that runs across difficulties in other ways is, on the one hand, a poor testament to the special reverence for this concept, a concept that lies too deep for one to be able to directly begin with it, to directly make use of it—as some imagine. On the other hand, it means to give up all understanding [*Begreifen*] if one wants to explain what is not understood [*ein Unbegriffenes*] through something else as little, or less, understood [*Begriffenes*]. For as familiar as this *word* is to many of us, who actually *thinks* [XI 180] something when he utters it. One would like to say: explain everything that you want through a revelation, but first explain to us what this itself is; make understandable for us the *precise process*, the fact, the event, which you have to think to yourself in the concept!

From time immemorial the real defenders of a revelation have restricted it to *a certain time*; thus they have explained the state of consciousness—the state that renders consciousness amenable to a revelation (*obnoxium reddit*)—as a transitory one, just as the apostles of the final and most complete revelation announce as an effect of it also the end of all extraordinary appearances and states of affairs, without which an actual revelation is unthinkable.

Christian theologians above all should be concerned to protect the revelation in this dependence on a special state that is to be presupposed to it, such that for them it is not, as has long since happened, dissolved into a merely *general* and rational relation, and such that, on the contrary, it is preserved in its strict *historicity*. Revelation, when such is assumed, presupposes a certain extraordinary state of consciousness. Every theory that treats of revelation would have to prove such a state independent of this revelation. Now, however, there cannot be found a fact out of which such an extraordinary state could be made evident other than mythology itself, and for this reason it would be far more likely that mythology be the presupposition of a philosophical understanding of the revelation than, vice-versa, mythology could be derived from a revelation.

From a philosophical standpoint we cannot place the hypothesis of revelation higher than any other that makes mythology dependent on a merely contingent fact. For a revelation accepted uncomprehendingly, as it can be taken no differently according to the present insights and philosophical means, is to be considered as nothing other than a purely contingent fact.

One could object to us that the relative monotheism from which [XI 181] we have all mythology proceed is also, up to now, a fact not yet understood. But the difference is that the hypothesis of revelation presents itself as a final one, which cuts off any further regress, while we in no way mean to conclude with that fact, but rather now take this fact that is historically established, and from this perspective—as we may assume—secured against every attack and consider it now straight away as a point of departure for a new development.

Accordingly, the following reflection will serve initially as a transition to a further development. That *One* who does not yet know his equal, and who is the ultimate *One* for the first humanity, comports itself however as the merely relative *One*, which does not yet *have* another outside itself, but yet can have one, and indeed such another one who will relieve him of his exclusive being. Thus, already with him the *foundation* is laid after all for successive polytheism [*successiven Polytheismus*]; he is, even if not yet known as such, according to his nature the first member of a future series of gods, of an actual successive polytheism [*Vielgötterei*]. From this, and this is now the next necessary conclusion, there ensues *the result that we know of no historical beginning for polytheism at all*—even taking historical time in the broadest sense. In the precise sense, historical time begins with the completed separation of the peoples. However, the time of the *crisis* of the peoples[3] precedes the completed separation. This time of crisis, as transition to the historical time, is to this extent properly pre-historical, but yet, to the extent that something happens and occurs in it too, it is only pre-historical in relation to the so-called historical time in the strictest sense—and so is in itself also historical; thus it is only relatively the pre-historical or historical time. On the other hand, the time of the calm, still unshaken unity of the human species—this will be the *ultimately pre-historical one*. Now, however, the consciousness of this time is already filled by that unconditioned, absolute *One*, which will subsequently be the first God of the successive polytheism. To that extent we know of no historical beginning for polytheism. To be sure, one might perhaps think it is unnecessary that the entire [XI 182] pre-historical time was filled with that God, and that, indeed, in this time there can still be thought an *earlier time*—where man still associated immediately with the true God—and a *later time* where it first fell prey to the relative *One*. If one wanted to make this objection, then the following would need to be remarked. With the simple concept of the ultimately pre-historical time every *before* and *after*, which one might think in it, is nullified. For if something could also still occur in it—and the assumed transition from the true God to the relative *One* would indeed be an occurrence—then it *would be* precisely not the ultimately pre-historical time, but rather would itself belong to historical time. Were there in it not *one* principle, but rather a series of principles, then it would be a series of actually differentiated times and thus it itself a part or stage of historical time. The ultimately pre-historical time is, *according to its nature*, the indivisible, absolutely identical time; and for this reason, whatever duration one ascribes it, it is to be considered only as a *moment*—that is, as time in which the end is as the beginning and the beginning is as the end, a type of eternity, because it itself is not a series of times but rather is only *one* time, which in itself is not an actual time, that is, a series of times, but rather only becomes time (namely, the past) relatively to that time following it. Now, if this is the case, and the ultimately pre-historical time admits *in itself* no further differentiation of times, then that consciousness of humanity—to which the relative *one* God is still the ultimately *One*—is the first *actual* consciousness of humanity, the consciousness *before* which it *itself* [humanity] knows of no other, in which it finds itself just as it finds itself, to which—according to time—no other is to be preconceived. And thus it follows that we know for polytheism no historical beginning, for in the first actual consciousness it is indeed not yet *actually* present (for no first member already forms for itself an actual series of consequences), but yet is present as *potentia*.

Given the otherwise so divergent course, the agreement here with David Hume can seem strange, in that Hume first asserted: *as far as we go back in history we find successive polytheism* [XI 183]. Thus in this we fully concur with him, even when it is to be deplored of the indefiniteness and even imprecision of his exposition[c] that the preconceived opinions of the philosopher here let the assiduity and precision of the historical researcher appear as dispensable. Hume proceeds from the totally abstract concept of polytheism, without considering it worth the trouble to penetrate into its actual character and into its various types, and then investigates, according to this abstract concept, how polytheism *could* have emerged into being. Here Hume has given the first example of that groundless type of Raissonement, which so often afterward—only without Hume's wit, spirit, and philosophical acumen—has been applied to historical problems, a Raissonement by which indeed—without looking around for what is historically or actually knowable—one attempts to imagine to oneself how the matter could have happened [XI 184], and then in a heartfelt way claims that it really *has* occurred in such a way.

In particular it is characteristic for his time how Hume neglects the Old Testament entirely, almost as if, for the sole reason that it is seen as a holy text by Jews and Christians, it lost historical value, or as if these texts for this reason—because they have been employed chiefly only by theologians and for dogmatic aims—cease to be a source for the knowledge of the oldest religious ideas, with which none is to be compared in purity as in age, and whose preservation, so to speak, is itself a miracle. Precisely the Old Testament has served to show us in what sense successive polytheism is as old as history. Not in the sense of a Humean polytheism, but rather in the sense that with the first actual consciousness also the first elements of a successive polytheism were already posited. Now, however, this is still merely the fact that cannot remain unexplained. That it must be explained means: this already mythological consciousness *potentia* too can only be one that *has become*, but as we have just seen, not one that has become *historically*. The process by which that consciousness has become, which we already find in the absolutely pre-historical time, can thus only be a *supra-historical* one. As we proceeded earlier from the historical time into the relative pre-historical time, then into the absolute pre-historical time, so also we see ourselves here obliged to proceed from the last to the supra-historical; and as earlier from the individual to the people, from the people to humanity, so now from humanity *to the original man himself*—for this original man only is to be thought in the supra-historical time. We see ourselves, however, obliged to a similar advance into the supra-historical time through another necessary consideration, through a question that was only withheld to this point because the time for its discussion had not yet come.

We have seen humanity unprethinkably in the relation to the relative One. Now, however, there is, besides the properly and the merely relative monotheism, which is monotheism [XI 185] only because it still conceals its opposite—apart from both there is a third: consciousness could nowhere be in any relation to God, neither to the true God nor to him who has to exclude another. Thus, of this—that it is in relation to God *at all*—of this the ground can no longer lie in the first actual consciousness; it can only be beyond it. But beyond the first actual consciousness there is nothing more to be thought except man, or the consciousness, *in its pure substance* prior to all *actual* consciousness, where man is not consciousness of *himself* (for this would not be thinkable without a *becoming* conscious, that is, without an *Actus*); thus, because he must yet be consciousness of *something*, he can only be consciousness of God, not bound up with an *Actus*, thus, for example, with a knowing or willing, thus the purely substantial consciousness of God. The original man is not *actu*, but rather he is *natura sua* that which posits God, and indeed—because God merely thought in general is only an abstraction, while the merely relative *One* already belongs to the actual consciousness—there remains for the primordial consciousness nothing other than that it is that which posits God in his truth and absolute unity. And so, indeed, if it is at all admissible to apply a term to such an essential God-positing, a term through which a scientific [*wissenschaftlicher*] concept is actually designated, or if we want to understand under monotheism just that positing of the true God in general, then—monotheism *would be the final presupposition of mythology*; but, as *you* now well see, first off a supra-historical monotheism, and second, not a monotheism of the human *understanding*, but rather of human *nature*, because man has in his *original* essence no other meaning but to be the God-positing nature because he only existed originally in order to be this God-positing creature—thus not the nature which is *for itself*, but rather the one that is devoted to *God*, as it were enraptured in God. For I gladly need everywhere the most proper and characteristic terms, and do not fear that one, for example, says here that that is a fanatical[4] teaching. For indeed the talk [XI 186] is not about that which man now *is*, or also only about that which he *can be*, since there lies in the middle of his primordial being and his current being the whole large, eventful history. Indeed, the teaching that maintained that man only *is* in order to posit God would be fanatical. This teaching of the immediate positing of God by man would be fanatical if one—after man has made the great step into reality—wanted to make this positing of God into the exclusive rule of his current life, as happens with the meditators, the

Yogis of India or the Persian Sufis, who, internally torn apart by the contradictions of their faith in the gods, or weary in general of being and thinking subordinated to *becoming*, practically want to strive back to that disappearance into God—that is, like the mystics of all ages find only the way backward, not however forward into the true knowledge.

It is a question that must be addressed not merely in an investigation into mythology, but rather in every history of humanity, how the human consciousness could from the beginning, indeed before all else, be concerned with representations of a religious nature, indeed entirely seized by such. But what occurs in so many similar cases—that by incorrectly stating the question one makes the answer itself impossible—has also happened here. One asked: how does consciousness come to God? But consciousness does not come to God. Its first movement, as we have seen, goes away from the *true* God. In the first actual consciousness there is only a moment of him (for we can also preliminarily view the relative *One* in this way), no longer he himself; thus because this consciousness—as soon as it emerges from its primordial state, as soon as it *stirs*—moves away from God, nothing remains but that this God originally is attached to this consciousness, or that consciousness has God *in* himself, in itself in the sense that one says a man has a virtue in itself, or more often, a vice in itself, by which one just intends to express that it is not something objective to him, not something that he wills, indeed not even something about which he knows. [XI 187] Man (always understood as the original, essential man) is in and, as it were, prior to himself; that is, before he is in possession of himself, thus before he has become something *else*—for he is already something different if he, returning to himself, has become object to himself—man, as soon as he simply *is* and still has *become* nothing, is consciousness of God. He does not *have* this consciousness; he *is* it, and precisely in the *non*-actus, in immobility, is he that which posits the true God.

We have spoken of a monotheism of the primordial consciousness, of which was noted that it 1) is not an accidental monotheism that has somehow become for consciousness, because it is one that is attached to the substance of consciousness; that it 2) is for this reason precisely not one that is to be historically presupposed, one that has become the lot of man or to the human species and was later lost to him. Because the God is one posited with the nature of man, he is not first in man with time; he is eternal to him because he has become along with his nature; 3) we will also have to admit that this monotheism of the original consciousness is not one that knows itself, that it is only a *natural* and *blind* one, which has first to become one that is known. Now, if following this determination someone further argued: with such a blind monotheism one cannot speak of a differentiation, of consciousness of the true God *as such* (that is, not as the formal God)—then this we can grant completely. Further, if one said: just as it rests on an absorption of the human essence into the divine essence it will suffice to designate that consciousness as a natural or essential theism—so we will also not argue against him, especially since with appropriate distinguishing between concepts and their designations it is necessary to posit theism as that which is in common and that which communally precedes, and the indifference, the equal possibility, of (actual) monotheism and polytheism; and our intention can indeed be none other than to let both the one and the other proceed from out of the original consciousness. To the question of which existed first, if polytheism or monotheism, we will in a certain sense answer: *neither of the two* [XI 188]. Not polytheism: in whose case it is self-evident that it is nothing original—everyone concedes this, for all seek to explain it. But, as we have already stated, a polytheism, which really is polytheism, can also not be understood with an original atheism of consciousness. So, would indeed monotheism be what is original? But this monotheism is not original either; to wit, not according to the concepts that the defenders of its priority attach to the word, and thereby mean either an *abstract* monotheism, which only excludes its opposite, out of which polytheism thus could never have emerged, or a *formal* one—that is, one resting on actual knowledge and differentiation. Thus, if we kept the word, then it is indeed only possible in this way, in that we answer: indeed monotheism, but one that is and is not [that which is original]; *is* now namely and so long as consciousness does not stir; is *not*, namely is not so that it could not become polytheism. Or, in a more determinate precaution against misunderstanding: indeed monotheism, but one that yet knows nothing of its opposite, and thus also does not know itself *as* monotheism, and neither one that has made itself already into the abstract monotheism—by excluding its opposite—nor one that is an already *actual* one, a self-knowing and self-possessing monotheism by virtue of having overcome its opposite and carrying it within itself as conquered. Now we indeed see: monotheism, which relates to both polytheism and the future formal monotheism—the latter resting in real knowledge—only as the possibility or matter that has a common relation [to both], is itself simply material monotheism, and the latter is not differentiable from simple theism, if this theism is not taken in the abstract sense of the moderns but rather in the one established by us, where it is just the equal possibility of either.

Thus this might be sufficient for the explanation of the question of in which sense we presuppose to mythology either monotheism or theism: 1) not formal, in which the true God as such is differentiated; 2) not an abstract one, which only excludes polytheism; for to the contrary it indeed still has it in itself. But from here on [XI 189] our entire investigation must take a different course. For this reason *allow* me once again to sum up, as a conclusion, a general view of that which was just dealt with.

Our ascensive examination led us ultimately to the first actual consciousness of mankind, but already in this, in the consciousness, beyond which mankind knows nothing, God has a determination. We find as content of this consciousness, at least as immediate content, no longer the pure divine Self but rather God in a determinate form of existence. We find him as the God of power, of strength, as El Schaddai—as the Hebrews called him—and as the God of heaven and earth. Yet the content of this consciousness is God in general, and indeed undoubtedly with necessity—God. This necessity must stem from an earlier moment; but beyond the first actual consciousness nothing more is to be thought than the consciousness in its pure substance. This consciousness is—not through knowing and willing, but rather according to its nature, essentially, and such that it is nothing else, nothing outside that— that which *posits* God, and as itself merely essentially that, it can also only be in relation to God in his essence, that is, in his pure Self. But now, however, furthermore it is to be immediately understood that this essential relation is precisely to be thought only as a moment, that man cannot persist in this being-outside-*itself*, that it must strive out beyond that state of being immersed in God in order to transform the relation into a *knowledge* of God, and thereby into a free relation. But it can only arrive at this relation in steps. When its primordial relation to God is sublated its relation to God is not for this ended *in general*, for it is an eternal, indissoluble one. Himself become *actual*, man falls prey to God in his actuality. Now, let us assume—in consequence of that which admittedly is not yet understood philosophically but is proved factually through our explanation of successive polytheism—let us assume that God is as much a *multiplicity* according to his own forms of existence as he is One according to his divine Self or essence, and then it is understood on what the successiveness of polytheism rests [XI 190] and toward which it aims. None of those forms is for itself equal to God, but if they form into a unity in consciousness, then this emerged unity, as one that *has become*, is also a monotheism attained knowingly, by consciousness.

A monotheism proper, one bound up with knowledge, is itself even historical only as result. For all that, consciousness will not immediately fall prey to the multiplicity of figures that succeed one another in consciousness—that is, not immediately to the decisive polytheism. With the first figure, those that follow, and thus polytheism, will only be given as *potentia*. This is that moment known by us historically, where consciousness completely and indivisibly belongs to the relative *One*, who is not yet in contradiction with the ultimate *One* but rather is to consciousness *like the latter*. In it, we said, mankind still worshipped the *One*—albeit unknowingly. The decisive polytheism now following is only the path to the liberation from the *One*'s one-sided power, only the transition to the relation that is supposed to be won again. In polytheism nothing is mediated through knowledge. On the other hand, monotheism, which, when it is knowledge of the true God as such and with differentiation, can only be a result, not that which is original— monotheism expresses the relation that man can have to God only in knowledge, only as one that is free. If, in the same context, Christ—where he announces[d] the worshipping of God in spirit and in truth as the future, universal one—has the liberation (σωτηρία) come from the Jews, then the context shows that this liberation according to Christ's meaning is the liberation or salvation from *that which* humanity worshipped without *knowing* it, and elevation to that which becomes *known*, and that is *only* to be known.[5] God in his truth can only be known; a blind relation to God in his mere actuality is also possible.

The meaning of this last development is: only in this way *can* mythology be understood [XI 191]. For this reason, however, it is not yet *actually* understood. Meanwhile we are also free from the *last* contingent presupposition—of a monotheism historically preceding mythology, a monotheism that because it could not be for humanity one that is self-invented, could only be a revealed one; and because this presupposition was the last remaining of all the earlier ones, we are thus now first free of *all* contingent presuppositions, and thereby of all explanations that deserve to be called merely hypotheses. Where, however, the contingent presuppositions and hypotheses stop, there begins science [*Wissenschaft*]. According to the nature of the matter, those contingent presuppositions could only be of a *historical* nature, but they have through our critique much rather proven themselves *unhistorical*. And it requires *no* presupposition, aside from the consciousness in its *substance* and the first movement, which is indisputably to be viewed as natural, that first movement through which consciousness receives that determination, by virtue of which it is subjugated to mythological succession. But *these* presuppositions are no longer of a historical nature. The limit of possible historical explanations was reached with the pre-historical consciousness of mankind, and there remained only the way into the supra-historical. The blind theism of the primordial consciousness, from which we proceed, is—as with the *essence* of man prior to all movement, thus also before all events—posited only to be determined as one that is supra-historical; and likewise that movement—through which man, posited from out of the relation to the divine Self, falls prey to the actual God—can be thought only as a supra-historical event.

Now, however, with such presuppositions the entire method of explanation of mythology is also altered. For, understandably, we will not yet be able to proceed to the explanation itself. But it may yet be tentatively seen which *method* of explanation is solely possible according to the just delineated presuppositions.

Thus, to begin with, how every merely contingent emergence into being is eliminated of itself with these presuppositions will become clear through the following considerations.

[XI 192] The ground of mythology is already laid in the first actual consciousness; thus, polytheism, according to its essence, already emerged in the transition to this consciousness. From this it follows that the act by *which* the ground for polytheism is laid does not itself fall into the actual consciousness, but rather lies outside of the latter. The first actual consciousness *exists* already with this affection, through which it is separated from its eternal and essential being. It can no longer go back into this being and can as little transcend this determination as it can transcend itself. For this reason this determination has something incomprehensible for consciousness; it is the unintended and unforeseen consequence of a movement that it cannot retract. Its origin lies in a region to which it no longer has access once separated from it. That which is incurred, the contingent, transforms itself into what is necessary and immediately assumes the figure of what is never again to be sublated.

The alteration of consciousness consists in this, that the ultimately *One* God does not live in it any longer, but instead only the relative *One* God. But the second follows this first one not contingently, but rather according to an objective necessity that we indeed do not yet understand, but for this reason are obliged no less to recognize as such (as objective) in advance. Thus with that first determination consciousness is simultaneously subjected to the necessary succession of representations, by which polytheism proper emerges into being. Supposing the first affection, the movement of consciousness through the succeeding figures is such a one in which thinking and willing, understanding and freedom, no longer have a part. Consciousness is unexpectedly involved in this movement in a mode now no longer comprehensible to it. The movement is related to that consciousness as a *fate*, as a *destiny* against which it can do nothing. It is a *real* power against consciousness—that is, a power that now no longer is under its authority, which [on the contrary] has taken hold of consciousness. *Prior* to all thinking it is already captivated by that principle whose merely *natural* consequence is successive polytheism and mythology.

Thus—to be sure, not in the sense of a philosophy [XI 193] that has man begin from animal obtuseness and senselessness, but indeed in the sense that the Greeks intimate by various very descriptive expressions such as θεόπληχτος, θεοβλαβής, among others, and thus in the sense that consciousness is subject to and, as it were, struck by the one-sided *One*—in this way, the oldest mankind indeed finds itself in a state of unfreedom, finds itself posited outside itself, which is to say outside its own self-dominion—it finds itself in a state that we, living under the law of an entirely different time, cannot immediately understand, a condition of mankind struck (*stupefacta quasi et attonita*) with a type of *stupor* and seized upon by an alien dominion.

The ideas through whose succession the formal polytheism immediately emerges, but also through which material (simultaneous) polytheism mediately emerges, produce themselves for consciousness *without its cooperation*, indeed against its will and—so that we definitely articulate the correct word, which brings to an end all earlier explanations that somehow assume *invention* in mythology, and that actually first gives us that which is independent of all invention, indeed *that which is opposed to all invention*, which we were already occasioned earlier to demand—mythology emerges into being through a (in view of consciousness) **necessary process**, whose origin is lost in the supra-historical and is concealed from it itself, a necessary process against which consciousness perhaps can resist in isolated moments, but which it cannot stop on the whole and can revoke and undo still less.

Accordingly, with this the concept of the *process* would be advanced a general concept of the manner of emergence, the former of which completely removes mythology (and with it our investigation) from the sphere in which all prior explanations maintained themselves. With this concept it is decided about the question of how the mythological ideas were meant in mythology's emerging into being. The question of *how* the mythological ideas were meant shows the difficulty or impossibility in which we find ourselves when assuming that they were meant as truth. For this reason then the first attempt is to interpret them figuratively; that is, to assume in them a truth, but a different one than they express immediately [XI 194]—the second attempt is to see in them an original truth, but one that has been *distorted*. But, rather, after the result just obtained one can open up the question of whether the mythological ideas were *meant* at all, namely, if they were object of an intent—that is, of a free holding for true.[6] So here also the question was incorrectly posed; it was posed under a presupposition that was itself incorrect. The mythological ideas are neither invented nor voluntarily taken on.—Products of a process independent of thinking and willing, they were of unambiguous and urgent reality for the consciousness subjected to this process. Peoples as well as individuals are only tools of this process, which they do not survey, which they serve without understanding it. It is not up to them to elude these representations, to take them up or not to take them up; for they do not *come* to them externally, but rather they *are* in them without them being conscious of how; for they come from out of the inner part of consciousness itself, to which they present themselves with a necessity that permits no doubt about their truth.

Once one has hit upon the idea of such a manner of emergence, then it is understood completely that the mythology considered merely materially seemed so puzzling, in that it is a known fact that also other things resting on a spiritual process, on a particular and internal experience, appear as alien and incomprehensible to those who do not have this experience, while it has an entirely comprehensible and reasonable meaning for him to whom the internal process is not hidden. The central question with respect to mythology is the question of meaning. But the meaning of *mythology* can only be the meaning of the *process* by which it emerges into being.

Were the personalities and the events that are the content of mythology of the type that, according to the assumed concepts, we could consider them possible objects of an immediate experience, and were gods beings that could appear, then no one would ever have thought to take them in a sense other than an *actual* one [XI 195]. One would have explained the belief in the truth and objectivity of these representations—the belief that we absolutely must ascribe to heathendom, should it not, in a different way, itself become a fable for us—simply out of an *actual experience* of that earlier mankind. One would simply have assumed that these personalities, these occurrences, have in reality happened and appeared to that earlier mankind in such a way, and thus were also true for it in its proper and actual understanding—just like the analogous appearances and encounters that are recounted by the Abrahamites, and which to us in the current state are likewise impossible, were true for them. Now, just precisely that which was not thought previously is made possible by the presently justified explanation; this explanation is the first that has an answer to the question: how was it possible that the peoples of antiquity were not only able to bestow faith in those religious ideas—which appear to us thoroughly nonsensical and contrary to reason—but were able to bring them the most serious, in part painful, sacrifices.

Because mythology is not something that emerged artificially, but is rather something that emerged naturally—indeed, under the given presupposition, with necessity—*form* and *content*, *matter* and *outer appearance*, cannot be differentiated in it. The ideas are not first present in another form, but rather they emerge only in, and thus also at the same time with, this form. Earlier in these lectures such an organic becoming was already demanded by us, but the principle of the process, by which alone it becomes explicable, was not found.

Because consciousness chooses or invents neither the ideas themselves nor their expression, mythology emerges immediately *as such* and in no other sense than in which it articulates itself. In consequence of the necessity with which the *content* of the ideas generates itself, mythology has from the beginning a *real* [*reelle*] and thus also *doctrinal* [*doctrinelle*] meaning. In consequence of the necessity with which also the *form* emerges, mythology is thoroughly actual—that is, everything in it is thus to be understood as mythology expresses it, not as if something else were thought, something else said. Mythology is not *allegorical* [XI 196]; it is *tautegorical*.[e] To mythology the gods are actually existing essences, gods that are not something *else*, do not *mean* something else, but rather *mean* only what they are. Earlier, authenticity [*Eigentlichkeit*] and doctrinal meaning were opposed to one another. But according to our explanation both authenticity and doctrinal meaning cannot be separated, and instead of relinquishing the authenticity to the benefit of a doctrinal meaning, or saving the authenticity, but at the cost of the doctrinal meaning, like the poetic view, we are rather, conversely, obliged through our explanation to assert and maintain the consistent unity and indivisibility of the meaning.

In order to show immediately in practice the foundational principle of the *unconditioned* [*unbedingten*] authenticity, let us recall that in mythology two moments were differentiated: 1) the polytheistic; [XI 197] in relation to this moment we will thus, after the repudiation of every inauthentic meaning, maintain that the talk is *actually* of gods; after the earlier explanations, what this means to say requires no repeated discussion. Only in the meantime the discovery has come to light that the process producing mythology already has its ground and beginning in the *first actual consciousness* of mankind. From this it follows that the representations of the gods could at *no* possible or presumable time have been left to that contingent emergence that is assumed in the usual hypotheses, and that, in particular, there remains for a presumably *pre*-mythological polytheism—as is in part presupposed by those explanations—so little time as for the reflections on natural phenomena, from which—according to Heyne, Hermann, or Hume—mythology is supposed to have emerged, for the first actual consciousness was, according to the matter, already a mythological one. That merely so-called polytheism is supposed to rest on contingent representations of invisible, supernatural beings; but there was never originally a part of the human race that was in the position to come to representations of the gods in such a way. This polytheism prior to mythology is therefore a mere figment of the schools. It is, we can say, *historically* proven that there could not be another polytheism prior to the mythological one, that there was never another polytheism besides a mythological one—that is, that one that is posited with the process proven by us, thus none in which there would not have been actual gods, that is, in which *God* would not have been the ultimate content. But mythology is not merely polytheism in general, but rather 2) historical polytheism, so much so that that which would not (*potentiâ* or *actu*) be polytheism historically could also not be called mythological. But in spite of this moment, the succession is to be understood as an actual one and the unconditional authenticity to be held on to firmly. It is a movement that *truly occurs*, to which consciousness is *in reality* subjugated. Even in the specifics of the succession, it is not arbitrariness, but rather necessity, that a particular god and no other precedes or follows some other god, and even in view of the special circumstances of those events, which happen in the history of the gods [XI 198], no matter how odd they may appear to us, in the consciousness the conditions out of which the representations of the same naturally arise will constantly be proven. In order to take on a comprehensible and graspable meaning, the emasculation of Uranus, the regicide of Kronos, and the other countless acts and events of the history of the gods require nothing other than to be understood literally.

One also cannot, as has often been attempted with revelation, differentiate *doctrine* and *history* and consider the latter as mere wording of the former. The doctrine is not *external to* history, but rather precisely history itself is also the doctrine, and conversely the doctrinal of mythology is contained precisely in the historical.

Considered objectively, mythology is as what it presents itself: *actual theogony*, the history of the gods. Because, however, actual gods are only those for which God lies as the ground, the final content of the history of the gods is the production of an actual becoming *of God* in consciousness, to which *the gods* are related only as the individual, productive moments.

Considered *subjectively*, or as according to its emergence into being, mythology is a *theogonic process*. It is 1) a process in general, which consciousness actually completes, namely, in such a way that it is obliged to tarry in the individual moments, and in the one following constantly hangs on to the preceding one, and thus *experiences* that movement in the proper sense. It is 2) an *actually* theogonic process; that is, one that stems from an essential relation of human consciousness to God, from a relation in which it, according to its substance, is what is God-positing, thus in virtue of which it is in general that which posits God naturally (*natura sua*). Because the original relation is a natural one, consciousness cannot emerge from this relation without being led back into it *through a process*. Hereby it cannot (I plead that this be noted) help but to appear as that which again *posits* God only *mediately* (indeed, precisely through a process)—that is, it cannot help but to appear as just the consciousness that produces God and thus as the theogonic one.

Lecture Nine

[XI 199] If, from the standpoint arrived at, we look back one last time at the merely *external* presuppositions with which one, in the earlier hypotheses, intended to understand mythology (indeed, revelation was also one of these), then it was indisputably an essential step to the philosophical consideration of mythology in general that its emergence was transferred into the *interior* of the original mankind, that poets or cosmogonial philosophers or adherents of a historically preceding religious doctrine no longer counted as inventors of mythology, but rather human *consciousness* itself was recognized as the true seat and the authentic principle of production of the mythological ideas.

In the whole development up to this point I have been at pains duly to indicate and recognize, in its place, every progress that the investigation owes to earlier researchers, and even from those views that could appear totally random to win a side by which they nevertheless presented themselves as necessary. It was also guaranteed by the method that no type of representation of mythology worthy of being mentioned was passed over. Already its title—a title that seemed to announce something similar to the intent and the content of the present lectures—occasions us to take special consideration of a text: we mean the text by the too soon departed *K. Ottfried Müller: Prolegomena to a Scientific Mythology (1825)*.[1] I found there the following statements, which could appear to agree [XI 200] with some of my own statements, presented four years earlier. "From the beginning, mythology emerged through the unification and mutual interpenetration of the Ideal and the Real,"[a] where under the Ideal is understood that which is thought and where under the Real is understood that which happens. Additionally, under that which happens he understands, as we will see, not the form of that which happens in mythology, but rather that which actually happens **outside** of mythology. The same author wants to know nothing of *invention* for the emergence of the myths—but in what sense? As he himself explains, in the sense in which invention "is supposed to be a free and intentional action, through which something *perceived as untrue* by the agent is supposed[b] to be draped with the illusion of truth." We have neither accepted nor repudiated invention in this sense. Müller, however, allows invention insofar as it is a communal one. This becomes evident by that which he assumes, "that a *certain* necessity has prevailed in the connection of the Ideal and Real in the myth, that the designers (that is, perhaps, the inventors?) of the myths *were led to this* (that is, to the myths?) *through drives that worked in common on all*, and that in the myths those various elements (Ideal and Real) grew together, without[c] that those, through whom it occurred, would even have perceived their differentiation, would have brought their difference to consciousness." Thus this would come back to that communal creative[2] drive (probably of a myth producing people), that we have earlier[d] likewise designated as a possibility but that, however, has also been eliminated there. It appears that this interpenetration of the Ideal and Real in their application to mythology (for, in any case, the scholarly man had indeed brought along the general thought from a philosophical school) presented itself to some researchers of antiquity as dark and mystical. [XI 201] For this reason O. Müller seeks to explain it through examples, and there we will clearly see his meaning. The first of these examples is drawn from the plague in the first book of the *Iliad*, where, famously, Agamemnon insults the priest of Apollo; then this priest asks the god to avenge him; the god immediately has the plague come, and where the *facta*—thus, that is, that the daughter of a priest of Apollo was demanded back in vain by the father, where the father was refused with disdain, upon which the plague broke out—and, where the facta are taken as correct, *"all those who were filled by the belief in Apollo's vengeful and punishing violence"* immediately, and each *of themselves* and with complete agreement, made the connection that Apollo had sent the plague at the request of his priest, who had been insulted by the refusal to give back his daughter, and each articulated this connection with the same conviction, as the facta (one sees here what that which has happened means to him) that he had seen himself.[3] From this it would seem to be gathered that the explanation presented, according to the own opinion of its author, was not supposed to encompass that which alone is puzzling, that is, how men came to the point where they were convinced of the existence of an Apollo and of his avenging and punishing violence, [and] thus the essence of the proper content of mythology itself. For that story in the first book of the *Iliad* belongs as little to mythology itself as the story of the *Legio fulminatrix* or other similar stories belong to the Christian teaching.[4] After I found this, I saw that O. Müller's prolegomenas have nothing in common with the Philosophy of Mythology.[5] This Philosophy of Mythology refers to that which is original, to the history of the gods itself, and not to the myths that first emerge in that a historical factum is posited in connection with a divinity; and because it does not at all refer to mythology proper, the O. Müllerian view could not also be mentioned under the earlier views of mythology. For the Philosophy of Mythology does not concern itself with this, with how these stories derived from mythology have emerged. If that were so, it would be like those instances when the discussion is about the meaning of Christianity and someone were to speak of the legends and wanted to explain how these came to be. Naturally, out of the abundance of the heart, the mouth speaks. When once filled with representations of the gods, they will have involved them in all situations, and thus also in all narratives, and thus indeed myths in O. Müller's sense will, without arrangement, without intention, emerge [XI 202] with a type of necessity.

Now, if in this whole development I have endeavored to be true to my predecessors, and have sought to give each his due, one will not be able to blame me if I also bring this justice to bear upon myself and vindicate to myself that first step—without which indeed I never would have been occasioned to hold lectures relating to mythology—of seeking the thought, the seat, the *subjectum agens* of mythology in the human consciousness itself. This thought, to posit human consciousness in the place of inventors, poets, or individuals in general, later received something corresponding in the attempt to make for the doctrine of revelation the *Christian consciousness* into the carrier and support of all Christian ideas; although herewith it appears that what was sought more were the means of getting rid of all objective questions, where the point with us, on the contrary, was to gain objectivity for the mythological representations.

Goethe opined, at the moment I do not know on which occasion: whoever wishes to achieve something in a work and not to be disturbed, he will do well to keep his plans as secret as possible. The least disadvantage that he has to expect in the opposite case is—if someone somehow happens to hold of him the opinion that he knows where a treasure is to be unearthed—that he may have to anticipate that many hope in haste and hurry to win the treasure before him, or, if they are quite courteous and reasonable, at the least indeed want to help him with the unearthing of it. Obviously, then, the public lecturer—who does not merely repeat what is long known—is in the worst position, in that he has almost thousands of people who share his knowledge, and whatever in Germany is once pronounced from the rostrum spreads in all sorts of manners and secret ways [XI 203], especially through transcribed volumes, into the farthest reaches, according to circumstances.[6] One has often misconstrued it of academic scholars, and admonished it almost as an acknowledgment of a dearth of ideas, and almost as base ill-will, when they did not comport themselves entirely with equanimity against unwarranted appropriation of their merely verbally disseminated thoughts. The first one could let slide, for no one is obliged to be rich in ideas, and poverty that is no one's fault is no shame. Concerning the other complaint, one should yet be so fair to consider that, for example, whoever has never been so fortunate to defend his fatherland with arms, whoever has never had a part in the public affairs of government or legislation, and to the *Dic cur hic* can in general only answer with his poetic creations or some scientific ideas, nevertheless has some right to retain purely the claim to all the latter, a claim that he believes to ground in his contemporaries or in posterity, just like then the most honorable spirits were not insensitive to this. The great poet just mentioned brings it up in his biography, when an acquaintance of youth used a mere sujet before him, and not at all as appears to me one especially worthy of envy. If one says that it is fitting for the rich man to let poverty have something of his wealth, then no one who has his own thoughts on scientific matters occurring in life, and who is used to stating them trustingly, will lack the opportunity to practice this Christian virtue in silence. Yet also this generosity has its limits, for by nothing else are so many ingrates produced. I am not speaking of the usual lack of gratitude, about which many teachers complain: perhaps here it just happens naturally, like when a magnetic pole at the point of contact gives rise to its opposite pole. But whoever has sold as his own the ideas of another, ideas that became known to him fortuitously—he becomes naturally that other's irreconcilable enemy. It is strange to hear from just those who believe not to be able to speak out vigorously enough against the pirate printing [*Nachdruck*], and from those who practice this shameful trade [XI 204]—it is strange to hear claimed by these people the most ignominious names, to hear recommended forebearance for the first printing [*Vordruck*], which though, in the case it could achieve its end, would be a far worse theft than the first. The error-filled editions are also brought to bear against the pirate printing [*Nachdruck*]; but it is not noticed in which form pilfered ideas come into the world, mostly so mauled and sullied that they could become disliked by the author himself. To use notebooks that are transcribed from a public lecturer who does not impart what is long known but rather new and specific ideas means to want to learn from this lecturer, but without acknowledging oneself as his student; but this means, at the same time, to seek to gain an advantage over competitors for whom either the occasion for such use is absent or who disdain such a usage; for even whoever is beware of material use has won an advantage, at least with respect to the method, the treatment, the manner of expression, if these are new and specific. If now, otherwise, all of this is less highly appraised, then it is so because at the end the true author always distinguishes himself, and instead of the *Sic vos non vobis*, the other claim comes true: *Sic redit ad dominum, quod fuit ante suum.*

Our last result was that mythology in general emerges through a process, especially through a theogonic process, in which human consciousness is held firmly through its essence. After this concept is won, precisely it immediately becomes—in consequence of the procedure followed in this entire investigation—again the departure point of a new development; indeed, that process will be the only object of the *science* [*Wissenschaft*] for which the discussions up to now have served as introduction. It will not have escaped you that we have so far only used that result to take into account and consider the *subjective* meaning of the process, that which it had for *the humanity involved in it*. Also this meaning had to be dealt with above all; for this entire investigation had proceeded from the question of what mythology originally means, that is, what it means to them for whom it emerged. Thus, whatever concerns this question [XI 205], a completely satisfactory explanation is reached and this investigation can be considered as closed. But precisely thereby are we summoned to the higher question, of what the process means not in relation to the consciousness subjected to it, but what it in itself means, what it objectively means.

Now, we have seen that the representations producing themselves in consciousness have a *subjective* necessity for the mankind affected by them, and likewise a subjective truth. Now, as *you* well see this would not prevent that these same representations would, *objectively* considered, yet be wrong and contingent, and also in this sense explanations can be thought of that one could not speak earlier because they first become possible in the current standpoint of subjective necessity. All earlier explanations stopped with their presuppositions within historical time; we have now established an explanation that goes back to a supra-historical process, and so here we find forerunners that could not be thought before. It is a very old opinion that derives heathendom, like all ruination in humanity, from the *fall of man* alone. This derivation can sometimes assume a merely *moral* tone, and sometimes a *pietistic* or *mystical* tinge. In every form, however, it deserves recognition on account of the insight that mythology cannot be explained without a *real displacement*[7] of man from his original standpoint. In this it agrees with *our* explanation; on the other hand the course of the explanation will be a different one, insofar as it finds especially necessary to draw on nature and to explain polytheism by the divinizing of nature. In the *manner that* it links mankind to the divinization of nature, the theological view differentiates itself from the famed analogous explanations; but with the divinization of nature it returns under a category of interpretations that was already there earlier. Man, fallen through sin into the sphere of attraction[8] of nature, and, sinking always deeper in this direction, conflates the created with the creator, which thereby ceases being *One* for him, and becomes many. This may be, in short, the content of this explanation—in its simplest form [XI 206]. Turned toward the mystical, it was able perhaps to more precisely articulate itself in the following way. To be sure, we must not proceed from an original, however masterly *knowledge*, but rather from a *Being* of man in the divine unity. Man is created in the center of the Godhead, and it is *essential* to him to be in the center, for only there is he in his true place. As long as he finds himself in this [center] he sees things as they are in God, not in the spiritless and unityless externality of the usual seeing, but rather as they are taken up step by step into one another, are thereby, in man as their head, and through him, taken up into God. However, as soon as man has moved away from the middle point and has removed himself, the periphery leads him astray, and that divine unity is confused, for he himself is no longer lord *over* things, but rather has himself sunk to the same level as them. However, as man intends to retain his central position and the intuition bound up therewith—while he already is in another place—there emerges that middle world, which we name a world of the gods, out of the striving and fighting to hang on to the original divine unity in that which is already disturbed and diverged, that world of the gods that is as it were the dream of a higher existence, a dream that man continues to dream for a certain time, after he has sunk from that higher existence. And this divine world emerges for him in fact in a nonarbitrary way as consequence of a necessity dictated to him through his original relation itself, the effect of which necessity persists up to the final awakening, where he, having come to self-knowledge, resigns himself to this extra-divine world, happy to have been released from the immediate relation that he cannot maintain and all the more eager to posit in its place one mediated, but one at the same time liberating for him.

In this explanation there is also a return to the primordial Being [*Urseyn*] of man: mythology is no less the consequence of a nonarbitrary process, to which man falls prey because he stirs himself from his original position. But as you yourself see, according to this explanation mythology would be only something false [XI 207] and also something merely subjective, namely, what exists in such representations, to which nothing real outside them would correspond, for divinized natural objects are no longer actual ones. But especially to be accentuated, however, would be the *contingency* that the drawing-on things brings into the explanation, while alone the manner in which we have reached the concept of the process brings with it that nothing is required for this process except consciousness, nothing outside the principles it itself posits and constitutes. It is not at all the things with which man deals in the mythological process by which consciousness is moved, but rather it is the *powers arising in the interior of consciousness itself*. The theogonic process, through which mythology emerges, is a *subjective* one insofar as it takes place in *consciousness* and shows itself through the generating of representations: but the causes and thus also the objects of these representations are the *actually* and *in themselves* theogonic powers, just those powers through which consciousness is originally the God-positing consciousness. The content of the process are not merely *imagined* potencies but rather the *potencies themselves*—which create consciousness and which create nature (because consciousness is only the end of nature) and for this reason are also actual powers. The mythological process does not have to do with natural *objects*, but rather with the pure creating potencies whose original product is consciousness itself. Thus it is here where the explanation fully breaks through into the objective realm, becomes fully *objective*. Earlier there was a point where we grouped together under the name irreligious all of the explanations dealt with until then, in order to oppose to them the religious explanation in general as the one that is alone still possible; now there is needed a still more general designation under which also the religious explanations rejected heretofore can be relegated to those earlier explanations that have been dealt with. We want to now call the *subjective* ones all explanations—including the religious ones that ascribe to the mythological representations a merely contingent or subjective meaning—that have come forth until now; these are the subjective explanations above which the *objective* explanation elevates itself as the ultimately alone victorious one.

[XI 208] The mythological process that has as causes the theogonic potencies in themselves is not of merely religious meaning in general but rather of *objectively religious* meaning; for it is the in themselves God-positing potencies that are effective [*wirken*] in the mythological process. But also herewith the final determination is not yet reached, for we have heard earlier of a monotheism that supposedly *has diverged* and splintered itself into polytheism. Thus indeed in the process it can be the theogonic potencies themselves, but themselves as such, that diverge in it and cause [*bewirken*] it through *divergence*. In this way mythology would then be only what is *deformed*, ruptured, and wrecked of the primordial consciousness. Under monotheism, which is supposed to have disintegrated into successive polytheism [*Vielgötterei*], a historical one was of course considered, a historical monotheism that is supposed to have been present in a certain era of the human race. Admittedly, we have now had to give up such a thought. But in the meantime we have accepted an essential, that is, potential, monotheism of the primordial consciousness. Thus at the least it could be this monotheism that destroyed itself in the theogonic process, and one could now say: the same potencies, which in their collective effectivity and in their unity make consciousness into what posits God, become in their *divergence* the causes of the process by which gods are posited and thus through which mythology emerges.

Now, initially however, how is the *true* unity [*Einheit*] supposed to destroy itself in the assumed process, since on the contrary it has been explained expressly that it is a destruction of the *false* singularity [*Einzigkeit*] as such, and this destruction itself is again only a *means*, only a transition, which could have no other end than the restoration of the true unity, the reconstruction and, in the last instance, the actualization of the same monotheism in consciousness, a monotheism that in the beginning was a merely essential or potential one?

However, one could object as follows. Mythology is essentially successive polytheism [*successiver Polytheismus*], and the latter can only emerge through an actual series of potencies, in which each of the previous potencies calls forth the following one [XI 209], the following potency is complemented through the previous one, and thus ultimately the true unity is again posited. But just this successive emergence of the moments that compose and restore the unity supposedly is a divergence after all, or at least presupposes their having diverged.

One could grant the last objection, but only by adding that this divergence does not happen in the process itself that produces mythology, for in this process the potencies only occur as successive *in order* to again produce and posit the unity. The *meaning* of the *process* is for this reason not a diverging, but rather, on the contrary, a coming together of the moments positing the unity; the process itself consists not in the separation but rather in the re-unification of those moments. Apparently a potency gives the impulse for this process, a potency that has seized consciousness exclusively—thus to the exclusion of the others—without this consciousness being cognizant of it. But just this potency that, to this extent, sublates the true unity transforms itself—again relieved of the exclusivity and subdued by the process—into that which posits the unity now no longer silently, but rather *actually*, or as I tend express it, *cum ictu et actu*, such that the monotheism posited hereby is to consciousness itself now also more *actual, more emerged*, and accordingly at the same time *more understood*, more objective. The false, by which the tension is posited and the process is initiated, thus lies *prior to* the process. For that reason, *in* the process as such (and this is the main point) there is nothing false, but rather *truth*. It is the process of the self-restoring and for this reason self-realizing truth; it is thus indeed not truth in the individual moment, for otherwise it would need no advance to one following, no process; but in this process itself the truth generates itself and therefore *is*— as a self-generating one—contained within this process: the truth that is the end of the process, that thus the process *in toto* itself contains as completed.

At any rate, if one found it impossible to find truth in mythology as it is, and for this reason decided at the most to perceive a *distorted* one in it [XI 210], then the impossibility stemmed from just the fact that merely the individual representations as such were taken, not in their succession, but rather in their abstraction—that is, because one did not raise oneself to the concept of the process. One can admit that the particular in mythology is false, but that does not mean that the whole is considered in its final sense, that is, in the process. Successive polytheism [*successiver Polytheismus*] is just the way to again produce the true unity; the polytheism of a simple series of a multitude of gods as such[9] is merely what is *accidental*, what sublates itself again in the whole (if one looks at it), and it is not the intention of the process. Accordingly, one could of course say that what is false in mythology is only present through a misunderstanding of the process, or it is found only in that which has been diverged in it, in that which is observed in it in isolation. But this then is a mistake of the observer who views mythology merely from the outside, not in its essence (in the process); it explains the observer's false viewpoint of mythology, but not mythology itself.

One could, in order to clarify this to someone, compare the moments of mythology with the individual propositions [*Sätzen*] of philosophy. Every proposition of a true system is true in its position, in its time—that is, grasped in the progressing movement. And each is false considered for itself or abstracted from the incessant progress. So there is unavoidably a point where it *must* be said: God is also the immediate principle [*Princip*] of nature. For what can be that would not be God, from which God would have to be excluded? For those with a narrow mind all this is already pantheism, and they understand under *everything* that God is, all *things*; but the pure causes stand above the things, the pure causes from which those things are first derived, and just for precisely the reason that God is *everything*, he is also the opposite of that immediate principle: for that reason the proposition [*Satz*] is true or false, depending on how it is regarded. *True*, when it has the meaning: God is the principle [*Princip*] of nature, but not in order to be it, but rather to again sublate [*aufzuheben*] himself as that principle and to posit himself *as* Spirit (here we already have three moments). It would be false, if it had the meaning: God [XI 211] is that principle, in particular, in a stationary or exclusive manner. In passing one can here explain to oneself how easily it comes to the weakest and otherwise most incapable minds, through an entirely simple trick, to transform the most deeply thought proposition [*Satz*] into a false one, in that they emphasize it *alone*—against the express explanation that it is not to be so taken—and pass over in silence what follows it, either intentionally or unintentionally, which indeed certainly happens more frequently, because they are altogether unfit to grasp a whole of any type.

"Thus, then, according to this opinion, polytheism would not be a false religion, because in fact in the end there is not any such thing?" What concerns the first statement, by our view mythology is only not in itself false: under the presupposition that it has it is true, as indeed nature also is only true under a presupposition. What concerns the other inference is that it is already explained that every moment of mythology is false that is not apprehended as *such a moment* and is thus apprehended *outside* its relationship to the others. Now, after that which has been already earlier suggested, one has to see in reality the various mythologies of the peoples only as *moments*, as moments of a process extending through the whole mankind. To this extent every polytheistic religion that has fixed itself in a people and has remained unchanged is, as such, a false one; that is, every polytheistic religion is indeed a false one, insofar as it is a moment exclusively positioned at that present time. But we are considering mythology precisely not in these singular moments; we are considering it *in toto*, in the uninterrupted interrelation, connection, coherence of its continual movement through all moments. As long as mankind, and thus also as long as every part of it, is immersed in the movement of mythology, and as long as it is—as I put it—carried by this stream it is on the way to truth. Only when a people excludes itself from the movement and cedes the continuation of the process to another people does it begin to be in error and in the false religion.

No single moment of mythology is the truth, only the process as a whole. Now, the various mythologies themselves are only different moments of the mythological process. Indeed to this extent [XI 212] every individual polytheistic religion is indeed a false one (false would be, for example, relative monotheism)—but polytheism considered in the entirety of its successive moments is the way to truth and to this extent truth itself. One could conclude from this: in this way the final mythology, uniting all moments, must be the true religion. And in certain ways so it is—namely, *to the extent* that the truth is at all reachable on the path of the presumed process, *which always has as its presupposition the estrangement from the divine Self*. Thus the divine Self is indeed not in the mythological consciousness but rather its identical image. The image is not the object itself but yet fully like the object itself; in this sense the image contains truth, but because it is not the object itself to that extent it also is what is not true. In the same way the *image* of the true God is produced in the final mythological consciousness, without it thereby being the case that the relation to the divine Self—that is, to the true God himself— would be given, the entrance to whom is first opened by Christianity. The monotheism at which the mythological process arrives is not the false monotheism (for there can be no false monotheism), but against the true monotheism, the esoteric monotheism, it is only the exoteric monotheism.

The polytheistic religions are, taken individually, the false ones, but in the sense that everything in nature sundered from the movement extending throughout everything—or to the extent that it is thrown out of the process and has remained as a dead residual—has no truth, namely, not *the* truth that it has in the whole and as moment of it. Not only those heathen peoples who have extended their existence up until our time, for example the Hindus, find themselves in an entirely foolish relation to the objects of their superstitious veneration; also the common Greek fundamentally had no other relation to the gods of his religion, once the religion became present and fixed. As such the false religion is always only a dead remnant—a remnant thus become meaningless—of a process *that in its entirety is truth*. Every praxis that rests on a [XI 213] now no longer known interrelation and continuity or a no longer understood process is a superstition [*Superstition*]. One has for a long time asked about the etymology, that is, about the original meaning, of this Latin word. Some maintained the word has first been used for the superstition [*Aberglauben*] of the survivors in relation to the shadows of the departed; there the subjects of the superstition were designated, but the main topic (the superstition itself) was not expressed. Still better would be to say that every false religion is only a *superstes quid*, the remainder of what is no longer understood. But certain gods, probably mysterious ones, were called[e] *dii praestites* by the Romans. Thus it can indeed be assumed that these same gods in an older form also were called *superstites* with the same meaning (principal gods).

Thus, according to what was just treated one could say that the polytheistic religions are like a whole that has become meaningless, and they are like the ruins of a collapsed system, but the *emergence into being* cannot be explained by such an analogy. The unity is not to be sought in a primordial system that was understood earlier; it is to be sought in the no longer understood process, which does not have merely subjective truth (for the humanity conceptually entailed with it), but rather the truth in itself, objective truth. And what till now has simply not been considered as possible, or, rather, has not even been *thought* of, results as a necessary consequence from [XI 214] the postulated method of explanation: that, namely, there is truth in mythology *as such*, that is, to the extent that mythology is a process, successive polytheism.

It cannot be undesired if I use this last result in order to impart to you a schema that grants a short overview of the various views as they present themselves when one takes as the main vantage point the *objective* truth. Only I note that it is natural if with this classification the views in part receive a different position than they had in the earlier development, which proceeded from the question of how the mythological representations were *intended*, where thus one could speak only of their possible subjective truth.

   A. There is *no* truth at all in mythology. It is: 1) either meant *merely* poetically, and the truth found in it is merely contingent; 2) or it consists of meaningless representations that ignorance produced, and which the poetic arts later developed and combined into a poetic whole. (*J. H. Voss*)

   B. There is truth in mythology, but not in mythology *as such*. The mythological is: 1) either a *mere form*, *disguise* of a) a historic truth (*Eumeros*), b) of a physical truth (*Heyne*); or 2) *misunderstanding*, *distortion*, a) of a *purely scientific* (essentially irreligious) truth (*G. Hermann*), b) of a religious truth (*W. Jones*) (*Fr. Creuzer*)

   C. There is truth in mythology *as such*.

[XI 215] You notice, self-evidently, the *progression* from A through B to C. The third view, however, is actually at the same time the unification of the two others, to the extent that the first documents the *authentic and proper* meaning, but with a rejection of all doctrinal meaning, while the other admits a *doctrinal* meaning, or that truth was intended, but that is present in mythology only either as a disguised or as a distorted truth. Finally the third sees in the authentically and actually understood mythology also its truth. Now, however, as *you* see, this *view* has first become possible only through the *explanation*. For only for the reason that we are obliged to assume in mythology a necessary emergence are we also obliged to perceive in it necessary content, that is, truth.

The truth in mythology is initially and especially a *religious* one, for the process by which it emerges into being is the theogonic process, and indisputably subjective—that is, for the mankind affected by the process it has only *this*, namely religious, meaning. But, also considered *absolutely*, does *it* have—and for this reason does the process by which it emerges also have—only this particular but no *general* meaning?

Consider the following. Those real (actual) powers by which consciousness in the mythological process is moved, [powers] whose succession itself is the process, have been determined as precisely the same powers through which consciousness is originally and essentially that which posits God. These powers that create consciousness, and, as it were, bring it into action—*can* these be other than the ones through which also nature is posited and created? Indeed, no less than nature is human consciousness something that has become, and nothing *outside* of creation, but rather its *end*. Thus the potencies must co-operate [*zusammenwirken*] toward it as a goal, potencies that previously effectuate [*wirken*] nature in the departure from and in the tension against each other. The powers arising again inside of consciousness—as we expressed ourselves earlier—and showing themselves as theogonic can for this reason be none other than the world-generating powers themselves, and just as they again *elevate* themselves, they are transformed from subjective powers—subjugated to consciousness as their unity—again into objective powers [XI 216], which take on once more, over and against consciousness, the quality of external, *cosmic* powers, which they had lost in their *unity*—that is, as they posited consciousness. As stated, the mythological process can only be the restoration of the sublated unity. But it can be *restored* in no other way besides that by which it was originally *posited*—that is, in that the potencies pass through all the positions and relations to each other which they had in the process of nature. Not that mythology would have emerged under an influence of nature, of which the interior of man is on the contrary *deprived* through this process; rather, the mythological process passes, *according to the same law*, through the same levels through which nature originally passed.

It is not in itself thinkable that the principles of a process that proves to be a theogonic one can be something other than the principles of *all* Being and *all* Becoming. Thus the mythological process does not have merely religious meaning—it has *universal* [*allgemeine*] meaning. For it is the universal [*allgemeine*] process that repeats itself in it; accordingly, the truth that mythology has in the process is also a universal [*universelle*] one, one excluding nothing. One cannot, as is customary, deny to mythology *historical* truth, for the process by which it emerges into being is itself a true history, an actual set of events. Just as little is physical truth to be excluded from it, for nature is just as much a necessary passage point of the mythological process as of the universal process. The content of mythology is not an *abstract*-religious one, like that of the common theistic tenets. The world lies in the middle between the consciousness in its mere essentiality and the consciousness in its actualization, between the unity merely posited essentially in it and the unity actualized in it. Thus, the moments of the theogonic movement do not exclusively have meaning for that movement; they are of *universal* meaning.

Mythology is known in its truth, and thus only truly known, when it is known in the process. But the process that repeats itself [XI 217] in it, only in a particular way, is the *universal*, the *absolute* process, and thus the true science of mythology is accordingly the one that presents the absolute process in it. But to present this process is the task of philosophy. *The true science of mythology is for this reason the Philosophy of Mythology.*

One may not distort the proposition, as occurred earlier with similar ones. The idea of the process is not supposed to be presented just in some concocted mythology, but rather in precisely the actual mythology. But it is not merely a matter of knowing a general *outline*; the main point is to know the moments in the contingent form that they have unavoidably taken on in reality. But from where else would one know of these forms than through historical investigation, which therefore is not lightly regarded by the Philosophy of Mythology, but rather is presupposed? The investigation of the mythological facts is initially the task of the researchers of antiquity. But the philosopher must remain at liberty to scrutinize if the facts are correctly and completely ascertained.

Furthermore, in the proposition "the *true* science of mythology is the Philosophy of Mythology" it is simply articulated that the other ways of considering it do not perceive the *truth* in mythology. They say this themselves, however, as they deny its truth, either in general or at least to mythology as such.

Right when the concept "Philosophy of Mythology" was first articulated, we had to recognize it as a problematic one—that is, as one that itself first stands in need of substantiation. For everyone is indeed free to bring the word philosophy, with the help of a following genitive, into connection with every object. In some countries a Philosophy of Culinary Art would perhaps not be anything striking, as we ourselves in Germany in earlier years received from a magnificent civil servant of Thurn and Taxis a Philosophy of the Postal System, this latter treated according to Kantian categories.[10] For its time, a very serviceable work from the well-known Fourcroy[11] carried the title: Philosophy of Chemistry, without distinguishing itself through any sort of philosophical quality, if one does not already want to take for such the elegance of the development and the logical coherence and structure [XI 218]. We Germans, however, to whom is given a measure for the meaning of this construction through the concepts Philosophy of Nature, Philosophy of History, Philosophy of Art, will do well to be careful not to apply it where it could somehow only express that there is clarity and method in the investigation, or that one intends to offer about the named object only philosophical thoughts in general. For clarity and method are requirements of every investigation; and who—who is otherwise capable of such—could not come up with philosophical thoughts about whatever object in the world!

The objective emergence into being, independent of human intent, thought, and will, also gives mythology an objective content, and with the objective content simultaneously objective truth. But this view, on which it depends if *Philosophy of Mythology* is a scientifically possible expression or a merely improper combination of words, was not to be presupposed. With its substantiation we found ourselves still *outside* the sphere of the announced science and at the standpoint of a mere preinvestigation, which indeed—so one might think after the fact—could also have reached its goal via a shorter path if one, proceeding right away from mythology as *universal* phenomenon, had immediately determined the necessary universality of the *causes*. But this conclusion would not have led immediately to *the determinate nature* of these causes, which nature likewise is now known to us. Furthermore, the conclusion was opposed by the explanations according to which the presupposed universality would still only be an illusory one, in that the affinity of the content in the various mythologies would be one mediated merely externally, by tradition from people to people. And this manner of explanation was not established by ordinary people, but rather by men who hold the opinion of having occupied themselves most fundamentally with this object on account of their profession, and whose acumen is recognized in other investigations. It was particularly necessary to overcome the aversion that many feel in advance [XI 219] against every intervention of philosophy, that is, those who, if one wanted to designate their views and explanations as unphilosophical, would simply have answered: our views are not *supposed* to be philosophical; we make no claim to this. Like the Belgians answered to the agents of Joseph II: *Nous ne voulons pas être libres*.[12] Thus these people had to be convinced of the untenability of their intended explanations by other means. And, indeed, even this business was not to be called an entirely unphilosophical one. For if, as Plato and Aristotle say, the philosopher loves preeminently what is worthy of amazement, then he is indeed in his calling when he everywhere pursues what is worthy of amazement, but especially where it is deformed and covered by false explanations, and he seeks to free it again from those veils and to reproduce it in its pure form. And also formally—because a mere enumeration did not suffice—this business was a philosophical one, in that the method was applied that seeks to reach the *true* through successive negation of the merely relatively-true, which precisely thereby is at the same time the relatively-false. The explanation only first became for us a Philosophy of Mythology at the point where no other presupposition remained possible except that of a necessary and eternal condition of human nature, a condition that, in its progression, transforms itself into a *law* for this human nature. And thus we have not advanced our concept from above to below, dictatorially as it were, but rather substantiated from the bottom up—*which alone is universally convincing*. Thereby, the other views have had to serve as conduit to the true one, because there cannot be any among them that did not have apprehended an *aspect* of the object, some moment that must be also understood and considered in the completed theory.

If the standpoint of the first part of our investigation chiefly was the *historical-critical* or *dialectical*, then no one will deem for badly utilized the time devoted to this, no one who knows what worth it has for all science [*Wissenschaft*] if even only a single matter has been investigated entirely from the foundation and with the exhaustion of all possibilities.

The concept "Philosophy of Mythology" is subsumed under the general concepts of a *theory* of mythology [XI 220]. One and the same matter can be the object of a merely external knowledge, where it deals merely with the *determinate being* of the matter, but not with the *essence*. If this knowledge raises itself to this, then it becomes theory. From this it is easy to see that theory is only possible of that in which there is a true essence. The concept of essence, however, is: to be principle, source of Being or of movement. A mechanical motor is not effective *out of itself*, and yet the word theory is also applied to a merely mechanical production of movement, while no one speaks of theory there where there is not even the semblance of an inner source of movement, of an internally driving essence.

Such an essence and inner principle is missing in mythology according to the earlier explanations, which for this reason could only be named theories very inappropriately. But a Philosophy of Mythology of itself entails that the explanation is a theory in the true sense of the word. The theory of every natural or historical object is itself nothing other than a *philosophical* consideration of it, whereby the point is to uncover the living seed, which drives toward development, or to uncover the true and actual *nature* in it.

At first view nothing seems more disparate than truth and mythology, as this also is expressed in the long-used words teaching of fables [*Fabellehre*][f]— thus nothing is more opposed than philosophy and mythology. But precisely in the opposition itself lies the definite challenge and the task of uncovering reason in just this which is apparently unreasonable, of uncovering meaning in just this which appears meaningless—and indeed not in the way in which this has only been attempted up to now, by virtue of an arbitrary differentiation, such namely that anything one was confident in asserting as reasonable or meaningful was explained as essential, everything else however merely explained as contingent, and counted as part of disguise or distortion [XI 221]. The intent must be, on the contrary, that also the form appears as a necessary and to that extent reasonable one.

Whoever sees in mythology only what is opposed to our usual concepts to such extent that mythology appears to him as it were as unworthy of all consideration, especially of all philosophical consideration, he had better consider that nature hardly still evokes amazement for the thoughtless person and for one dulled by the habit of what he sees every day, but that we can think to ourselves very well a spiritual and ethical disposition for which nature would have to appear just as amazing and strange as mythology, and no less unbelievable. Whoever would be accustomed to living in a high spiritual or moral ecstasy could easily ask, if he directed his look back onto nature: what is the purpose of this stuff, uselessly lavished for fantastic forms in the mountains and cliffs? Was a God or some moral being able to fancy himself in such a production? What is the purpose of these forms of animals, which look to us in part fantastic, in part monstrous, in whose being, by which for the most part no goal can be divined, we would not *believe* if we did not see them before our eyes? What purpose in general is there in the great unseemliness in the actions of animals? What purpose in general is there in this entire corporeal world? Why is there not a simple, pure spirit-world, which would seem to us completely conceivable? Yet we cannot refrain from seeking the original intelligence [*Verstand*], the meaning of its initial emergence, in the nature that has become unintelligible to us. Certainly, many who see in mythology only a senseless and in itself tasteless teaching of fables cannot think worse of it than many philosophers, jealous of the Philosophy of Nature, considered the predicates of nature—namely, as senseless, unreasonable, un-divine, and such things. How many more, of course, must judge the same of mythology. For this reason it would not be surprising if it did not in the beginning of the Philosophy of Mythology go much differently than with the Philosophy of Nature, which just recently has been recognized generally as a necessary element of philosophy in general.

There are objects that philosophy must consider outside of all relation to itself [XI 222]. To these belongs everything that has no essential actuality in itself, which is only something in the arbitrary opinion of men. The mythological process, however, is something that has occurred in humanity independent of its intent and opinion. It is the same with everything merely *made*. But mythology is a natural, necessary plant. We have admitted that it could be treated poetically and even expanded, but it thereby acts like language, which can be used and expanded with the greatest freedom, and, within certain limits, constantly enriched anew with new inventions, but the basis is something into which human invention will have not reached, which is not made by *humans*.

Moreover, that with which philosophy has nothing to do is everything that is corrupt, distorted; only what is original has meaning for philosophy. Although it might be, as in everything that has gone through human use, that individual pieces that have come unhinged find themselves in various systems of the gods, mythology itself has not emerged through deterioration but rather is the original product of the consciousness striving to restore itself.

A third matter in which philosophy cannot find and know itself[13] is that which is the boundless, that which is without end. But mythology is a true totality, something complete, something held in certain limits, a world for itself; the mythological process is a phenomenon of such complete course, like perhaps in a physical process a sickness that takes its regular and natural course, which is to say like a sickness overcoming itself and restoring itself to health through a necessary striving; a movement that, proceeding from out of a determinate beginning through determinate middle-points to a determinate end, completes and concludes itself on its own.

Ultimately, what is dead, stagnant, is opposed to philosophy. But mythology is something essentially mobile and indeed is something essentially mobile of itself according to an immanent law, and it is the *highest* human consciousness that lives in it and that, by overcoming the contradiction itself, in which it is entangled, proves itself as true, as *real* [*reell*], as necessary.

[XI 223] *You* see, the expression Philosophy of Mythology is entirely proper and understood just like the ones similar: Philosophy of Language, Philosophy of Nature.

The expression has something awkward about it, to the extent that some already understand under mythology itself the *science* [*Wissenschaft*] of the myths. The expression could have been avoided had I intended to say: philosophy of the mythical world, or something similar. Moreover, it is not unknown to all who are informed that the word mythology is likewise employed in the objective sense for the whole of the mythological representations themselves.

As long as it was still a possible thought to consider mythology as a whole that has come undone from its continuity, a whole for which an ancient philosophy was the foundation, one was able to understand under the Philosophy of Mythology what had perished in it, which one would have intended to bring to light or to restore from its pieces. This misunderstanding is no longer possible.

If it was only a question of laying claim for philosophy to a certain influence on the treatment of mythology, then it would not have stood in need of the detailed substantiation. The influence has already long been admitted. If it is not a scientific and deep philosophy, then it is a random and superficial one that, with the occasion of mythology, can at least be interrogated about the conditions of the human species that are to be presupposed of mythology. Only first with its *own* inner-historical formation did philosophy receive a relation to the interior of mythology, only since it itself began to progress through moments, only since it explains[g] itself as *history* at least of self-consciousness, a method that was later expanded and has continued being effective until now. The reference became *real* as nature was taken up into philosophy as a necessary moment of the development.

Mythology indisputably has the closest affinity with nature, with which it, besides its generality, also has this in common: to be a world closed off in itself, and to be a past in relation to us [XI 224]. Soon a certain identity of the content is unmistakable. It could count as an acceptable idea to see mythology as a nature elevated into the spiritual realm through an enhancing refraction.

Only the means were missing to make the enhancement conceivable. Undoubtedly, in this sense earlier explanations would have been more meaningful had there not been such a lack of natural philosophical ideas. But unavoidably the mythological research also had to take on a different meaning through a philosophy in which—in a not expected way—what is natural assumed at the same time the meaning of something divine.

Among the modern treatments of mythology, those may well be differentiated that have received already their first impulse from philosophy, which one, because it had in the first place again taken up the element of nature, also named in general or as such (although wrongly) Philosophy of Nature [*Naturphilosophie*]. However, this connection contributed in a doubly negative way to the first attempts. Once, in that they, proceeding from a philosophy itself still in the process of becoming, and led more by the general desire excited by this philosophy than from scientific concepts, themselves were expanded unduly and uncontrollably and into unmethodical combinations; and second in that they had to take their part in the fanatical hate that that philosophy excited in a part of the earlier presumed possessors of science and philosophy.

Earlier I happily would have made mention of a man who will always be counted among the curiosities of a certain transitional period of our literature, the well-known *Johann Arnold Kanne*,[14] whom I have known as having a considerably witty temperament and simultaneously one capable of the highest ideas, but on to whom however was at the same time yoked by a strange lot of fate the destiny to give way under the burden of a full, extensive philological erudition, but one for the most part subtle and too meager in the fullness of larger facts. Indeed, it was least of all understood how he believed to be able to serve Christianity with *that type of* erudition, a Christianity for which certainly in our time such means are of no help, unless it can be represented in simple, large traits as victorious truth overall [XI 225]. In a later impulse—as it appeared, touched by the feeling of vanity of such efforts—he sought angrily to cast from himself this entire plunder of erudition. But to no avail; for in his last writings he still returned to the same erudite combinations and analogies that, even if they are true in the same proportion as they are mostly bizarre, in the end prove nothing. Among his writings—which one cannot consider from the given point of view without a type of melancholy and which one is nearly tempted to compare with the treasure of a beggar, that in the end despite the greatest weight consists mostly of copper coins and pennies—the *Pantheon of the Oldest Natural Philosophy*[h] may be his most meaningful work relating to mythology; one still purely philological, but worthwhile because of its many scholarly notes and remarks, is the *Mythology of the Greeks*,[i] which was begun earlier but not completed.

It would be desirable that one of those who stood nearer to him would attempt to bring out in an understandable way his basic view of mythology.

Given the notorious condition of his writings, this was impossible for me. For this reason his name could not be mentioned along with any of the views that came up earlier, not even with that view that I called the mystical. According to the whole context of his earlier way of thinking, in which his earlier mythological works are still written, I believe to be able to assume only that he based mythology on a monotheism—or rather a pantheism—that is deeper than a merely *historical* monotheism. Now, in any event, this should not be forgotten of him, even if no one was able to benefit from his presentation or actually feel themselves aided by it.

A special good fortune happened to mythology in that [XI 226], after publications that remained transitory and without effect, a mind like Fr. Creuzer directed his efforts toward it, who through a classically beautiful presentation, through a real and extraordinary erudition, which was furthered by a deep, central intuition, spread and solidified in the widest circles the conviction of the necessity of a higher view and treatment of mythology.

It was inevitable that the insipid, half-baked view, which in certain scholarly circles had still maintained itself, rose up against this. If it could not with all noise and uproar (as *Voss* in particular knew to whip up) hope to win adherents still in our time, then it could at least count on temporarily *casting doubt*—within the less educated and thoughtful part of the public, and through the means of certain traditional calumniations—on all attempts to consider mythology from higher points of view or set it in connection with general investigations.[j]

However, such activity rather had the upshot that now also this part of scientific [*wissenschaftlich*] research that until then had kept itself in relative isolation, and for the most part in a customary insularity, was taken up into the general movement, into the great scientific struggle of the time. One felt that with this question there was more at stake than merely mythology.

The controversy over origin, meaning, and treatment of mythology showed itself as analogous to that controversy that in other areas was simultaneously carried on over questions of the highest and most universal importance, as so apparently analogous that the participation, which the latter controversy excited, did not of itself have to expand also to the former controversy. If every science can congratulate itself when it begins to be included into the circle of higher literature, then especially after Creuzer's effort mythology can be pleased by the advantage of belonging among the objects in the face of whose exploration it is as it were allowed to none to remain indifferent [XI 227], to none who is accustomed and capable of envisaging the great questions, the ones decisive for humanity.

Now, however, if through precisely the experiences heretofore it has been most decisively established that a satisfactory, generally convincing conclusion to this investigation is not to be reached with merely empirical or contingent assumptions, and that a result independent of an individual mode of thinking is only to be expected when one succeeds in leading mythology back to presuppositions of a universal nature and in deriving it as a necessary consequence from out of such presuppositions: then the idea of a Philosophy of Mythology at the same time thereby appears also as one substantiated and required through time and through earlier endeavors.

But no progress is possible in any direction without more or less affecting another direction. A Philosophy of Mythology cannot emerge into being without having an expanding influence on other sciences [*Wissenschaften*]. The Philosophy of History and the Philosophy of Religion initially present themselves as such sciences. Thus in the next lecture the topic must be the effect that the tentatively attained result has already on these sciences.

Lecture Ten

[XI 228] When a new science enters into the circle of those well-known, accepted ones, then it will find in them points with which it is connected, at which it is almost expected. The order in which from out of the totality of possible sciences some emerge and are fashioned prior to others will not consistently be that of their inner dependence on one another, and a science that is closer to the immediate need can have been fashioned throughout a long time, can even be highly developed in many ways, before it makes with gradually more stringent demands the discovery that its premises lie in another science not yet heretofore present, that another actually would have had to precede it, one that has not yet been considered. On the other hand, no new science can emerge without expanding the realm of human knowledge *in general*, without filling up the deficiencies and holes in those already present. Accordingly, here it is fitting that—after it is substantiated as a possible science—it is determined for every science at the same time its position and its circle of influence in the whole of sciences, thus its relationship to these in general. So then it is also fitting if we show for the Philosophy of Mythology the side by which it is connected and interrelated with other sciences long sought or in the process of cultivation, and by which it is itself capable of having an increasing effect on them.

Now, through the substantiation that the Philosophy of Mythology received, at least one great fact [XI 229] is initially won for human knowledge: the existence of a theogonic process in the consciousness of the original humanity. This fact unlocks a new world and cannot fail to expand human thinking and knowledge in more than one sense. For initially at least, everyone must feel that in particular there is no secure beginning of history as long as the darkness that covers *the first events* is not dispersed, as long as the points are not found on which the great mysterious web we call history was first set up. Thus it is *history* to which the Philosophy of Mythology first has a relation; and it is not to be made light of that through it we were placed in the position of filling a for science heretofore completely empty space—pre-historical time, of which nothing could be known, and to which one knew to give a content at most through empty inventions, fantasies, or arbitrary assumptions—with a *series of real concrete events*,[1] with a movement full of life, with a *true* history [*Geschichte*], which in its way is no less rich in varying incidents, in scenes of war and peace, in struggles and upheavals, than the history generally called by that name. In particular, the fact cannot remain without effect on 1) the Philosophy of History, 2) on all those parts of historical research that are somehow in the position to concern themselves with the first beginnings of human things.

The initial impulse for a Philosophy of History, and the name itself, came like much else from the French, but the concept was expanded beyond its first meaning already through Herder's famous work; right at the beginning, the Philosophy of Nature posited, vis-à-vis itself,[a] the Philosophy of History as the other main part of philosophy, or as applied philosophy, as it was expressed at that time. In the immediately succeeding time there was also no lack [XI 230] of formal discussions about the concept. The idea of a Philosophy of History continually has enjoyed great favor: it has even not lacked in elucidations. Yet I do not find that one has come to terms even with the concept.

I am initially drawing attention to this: that already that construction—Philosophy of History—explains history as a whole. It was first articulated in the last lecture that what is unfinished, what is limitless in all directions, has as such no relation to philosophy. Now, one above all could ask according to which of the previous views history is something settled and ended. Does the future not also belong to history, considered as a whole? But is there anywhere in that which has presented itself until now as Philosophy of History a thought by which an actual conclusion of history would be given—I do not claim to say a satisfying conclusion? So, for example, the actualization of a complete system of right,[2] the complete development of the concept of freedom, and everything similar, is in its poverty at the same time too groundless for the mind [*Geist*] to be able to find a point of rest in this. I wonder if a conclusion has been considered here at all, and if not, on the contrary, everything amounts to history having no true future, but that rather everything just continues infinitely, since a progress without limits—but for just this reason at the same time senseless progress—and a progress without cease and pause, by which something truly new and different would begin, belongs to the articles of faith of the present wisdom. Because, however, it is obvious that what has not found its beginning also cannot find its end, we will confine ourselves merely to the past and ask if from this perspective history for us is a whole and something completed, and not rather—according to all views up to now tacitly or expressly explained—the past just as the future is a time proceeding steadily into the infinite, a time limited and differentiated in itself through nothing.

Indeed, one differentiates in the past in general: *historical* and *pre-historical* time. And so one seems in this way to posit a difference. But the question is if this difference is a more than merely *contingent* one [XI 231], if both times are *essentially* different and not at base only one and the same time, whereby the pre-historical time cannot prove to be an actual boundary for the historical time, for it could only be that boundary if it were an *internally* other and different time from this one. But, following the usual concepts, is there really something *different* in the pre-historical time than the historical time? By no means; the entire difference is merely the external and contingent one that we know something of the historical time and know nothing of the pre-historical time: the latter is not actually the *pre-historical* time [*vorgeschichtlichen*], but rather merely the one *prior to historical accounts* [*vorhistorische*].[3] But can there be anything more contingent than the lack or the presence of written and other monuments or relics that inform us of the affairs of a time in a believable and sure fashion? After all, there are even within the time called historical entire stretches for which we lack suitably certifiable reports. And we are not even of the same opinion about which of the monuments and relics are worthy of historical value. Some refuse to let the Mosaic writings count as historical documents, while they confer historical standing to the oldest historians of the Greeks, for example Herodotus; others consider these also as not fully valid, but rather say with David Hume that the first page of Thucydides is the first document of true historical account [*Historie*]. The pre-historical [*vorgeschichtlich*] time would be an *essentially*, an internally different time, if it had a different *content* than the historical [*geschichtliche*] time. But in this respect what difference could one establish between both? According to the concepts commonplace up to now, I would know of none, other than that perhaps the affairs of the pre-historical time are meaningless, those of the historical time, however, meaningful. This would probably also arise from the following, that by a popular analogy, for whose invention it admittedly did not take much, the first era of the human species is seen as its childhood. Certainly also the small encounters from the childhood of a historical individual are given over to oblivion. Accordingly, the historical time would begin with the *meaningful* affairs. But what here is meaningful, what unmeaningful? [XI 232] It must nonetheless occur to us that that unknown land, that area inaccessible to historical narrative, in which the final sources of all history [*Geschichte*] are lost, conceals from us precisely the most meaningful events, the most meaningful because they are decisive and determinant for the entire aftermath.

Because there is no true, that is, internal difference between the historical and pre-historical time, it is also impossible to draw a solid border between both. No one is able to say where the historical time begins and the other ends, and those compiling Universal History are in a noticeable difficulty about the point with which they should begin. And naturally this is so, for the historical time has for them no actual beginning, but rather *at bottom* and according to the nature of the object goes back completely indefinitely; everywhere there is only *one kind* of time that uniformly is never limited nor is to be limited anywhere.

Certainly, in that which is so unresolved, without end, reason cannot know itself. Accordingly, up to this point we have never been so far away from anything as we are from a true Philosophy of History. We miss what is best, namely, the beginning. Nothing is accomplished with the empty and cheap formulas of Orientalism, Occidentalism, and similar ones—for example, that in the first period of history the infinite was dominant, in the second the finite, [and] in the third the unity of both—or in general with a mere application to history of schemas taken from elsewhere, a procedure into which just that philosophical writer[4] who had criticized it most loudly fell in the coarsest manner as soon as he himself reached the real [*Reelle*] and was abandoned to his own faculty of invention.

Through the preceding investigations, directed to an entirely different object, the time of the past has also in the meantime won for us another figure, or rather first a figure at all. It is no longer a boundless time into which the past loses itself; rather, it is the case that history settles and divides itself for us into *times actually and internally different from each other*. How? The following considerations may more clearly show this.

In that the historical time has been determined as the time of the completed separation of the peoples [XI 233] (as it begins for every individual people with the moment where it has declared and decided itself as such), the content of the pre-historical time—also merely considered externally—is different from the content of the historical time. That pre-historical time is the time of the cision or crisis of the peoples, of the transition to the separation. But this crisis is itself again only the external appearance or consequence of an inner process. The *true* content of the pre-historical time is the emergence of the formally and materially separate systems of the gods, thus of *mythology in general*, which in the historical time is already something finished and present, thus something that is historically past. Its *becoming*—that is, its *own* historical determinate being—was completed by pre-historical time. A converse eumerism is the right point of view. Not as Eumeros taught does mythology contain the events of the oldest history, but rather, conversely, mythology in emergence, that is, actually the process by which it emerges—this process of mythology in its emergence is the true and only content of that oldest history. And if one raises the question of by what was that time filled, that time so silent against the din of the later time, that time appearing so poor and empty of events, then it is to be answered: this time was filled by those inner processes and movements of consciousness, which accompanied or had as consequence the emergence of the mythological systems, of the doctrines of the gods, and whose ultimate result was the separation of humanity into peoples.

Accordingly, the *historical and pre-historical time are no longer merely relative differences of one and the same time; they are two times essentially different and set apart from one other, mutually exclusive times*, but also for this reason mutually limiting times. For between both there is the essential difference that in the pre-historical time the consciousness of mankind is subjugated to an inner necessity, to a process that as it were removes mankind from the actual and external world, whereas every people that has become one through an inner decision also is set out of the process *as such* through the same crisis and, free of the process, now abandons itself to that series of acts and actions [XI 234] whose more external, worldly, and profane character makes it into a historical time.

Thus the historical time does not continue into the pre-historical time but rather, to the contrary, is cut off and bounded by the latter as a fully other time. We name it a fully other time, not that it would not be in the broadest sense also historical, for also in it something great happens, and it is full of events, only of an *entirely other type*, events that are subject to an *entirely different law*. In this sense we have named it the relatively pre-historical time.

This time, however, by which the historical time is completed and limited, is itself also again a determinate time and thus also for its part limited by another. This other, or, rather, *third* time cannot again be one in some way historical, and thus can only be the *absolutely pre-historical time*, the time of the complete historical immutability. It is the time of the still undivided and unified humanity, which, because it is related to the following time only as a moment, as a pure *point of departure*—to the extent, namely, that there is in it no true succession of events, no succession of times, as is the case with both of the others—itself does not stand in need of another limiting. In it, I said, there is no *true* succession of times: by this is not meant that in it nothing at all happens, as a good-natured man has interpreted it. For obviously, also in that plainly pre-historical time the sun rose and set, men laid down to sleep and rose again, married and let themselves be wooed, were born and died. But in this there is no progression and thus no history, like the individual in whose life yesterday is like today and today like yesterday—whose existence is a circle of uniform and repeating turns—has no history. A true succession [*Aufeinanderfolge*] is not formed by events that disappear without trace and leave the *whole* in the condition in which it was before. Thus, for the reason that in the absolutely pre-historical time the whole is, at the end, as it was in the beginning, thus because in this time [XI 235] itself there is no longer a succession of times, because it (also in this sense) is only One time, namely (as we expressed ourselves), the *simply identical* and thus basically *timeless* time (perhaps this indifference of the passing time is captured by the memory through the unbelievably long life span of the oldest races [*Geschlechter*])—for this reason, I say, it itself does not again stand in need of the limitation by another. Its duration is indifferent; shorter or longer is the same. Therefore, with it not merely *a* time, but rather *time in general* is limited; it itself is the ultimate to which one can go back in time. Beyond it there is no step other than into the *supra-historical* [*Übergeschichtliche*]; it is a time, but one that *itself* is already no longer *a time* but rather only a time in the relation to what follows. In itself it is no time, because in it there is no *true before* and *after*, because it is a type of eternity, as also the Hebrew expression (*olam*) indicates, which word is used for it in *Genesis*.

Thus it is no longer a wild, inorganic, boundless time into which history runs for us; it is an organism, it is *a system of times*, in which for us the history of our species is enclosed. Every member of this whole is its own self-sufficient time, which is limited not by a merely *preceding* time, but rather by one essentially *different* from it, a time *removed* from it, up to the last one, which no longer stands in need of limitation because there is no longer time (namely, no series of times) in it, because it is relative *eternity*. These members are:

absolute pre-historical [*absolut-vorgeschichtliche*],
relative pre-historical [*relativ-vorgeschichtliche*],
historical [*geschichtliche*] time.

One can differentiate history [*Geschichte*] and history [*Historie*] as the accounts of things: the first is the series of the events and occurrences themselves; the second is the account of them. From this it follows that the concept of history [*Geschichte*] is more expansive than the concept of history [*Historie*] as the accounts of events. To this extent one could simply say pre-historical time [*vorgeschichtliche*] instead of absolutely pre-historical [*vorgeschichtliche*], and pre-historical [*vorhistorische*] time instead of relative pre-historical [*vorgeschichtliche*]; and the series would then be this:

a) pre-historical [*vorgeschichtlich*], [XI 236]

b) pre-historical [*vorhistorische*],

c) historical [*historische*] time

Only one would have to be careful in thinking that there is between the last two only the contingent difference, lying in the word, that we have accounts of the latter [*historische*] one, and not of the former [*vorhistorische*] one.

With a historical time that goes on boundlessly, the door is opened to every caprice; true is not differentiated from false, insight from arbitrary assumption or imagination. Enough examples of this could be shown from the investigation concluded by us. Hermann, for example, denies that a theism invented by men themselves could have preceded mythology, and he places great value that this could not have been. However, the very same man has nothing against, and in fact himself assumes, that such a theism was indeed instead invented some millennia later; so, in his opinion, prior to mythology there was only missing the time for such an invention. But, now, as has already happened to the history of the earth as a consequence of geological research (which Hermann, however, more probably knew from priest Ballenstädt's primordial world than from Cuvier),[5] this same man simultaneously voices the hope of likewise seeing,[b] by the research into antiquity, the history of man further enriched with an abundant addition of indeterminately earlier eons.

However, to those who have at their disposal a time as beautiful as the one Hermann reserves to himself, there cannot be lacking the time for any possible invention, which they would otherwise be inclined to ascribe to the primordial world. Thus Hermann would not be able to refute anyone who would assume an earthly primordial system of wisdom, of which for the few survivors of an earlier human race—a human race that, overtaken by one of those catastrophes that according to Hermann's opinion repeat themselves from time to time in the history of the earth (and one of which also stands[c] before us in the future), for the most part would have been buried with all of its knowledge [XI 237]—there would have been left only ruins and meaningless fragments, of which mythology now consists. If it is fitting and proper to true science to encompass everything as much as possible within defined boundaries and to enclose everything within the limits of conceptuality, then on the other hand with a time taken as boundless no type of arbitrary assumption is to be excluded; if it is only barbaric peoples that have fallen into heaping up millennia upon millennia, and if it can likewise be only a barbaric philosophy that strives to maintain of history an extension into the boundless, then it can only be desired by the lovers of true science to see established such a definite *terminus a quo*, such a concept cutting off every further regress, like that of our ultimately pre-historical [*vorgeschichtlichen*] time.

If one takes history in the broadest sense, then the Philosophy of Mythology itself is the first, and thus most necessary and indispensable, part of a Philosophy of History. It is no use to say that the myths contain no history. As myths that *actually* once were emerged, they are themselves the content of the oldest history, and yet, even if one intends to restrict the Philosophy of History to historical time, it must appear impossible to find a beginning for it or to make any kind of progress in it if that which this (the historical time) posits as the past of itself remains fully incomprehensible to us. A Philosophy of History that knows no beginning of history can only be something completely groundless and does not deserve the name of philosophy. Now, however, what is valid for history as a whole must likewise be valid for every particular historical research.

Regardless of the intent in which our investigations go back into the primordial times of our species, whether it be on account of its beginnings in general, whether it be to investigate the first beginnings of religion and of civil society [XI 238], or the sciences and arts, ultimately we always encounter that dark place, that χρόνος ἄδηλος, which is only occupied by mythology. For that reason, for some time it had to be the most pressing demand for all sciences coming in contact with those questions that this darkness be overcome, that place be made transparent and clearly knowable. Meanwhile, and because one cannot dispense with philosophy for those questions concerning the origin of the human species, a shallow and base Philosophy of History quietly exerted an only all the more definite influence on all research of this type. One recognizes this influence in certain axioms that are presupposed everywhere and consistently with the greatest naïveté, and as though something different were not even conceivable. One of these axioms is that all human science, art, and culture had to proceed from the lowest beginnings. In conformity with this axiom, a well-known, now dead historical researcher, at the occasion of the underground temples of Ellore and Mavalpuram[6] in India, makes the edifying reflection: "Already the naked bush Hottentots make drawings on the walls of their caves; from there to the richly decorated Indian temples, what steps!"—"And yet," the learned historical researcher continues, "art also had to tread them."[d] But, on the contrary, according to this view an Egyptian, an Indian, a Greek art would never and *at no time* have been possible. Imagine whatever expanses of time and reserve to oneself to add to the imagined times however many more millennia: according to the nature of the matter it is impossible that art ever and at any putative time reached such heights from such entirely negligible beginnings. And certainly even the historian mentioned would not have taken on the issue of determining the time in which art was able to traverse such a distance. He could just as well have stated how much time is necessary for something to emerge from nothing.

[XI 239] One will indeed object that that axiom cannot be attacked without touching on the great principle, considered sacrosanct as it were, of the constant progress of the human species. But where there is progress there is a point of departure, a where-from and a where-to. That progress, however, does not, as one thinks, go from the small into the great; rather, vice-versa, everywhere what is great, the gigantic, forms the beginning, and what is formed organically, brought into constriction, only follows afterward. Homer is of such greatness that no later time was in the position to produce something similar to him; even a Sophoclean tragedy would have been an impossibility in the Homeric age. The epochs do not differentiate themselves from each other by a mere more or less of a so-called culture; their differences are internal, are differences of essentially or qualitatively varying principles that follow each other and each of which in its epoch can achieve the highest development. This entire system, which history itself most clearly contradicts, with which even its adherents are actually preoccupied only in thought, and that none of them was able to execute or has even tried to execute, ultimately rests on the opinion—not derived from facts but rather deriving itself from incomplete research and probing—that man and mankind was exclusively left to itself from the beginning on, that it blindly, *sine numine*, and having surrendered to the most basest contingency, almost fumblingly, sought its way. This is, one can say, general opinion. For the believers in revelation, who seek in the revelation that which guides, that *numen*, find themselves in part in a decisive minority, and in part they can prove that guidance only for a very small part of the human species. And it always remains strange that the people of the true God had to seek the architect of their temples in the Phoenicians. But by what were these other peoples raised, through what were they prevented from losing themselves in the fully senseless, through what were they elevated to the greatness that we cannot deny to their conceptions? If it was not mere *chance* that let the Babylonians, Phoenicians, [and] Egyptians find the way to their elaborate and in part astounding structures [XI 240], then something else must have intervened, *something different* but yet analogous to revelation. Heathendom does not form a mere negation to the revealed religion but rather something positive of another type. This something other and yet something analogous was precisely the mythological process. It is positive, real powers that govern in this process. This process too is a source of inspirations, and only from such inspirations can the in part colossal productions of that time be understood. Works like the Indian and Egyptian monuments do not emerge like stalactite caves, merely through the course of time. The same power that internally created the in part colossal conceptions of mythology produced—when directed outwards—in art the bold undertakings exceeding all standards of the later time. The power which in the mythological representations raised human consciousness above the limits of actuality was also the first teacher of the great, the meaningful, in art, and also the power that, like a divine hand, lifted humanity out of and above the inferior levels—levels, however, that are logically to be thought in advance—and that still inspired in the later products of antiquity a greatness that has remained until now unreachable by the modern time. For as long, at least, as a heightened and expanded consciousness has not again won a relation to the great powers and forces, a relation in which antiquity found itself without its own doing, it will always be advisable to stick to that which feelings and refined sense can create from immediate reality. Indeed one speaks, just like of a Christian philosophy, also of a Christian art. But art is everywhere art and as such is originally and according to its nature worldly and heathen, and has for this reason also not to seek out in Christianity that which is particular in it, but rather that which is universal in it—that is, to seek out that which constitutes its connection and interrelation with heathendom. Provisionally, it is to be considered a good turn when art selects from out of the objects that revelation offers it those that go beyond the limitedly Christian, events such as the confusion of language [XI 241], the emergence of peoples, the destruction of Jerusalem, and others in which the artist does not first have to emphasize the great, universal context.

Although I cannot actually now tarry with this object, I will nevertheless remark that the Philosophy of Mythology also forms an indispensable foundation for the *Philosophy of Art*, just as it has a necessary relation to the Philosophy of History. For it will be essential, even one of its first tasks, for this Philosophy of Art to concern itself with the first *objects* of artistic and poetic presentations. Here it will be unavoidable to require, as it were, a poesy [*Poesie*] *originally* preceding all plastic and compositional art, namely, one originally inventing and producing the raw material. But something that can be seen as such an original production of ideas preceding all conscious and formal poetry is found only in mythology. Now, if it is inadmissible to have it itself emerge into being from out of the art of poetry [*Dicht-Kunst*], then it is for this reason no less apparent that it relates itself as such an original poesy to all later, free productions. For this reason in every comprehensive philosophy of art a main section will have to discuss the nature and meaning of mythology, and to this extent its emergence into being, just like I had included a chapter in my lectures on the Philosophy of Art[e] held more than fifty[7] years ago, a chapter whose ideas frequently were reproduced in the later investigations into mythology. Among the causes through which Greek art was so extraordinarily fostered, the constitution of its particular *objects*—that is, particularly of the *objects* given to it through its mythology—undoubtedly stands at the top, objects that on the one hand belonged to a higher history and different order of things than this merely contingent and transient order, from which the later poet has to take his characters, and, on the other hand, stood in an internal, essential, and lasting relation to nature. Philosophy still has to show the possibility of what from the standpoint of art has always been perceived as necessity, namely, the necessity of actual beings, which do not merely signify, but rather *are*, at the same time, *principles, universal and eternal concepts*. [XI 242] Heathendom is intrinsically foreign to us, but the height of art alluded to is also not to be reached with the misunderstood Christianity. It was too early to speak of a Christian art, at least under the inspirations of the one-sided romantic disposition. But how much else does not precisely depend on the *understood* Christianity, and in the present confusion does not everything, knowingly or unknowingly, press toward this understanding?

Every work of art stands all the higher the more it at the same time awakens the impression of a certain necessity of its existence, but only the eternal and necessary content overcomes, as it were, the contingency of the work of art. The more the *in themselves* poetic objects disappear, the more contingent the poetry becomes; itself not conscious of any necessity, it has all the more the desire to hide its contingency through endless production, to give itself the appearance of necessity. Even in the case of the most demanding and exacting works of our time we cannot overcome the impression of *contingency*, while in the works of Greek antiquity not merely necessity, truth and reality of the *object*, but rather also the necessity, that is, truth and reality of the *production* is articulated. With these works one cannot, like with so many works of a later art, ask the question: Why, for what reason is it there? The mere multiplying of productions cannot raise a mere semblance of life to actual life. Also, in such a time one does not so much need particularly to promote the production, for what is contingent has, as said, of itself the tendency to appear as what is necessary, and for this reason the inclination to multiply itself into the unbounded and limitless, just as we can[f] perceive today such a truly endless and purposeless producing in the poetry that is not promoted by anyone. [XI 243] *Byron* seeks that higher, *in itself* poetic world, seeking in part to penetrate into it with violence, but the skepticism of a wretched time, which laid waste to his heart also, does not allow him any faith in its forms and figures.

Writers of spirit and knowledge have already long ago highlighted the contrast of antiquity and the modern era, but more in order to advance the so-called romantic poetry than to penetrate into the true depth of the ancient time. If however it is no mere manner of speaking to speak of antiquity as its own *world*, then one also will have to grant to it its own principle, and one will have to expand the thoughts of it to the point of recognizing that the mysterious antiquity was subject to a different law and other powers than those by which the present time is dominated—and indeed the higher we ascend all the more definitely. A psychology that is derived merely from the conditions of the present, and perhaps itself has known merely to take superficial observations from this present, is as little constituted to explain appearances and events of ancient time as the laws of mechanics—which are in force in the rigidified nature that has already come into existence—are applicable to the time of the original becoming and of the first living emergence into being. But it would indeed be the shortest way once and for all to banish as mere myths these appearances into the realm of the unreal, with insipid hypotheses to evade the most substantiated of facts, especially of the *religious* life of the ancients.

The theogonic process in which humanity involves itself with the first actual consciousness is essentially a religious process. If from this side the established fact is chiefly important for the *history of religion*, then it can also not keep from being a powerful influence on the *Philosophy of Religion*.

It is a beautiful peculiarity of the Germans that they have concerned themselves with this science so unremittingly and enthusiastically [XI 244]. If this science therefore is not more and perhaps even less sure than some others of its concept, scope, and content, then this might—not to mentionn that according to the nature of the matter there are in no other science so many dilettantes, and thus in no other is there so much that is botched as in the study of religion—in part derive from the fact that it constantly has kept itself in too great a dependence on the course of philosophy in general, whose movements it repeated helplessly in itself, while it would well have been possible for it to win a content independent of philosophy and thus to act reciprocally on this philosophy and expand it.

Now, such a possibility might actually be given to it through the result of our investigation of mythology, in which a religion independent of philosophy and reason, just as of revelation, has been proven. For if we assume the correctness of a statement by G. *Hermann*, who we again gladly introduce as a man who speaks out clearly and decisively, and if it is assumed that there is no other religion than either that which is derived from a presumed revelation or the so-called natural religion, which is however only a philosophical one, and thus a declaration whose meaning is that there is *only* a philosophical religion: then we would not in fact know how the Philosophy of Religion would be able to differentiate and maintain itself as a particular science (which it should be, after all). For undoubtedly the merely philosophical religion would already be taken care of through the General Philosophy, and to the Philosophy of Religion, if it did not give up on all objective content, would therefore be left nothing other than to repeat in itself a part or a chapter of the General Philosophy.

Now, in opposition to that statement, we have shown—and indeed without in any way proceeding from a philosophy, in consequence of merely historically grounded conclusions—that there is, besides those religions set there alone in opposition, a mythological religion independent of both. Moreover and in particular we have shown that it itself precedes in time every revelation (if one assumes such), and in fact itself first mediates this revelation, [XI 245] and accordingly is undeniably the first form in which religion at all exists, and is for a certain time the *universal* religion, the religion of the human species [*Geschlecht*], against which the revelation—regardless of how soon it appears on the scene—is however only a partial phenomenon, limited to only one particular race [*Geschlecht*], and for millennia long, comparable to a dimly shining light, unable to break through the darkness resisting it. Further, we have thereafter explained that mythology, as the unprethinkable religion of the human race, and to this extent also the religion of the human race anticipating all thought, is only comprehensible from the *natural* God-positing of consciousness, which cannot step forth out of this condition without falling prey to a necessary process through which it is led back into its original position. As having emerged from such a condition only mythology can be called the *naturally self-producing* religion, and for this reason also should alone be called the *natural* religion, but the rational or philosophical religion should not be given this name, as has happened until now for the reason that one named natural everything in which no revelation takes part, and knew only to set reason in opposition to revelation.

This determination of the mythological religion as the natural religion here has a deeper meaning than what now is generally said: that mythology is the natural religion, by which most people only want to say that it is the religion of men who cannot raise themselves above the created and to the creator, or of men who have deified nature (explanations whose insufficiency has been sufficiently shown). Some however even understand under natural religion only the first stage of the mythological religion, namely, that one where, as they say, the *concept* of religion, and thus God as the object of this concept, is still entirely concealed by nature, is submerged in it. As far as this explanation is concerned, we have shown on the occasion of the *notitia insita* that mythology could not emerge into being from the mere actualization of a *concept* (even if this actualization was perhaps thought of as necessary), because it must rather rest on an *actual*, real relation of the human essence to God, out of which alone a process independent of human thought can emerge [XI 246], a process that in consequence of this origin is to be called a natural one for mankind. Thus in this sense the mythological religion is for us the natural religion.

We could just as well call it the *wildly growing religion*, just as the great apostle of the heathens calls[g] heathendom the wild olive tree and has called Judaism—as one founded on revelation—the tame olive tree, or just the *wild religion*, in the sense in which in German one has called the natural fire of heaven the wildfire and the naturally warm springs the wild springs.

No fact, however, is isolated; with every fact newly disclosed others already known, but perhaps not cognized, appear in a new light. No true beginning is without consequence and progress, and the natural religion of itself and already on account of the opposition has as its consequence the revealed religion. So also have we found it to be already earlier. The blindly emerging religion can be without presupposition, but the revealed religion, in which there is a will and purpose, requires a ground and therefore can only be in the second position. If one had to recognize the mythological religion as one independent of all reason, then with respect to the revealed religion one will be all the less able to avoid doing the same, as the assumption in the case of the latter in any event is already a mediated one; the recognized reality of the one has the other as consequence, or at least makes it comprehensible. If the revealed religion is explained as the supra-natural [*übernatürliche*] one, then it becomes through the relation to the natural religion to an extent natural itself, where on the other hand then admittedly the wholly unmediated supernaturalism [*Supernaturalismus*] can only appear as unnatural.

Thus with the presupposition of the natural religion the whole position and status of the revealed religion is changed; it is no longer the only religion independent of reason and philosophy, and if one calls rationalism the type of thinking that comprehends none other than a rational relationship of consciousness to God, then first opposed to this relation is not the revealed religion but rather the natural religion.

[XI 247] In general, in a whole of interrelated concepts no single one can be correctly determined as long as one is missing or not correctly determined. The revealed religion is in the historical order only just the second, and thus already mediated form of the *real* religion—that is, of the religion independent of reason. This independence it has in *common* with the natural religion; for this reason its difference from the philosophical religion is only its *generic* difference, not its *specific* difference, as one has assumed up to now. No concept, however, can be completely determined by its merely generic difference. It is common to both the revealed and the natural religion to have emerged into existence through a real process, not through science [*Wissenschaft*]. Their specific difference is, in the one, that which is natural in its course of events, in the other that which is supra-natural. But that which is supra-natural becomes comprehensible through its relationship to that which is natural. The main point is that it does not exist in mere ideas.

Now, Christianity presents itself as the liberation from the blind power of heathendom, and the reality of a liberation is measured according to the reality and power of that from which it frees itself. Were heathendom nothing actual, then also Christianity could be nothing actual. Conversely, if the process to which man has been subjected in consequence of his stepping forth from the original relation, if the mythological process is not something merely *imagined* [*Vorgestelltes*], but rather something *which actually happens*, then also it cannot be ended through something that is merely in the imagination, through a doctrine, but rather it can only be sublated through an *actual process*, through an act independent of and in fact surpassing human imagination. For only an *act* can stand in opposition to the process, and this act will be the content of Christianity.

For the Christian theologians almost their entire science has dissolved itself into the so-called apologetics, with which however they have not come to grips and that they always begin again from the beginning, as proof that they have not found the point where it could be tackled with success in our time. This point can only lie in the presupposition of all revelation, in the religion that emerged into existence blindly. But even if [XI 248] they completely refrained from transitioning from the faint-hearted defensive position—to which they have been repelled—back to an aggressive defense, the defense of particulars would meet more easily resolvable difficulties if they would notice that revelation also has its material presuppositions in the natural religion. It does not itself *create* the *matter* in which it takes effect; rather it finds it as independent of itself. Its formal meaning is to be the overcoming of the merely natural, unfree religion; but for just this reason it has this religion in itself, like that which sublates has the sublated in itself. The assertion of this material identity cannot count as impious or unchristian, if one knows how decisively just this assertion was formerly recognized precisely by the most orthodox view. If it was permitted to see in heathendom distortions of revealed truths, then conversely it is impossible not to permit viewing in Christianity the heathendom that has been set in the right place. Besides, who in addition would not know how much in Christianity has appeared as a heathen element to those who want to know only of a rational religion, a heathen element that according to their opinion should be eliminated from the pure, that is, rational, Christianity? After all, the affinity of both showed itself already in their common external fate so that one sought to rationalize both (mythology and revelation) through a totally equal differentiation of form and content, of what is essential and what is merely time-appropriate raiment—that is, one sought to bring both back to a reasonable meaning, or what appears to most as a reasonable meaning. But precisely with the excised heathen meaning would also all reality be taken from Christianity. To be sure, the latter is the relation to the Father and the worship of him in spirit and in truth; in this result everything heathen disappears—that is, everything that is not in relation to God *in his truth*; but without its presuppositions this result does not have any empirical truth. Whoever sees me, sees the Father, Christ says; but he adds: I am the *way*, and no one *comes* to the Father except through me.

Let us finally have a universal principal decide [this matter]. [XI 249] This principle is that actual religion cannot be different from actual religion. If, now, both natural and revealed religions are actual religion, then according to the last content there can be no difference between them both. Both must contain the same elements, [and] only their *meaning* in the one will be different from that in the other; and because the difference of both is only that the one is the naturally posited religion, and the other the divinely posited one, then *the same* principles that are merely natural in the one will be taken as divine in the other. Without preexistence Christ is not Christ. He existed as a natural potency before he appeared as a divine personality. With respect to this we can also say of him that he was in the world ($ἐν τῷ χόσμῳ ἤν$). He was a cosmic potency, even if for himself he was not *without* God, as the apostle says to former heathens: you were *without* God (you had no immediate relation to God); you were in *the world* (in that which is not God, in the realm of the cosmic powers).[h] For these same potencies, in whose unity God Is and reveals himself—precisely these potencies in their disjunction and in the process are external to the divine, are the merely natural powers, in which God admittedly is not everywhere not in existence, but yet is not existent according to his divinity, thus not according to his *truth*. For in his divine self he is One and can be neither Many nor enter into a process. *There is coming a time*—Christ says in the aforementioned passage—and it is indeed namely now, according to the beginning, in which the true worshippers will worship the Father in spirit and truth; thus until this time the Jews too do not worship the Father in spirit, and the path to him in his truth was opened to both, to those who were near and to those who were far,[i] to those who stood under the law of revelation just as to those who stood under the merely natural law; which makes clear that there was also something in revelation through which consciousness of God was restrained in spirit [XI 250], and that Christ in his appearance is therefore precisely the *end of revelation* because he removes this being that alienates from God.

This much on the relationship of the revealed to the natural religion. But, if now that which has been developed up till now has been developed correctly, then you yourselves will understand that for the philosophical religion there remains in this series no position other than the third one. What then would this position have to be? If we also apply the already articulated principle to it, that essentially and according to the content actual religion cannot be differentiated from actual religion, then the philosophical religion actually can only be religion if it had in itself the factors of the actual religion, factors as they are in the natural and revealed religions, and had it no less than the natural and revealed religions have them: only in the *manner* in which it contained these factors could it have its difference from them—and furthermore this difference could not be other than that the principles that in the one are effective without being understood would be understood and comprehended in this one. The philosophical religion, far from having the right, through its position, to cancel the preceding religions, would thus through precisely this position have the task, and through its content the means, to comprehend those religions independent of reason, and indeed as such, and, accordingly, in their whole truth and actuality [*Eigentlichkeit*].

And now *you* well see: precisely such a philosophical religion would be necessary for us in order also to comprehend as possible—and therefore to comprehend philosophically—that which we see ourselves pressed to perceive as actual in mythology and thus in order to arrive at a Philosophy of Mythology. But this *philosophical religion does not exist*, and if, as indeed no one will deny, it could only be the last product and the highest expression of the completed philosophy itself, then we may well ask where we might find the philosophy that would be in the position to make comprehensible, that is, to explain as possible, what we perceived in mythology, and also mediately in revelation—a *real* [*reales*] relation of the human consciousness to God, while philosophy knows *only* of rational religion [XI 251] and of a *rational* relation to God and sees all religious development only as a development of the *idea* [*Idee*], to which also Hermann's statement belongs: that there is *only* philosophical religion. We admit this observation about the relationship of our view to the prevailing philosophy, but we cannot perceive in this any decisive objection against the correctness of our earlier development or the truth of its result. For in this entire investigation we have not proceeded from any preconceived view, least of all from a philosophy; thus the result is one that has been found and solidified independently of all philosophy. We have not taken up mythology at any other point other than where everyone finds it. For us philosophy was not the measure according to which we repudiated or accepted the views that presented themselves. Every type of explanation was welcome, even the one most distant from all philosophy, *if only it actually explained*. Only in steps, in consequence of a purely historical development visible to everybody, did we reach our result, in that we presupposed that for this object will be true also what Baco had shown with respect to philosophy: through successive exclusion of that which is proven as false, and through the purification of that which is fundamental truth from the false that clings to it, the true will be finally enclosed into such a narrow space that one is to a certain extent necessitated to perceive and declare it. Accordingly, not so much eclectically but rather on the path of a progressive critique gradually removing everything historically unthinkable, we have reached the point where only *this* view of mythology remained, which to grasp philosophically will now first be our task.

But indeed—given the dependence in which most find themselves with their philosophical concepts and their capacity to comprehend in general, it is to be expected that many will find reasons in the philosophy familiar to them not to accept the view articulated. This does not justify them immediately objecting against it, for this view itself is mere result after all; if they want to object against it, then they must find in the earlier deductions and conclusions something that justifies an objection [XI 252], and this too cannot be a mere corollary matter, any random detail (for how easy is it for something to be amiss there where so much and so much that is different is touched upon); it would have to be something that could not be removed without dissolving the whole web of our conclusions.

Since our view is so independent of philosophy it also cannot be contradicted because it does not accord with some sort of philosophical view (even if it were the almost universally valid one), and if no present and available philosophy is able to deal with this phenomenon, then it is not the once present and unmistakably known phenomenon that would have to let itself be brought back to the measure of some given philosophy, but rather conversely the factually grounded and substantiated view, whose unfailing effect on individual philosophical sciences we have shown, can claim to possess the power also to expand *philosophy* and *the philosophical consciousness itself* or to determine them to an expansion beyond their current limits.

Author's Notes

Lecture One

a. *Od.* XIX, 203.
b. *Aurae temporum meliorum, quae in fistulas Graecorum inciderunt.*
c. Οὑτοί εἰσιν οἱ ποιτ̄σαντες Τηεογοίην Ἑλλησιν. II, 53.
d. Wolfii *Prolegg. ad Homer.* p. LIV. not.
e. *Theog.* v. 881 ss. Αὑτάρ ἐπεί ρα πόνον μάχαρες Τηεοί ἐξετέλ-εσσν,/ Τιτήνεσσι δέ τιμάων χρίναντο βιῆφι,/ Δή ρα τοτ̄ ὠτρυνον βασιλευέμεν ἠδέ ἀνάσσειν Γάιης φραδμοσύνησιν ὀλύμπιον εὐρύopa Zῆν Ἀθανάτων ὁ δέ ψοισιν ἑῦ διεδάσσατο τιμάς. [The relevant passage from the *Theogony* follows: "And when the divine gods ended their toil, and had settled violently their struggle with the Titans for honor, at Earth's behest they urged far-seeing Olympian Zeus to reign over and rule them. Thus he divided their rank and dignities among them—Trans.] Herodotus's expressions are οὑτοι (Hesiod and Homer) δέ εἰοι — τοίσι Τηεοίσι τάς ἐπωνυμίας δόντες χαί τιμάς τε χαί τέχνας διελόντες. C.f. *Theogon.* V. 112. Ὡς τ̄ ἀφενας δάσσαντο χαί ὡς τιμάς διέλαντο. With the many discussions to which Herodotus's passage has given occasion, one can only be amazed that, to my knowledge, it has never been thought in those of Hesiod.

f. *Posthumous Writings*, Part XI, p. 190.
g. Those who, from the other side, have their reasons to isolate what is Greek as much as possible and keep distant from every general connection have invented the name *Indianophile* for the others who desire the explanation for everything in the Indian. I did not wait for this coinage in order to explain myself, in the essay on the deities of Samothrace, against every derivation of the Greek representations from the Indian; this happened itself

prior to the well-known declaration in Goethe's *West-Eastern Divan*. There (p. 30) it is definitely expressed that the Greek system of the gods in particular is to be traced back to a higher origin than the Indian representations. Had the first concepts not come to the Pelasgians (from whom everything Hellenic proceeded) from such outflows—that is, not, on the contrary, from out of the source of mythology itself—their representations of the gods would never have been able to unfold into such beauty.

h. *Lib.* II, c. 79.

LECTURE TWO

a. As is well known, allegory is from ἄλλο (an-other) and ἀγορεύειν (to say).

b. *Quae est enim gens, aut qoud genus hominum, qoud non habeat sine doctrina anticipationem quondam deorum? quam appellat πρόληπψιν Epicurus, id est anteceptam animo rei quondam informationem, sine qua nec intelligi quidquam, nec quaeri, nec disputari potest.* Cicero, *de nat. Deor*, I, 16.

c. *Cum non instituto aliquo, aut more, aut lege sit opinio constituta, maneatque ad unum omnium firma consensio, intelligi necesse est, esse deos.* Ibid., 17.

d. Kant, where he speaks of the former theory of phlogiston, mentions a young American savage who, asked about what astonished him so very much about the English beer that flowed forth as foam from out of an unearthed bottle, gave the answer: *I am not astonished that it comes out; I only wonder how you were able to put it in.*

e. The writings of *Dornedden* (one of the former Göttingen lecturers), the *Phamenophis* and others, according to which the whole Egyptian system of the gods is only a calendar system, a veiled representation of the yearly motion of the sun and of the change, posited with that, of phenomena in the course of an Egyptian year.

f. *De origine et causis Fabularum Homericarum* (*Commentt. Gott. T.* VIII).

g. *Nec vero hoc (per fabulas) philosophandi genus recte satis appelatur* **allegoricum,** *cum non tam sententiis involucra quaererent homines studio argutiarum, quam qoud animi sensus quomodo aliter exprimerent non habebant. Angustabat enim et coarctabat spiritum quasi erumpere luctantem orationis difficultas et inopia, percussusque tanquam numinis alicujus afflatu animus, cum verba deficerent propria, et sua et communia, aestuans et abreptus exhibere ipsas res et repraesentare oculis, facta in conspectus ponere et in dramatis modum in scenam proferre cogitata allaborabat.* Heyne l. c. p. 38.

h. Plato, *Phaedr.*, p. 229; *De Rep.*, III, p. 391. D.

i. Cicero, *De Nat.*, D. L. III, c. 24. **Magnum molestiam suscepit** *et minime necessariam primus Zeno, post Cleanthes, deinde Chrysippus com-*

mentitiarum fabularum reddere rationem, vocabularum, cur quique ita appellati sint, causus explicare. Quod cum facitis, illud profecto confitemini, longe aliter rem se habere atque **hominum opinio** *sit: eos enim, qui Dii appellentur,* **rerum natura esse**, *non figuras Deorum.*

j. *Alia quoque ex ratione, et quidem* **physica**, *magna fluxit multitudo Deorum; qui* **induti specie humana** *fabulas poetis suppeditaverunt, hominum autem vitam superstitione omni referserunt. Atque hic locus a Zenone tractatus, post a Cleanthe et Chrysippo pluribus verbis explicatus est. etc.* Cicero l. c. c. 24.

k. Compare B. Cousin's remarks in the two articles about Olympiodor. *Journal des Savants*, Juin 1834. May 1835.

l. *Dissert. de Mythol. Graecorum antiquississima*. Lips. 1817.

m. *On the Essence and Treatment of Mythology*. Leipzig 1819. p. 47.

n. Ibid., p. 107.

o. Ibid., p. 47.

p. Ibid., p. 38. 101.

q. *Voyage dans l'Amerique méridionale* T. II, p. 186. 187.

r. *On the Essence and Treatment of Mythology*, p. 140.

s. *Letters on Homer and Hesiod*, by G. Hermann and Fr. Creuzer, Heidelberg, 1818, p. 17.

t. The ὁ δῖος αἰθήρ of Prometheus in Aeschylus (p. 88, compare the other immediately following appeals) would only have been mentionable in the same sense.

LECTURE THREE

a. Following the meanings of the word in Hebrew, one is led likewise to the concept of *ability* or of the subject (*ejus, quod substat*).

b. *Letters on Homer and Hesiod*, by G. Hermann and Fr. Creuzer. Heidelb. 1818. p. 14. 65, and passim.

c. Ibid. p. 14, 65, and passim. *Dissert*. cit. p. IV.

d. *Dissertatio de Historiae Graceae primordiis*, in which the principal of exposition previously applied to the *Theogony* is also applied to the mythical history of Greece.

e. M. s. **Azara**, *Voyages etc*. T. II, p. 44, where it is said of the Pampas: *ils ne connaissent ni religion, ni culte, ni soumission, ni lois,* **ni** *obligations, ni récompenses, ni châtiments*; the same is said on p. 91 of the Guanas; and on p. 151 of the Lenguas: *ils ne reconnaissent ni culte, ni divinité, ni lois, ni chefs, ni obéissance, et* **ils sont libres en tout**; and the same of the M'bajas, on p. 113, where one also sees what the case is with the so-called Kaziks, who were charged with these savages by the other residents (who were found in a civil constitution), the Kaziks who (c.f. p. 47) have neither the right to order, nor to punish, nor to require anything at all, but, however, enjoy a certain respect from the others, who usually agree in collective meetings with their opinion, and follow them—not as masters, or out of some feeling of duty, but rather because they ascribe to them more understanding, acuity, and physical power than they themselves. With the Charruas no one is obliged to participate in the execution of an issue that has been decided upon, not even the person who proposed it. The parties themselves deal with their conflicts, usually through fist-fights. Ibid., p. 16.

Lecture Four

a. One compares the article *"Existence"* in the French *Encyclopedia*, from which a good deal in later, popular explanations of the first origins of the representations of the gods seems borrowed. The article is by Turgot.

b. *A.P.* 391 ss.

c. C.f. the critique of it printed again prior to the German translation of the above-named work, in the *Göttingen gel. Anzeigen*.

d. One compares, among others, the remarks of the French translators.

e. Because the fact is important for the conclusion, the conclusive passages may stand here. One passage, in which the writer explains himself generally, is the following: *Les ecclésiastiques y ont ajouté une autre fausseté positive en disant, que ce peuple avait une religion. Pursuadés, qu'il était impossible aux hommes de vivre sans en avoir une bonne ou mauvaise, et voyant quelques figures dessinées ou gravées sur leurs pipes, les arcs, les bâtons et les poteries des Indiens, ils se figurèment á l'instant, que c'étaient leurs idoles, et les brulèrent. Ces peuples emploient aujourd'hui encore les mêmes figures, mais ils ne le font que pour amusement,* **car ils n'ont aucune réligion.** *Voyages* T. II, p. 3. Of the Payaguas, among others, he explains likewise; p. 137: *Quand la tempête ou le vent renverse leurs huttes ou cases, ils prennent quelques tisons de leur feu, ils courent á quelque distance contre le vent, en le menaçant, avec leurs tisons. D'autres pour épouvanter la tempête donnent force coups de poing en l'air; ils en font quélquefois autant, quand ils aperçoivent la nouvelle lune; mais, dissent-ils, ce n'est que pour marquer leur joie: ce qui a donné lieu à quelques personnes de croire, qu'ils l'adoraient: mais le* **fait positif** *est, qu'ils ne rendent ni culte ni adoration* **à rien au monde** *et* **qu'ils n'ont aucune réligion.**

f. *A bien considérer la chose, cette pretendue Religion n'est en effet* **qu'un Athéisme superstitieux,** *les objèts du culte qu'elle établit, n'ont pas le moindre rapport avec l'idée que nous nous formons de las Divinité*. Histoire naturelle de la Religion, p. 25. These and the following passages are cited according to the [good] French translation.

g. Ibid., p. 35.

h. *Origine des tous les Cultes*.

i. *Les Ruines*.

j. *Histoire nat. de la Rel.* p. 110.

k. Ibid., p. 5.
l. Ibid., p. 8–10.
m. Ibid. p. 45f.
n. *On the Essence and Treatment of Mythology*, p. 25f.
o. § 6 and § 7.
p. In a letter to his brother (*Coll. Writ.* XXX, p. 523) Lessing himself speaks of the *Education of Man* in a way that indicates that it did not suffice for *him*: "I have, it is said, sent him (the book tradesman Voss) the *Ed. of Man*, which he shall extend for me to a half-dozen sheets. Indeed, I can fully send the thing into the world because *I will never know it for my own work*, and yet many have been desirous for the whole plan."—If one wanted to conclude from the emphasized words that Lessing is not at all the penner, then really the opposite might follow from this. In that he says he will never know it as his own work, he admits precisely that it *is* his work. Even the great author, and precisely one such as Lessing, can publish a work that does not satisfy him (and if the *Ed. of Man* could satisfy in general a mind like Lessing, even in wider relation, did he not have to consider its content as something that is provisionally established, in whose future position something entirely different, yet not for the present realizable, would have to step?)—I say, an author like Lessing can publish such a work, even as a transition and step toward a higher development.
q. C.f. the passage in my essay *On the Deities of Samothrace* (p. 30); which, moreover, as the context indicates, should contain no claim, but rather should only contrast the view posited there—which keeps merely to the letter of the Mosaic writings—with another one *as likewise possible*. Additionally, the author was at the time certainly more concerned with the material aspect of mythology and still distanced from himself the formal questions that were first articulated in the present lectures.
r. *Symbolism and Mythology of the Ancient Peoples, especially of the Greeks*. Part VI, 3rd edition. In the preparation of the present lectures the second edition is used. What is recommended to students is the excerpt (appearing in the same publication) of the work by *Moser*, which contains without exception everything essential in one volume. The French revision, by *Guigniant* (*Religions de l'Antiqué, Ouvrage traduit de l'Allemand du Dr. F. Creuzer refondu en partie completé et developpé*. Paris 1825. Part III), which has appended a bit that is new and valuable, is most highly worth attention.
s. One could also perhaps compare mythology with a great piece of music that continued to play to a great number of people who lost all sense for its musical coherence, rhythm, and measure and for whom, as it were, it could only appear as an entangled mass of cacaphonies; yet the same piece, artfully executed, would once again immediately reveal its harmony, its coherence, and its original intelligence.
t. *Letters on Homer and Hesiod*, p. 100–01.

Lecture Five

a. In Hindi a caste is called *Jâti*, but also Varna, color. See *Journal Asiat*. Tom. VI, p. 179.
b. Herodot. L. II, c. 104.
c. Compare the well-known writings of *Dr.* Schnurrer, who, unfortunately, has passed prematurely away.
d. *1. Mos.* 11.
e. One compares the well-known fragments of *Abydenus* in *Eusebius* in the first book of his *Chronikons*; the Platonic story *Politicus*, p. 272. B., where the same at least faintly shines through.
f. *Jerem.* 51, 7.
g. Precisely this meaning is to be noticed with the Apostle Paul, *1. Cor.* 14, 11: Ἐὰν μὴ εἰδῶ τὴν δύναμιν (meaning, sense) τῆς φωνῆς, ἔσομαι τῷ λαλοῦντι βάρβαρος χαὶ ὁ λαλῶν (ἐν) ἐμοὶ βάρβαρος, which Luther translates as: "I will be ungerman to the speaker, and him there speaking will be ungerman to me." According to this usage, even that one is a βάρβαρος who speaks unintelligibly, without being an *extraneus*. Cicero too opposes *disertus* to the *barbarus*. Likewise, with Plato, βάρβαρίξειν utters something unintelligible: ἀπορῶν χαι ʹβάρβαριξειν. *Theaet.* 175. D.
h. In the Arabic translation of the N. T. the word *balbal* is also used for ταράσσειν (τὴν ψυχήν). Acts. 15, 24. — From the same sound-imitation comes the Latin *balbus, balbutiens*, the German *babeln, babbeln* (Swabian) = *plappern*; French: *babiller, babil*.
i. Τὸ Ἀττιχὸν ἔθνος, ἐὸν πελασγιχὸ, ἅμα τῇ μεταβολῇ τε ἐς Ἑλληνας χαὶ τὴν γλῶσσαν μετέμαθεν. L. I. c. 57.
j. For this reason, in the lectures on the *Philosophy of Revelation* I named the phenomenon at Pentecost "the inverted Babel," an expression I later found in others. At that time Gesenius's suggestion in the article "Babylon" in the *Halle'schen Encyclopedia* was unknown to me. Moreover, this contrast was not uncommon to the early fathers of the church, a contrast that to this extent indeed has a claim to count as a natural one. Another parallel from the Persian doctrine—where the diversity of languages (ἑτερογλωσσία) is described as a work of Ahriman, and the unity of the languages is proclaimed for the era of the reestablishment of the pure kingdom of light, after the defeat of Ahriman—is mentioned in the *Philosophy of Revelation*.
k. Thus a true γλώσσαις (in the plural) λαλεῖν; also in Corinth something entirely different than the ἑτέραιςλώσσαις λαλεῖν, whose explanation contains the following: Ὅτι ἤχουν εἰς ἕχαστος τῇ ἰδίᾳ διαλέχτῳ λαούντον αὐτῶν, and that is only possible if the language that is spoken is *instar omnium*, not merely when the various languages reciprocally lose their tension and exclusivity. Whoever speaks in this way is βάρβαρος to the apostle, in the sense of the passage already mentioned.
l. Famously, Hermann explains it from ποτὸν (πόσις) and εἴδεσθαι, *qoud potile videtur, non est.* (Unless I err, instead of *potile*, *potabile* should

be there. For the ocean water is actually, like everything fluid, *potile*, something drinkable in a general sense; on the other hand, only *potabile* appears to be drinkable in a specific sense, agreeable to the human taste.)

m. The well-known adj. *mesquin* is a purely Arabic word, which migrated from Spanish to French.

n. According to a passage of the Pentateuch (5. *Mos.* 32, 8) the peoples are *divided and handed out* by the All-Highest (with respect to individual gods the Hebrew word usually has otherwise a dative after it); the Platonic is similar: τότε γάρ (in the first age of the world) αὐτῆς πρῶτον τῆς χυχλώσεως ἦρχεν ἐπιμελούμενος **ὄγης** ὁ θεός, ὡς νῦν **χατὰ τόπους** ταὐτὸν τοῦτο ὑπο ʼθεων, ἀρχόν-των πάντη τὰ τοῦ χόσμου μέρη διειλημμένα. *Politic.* p. 271. D.

o. Herod., *Lib.* II, c. 104.

p. *Ils parlent ordinairement beaucoup de la gorge et du nez, le plus souvent même il nous est impossible d'exprimer avec nos lettres leurs mots ou leurs sons.* Azara, *Voyages* T. II, p. 5, with which are to be compared pp. 14 and 57.

q. Πρῶτοι μὲν ὧν ἀνθρώπων, τῶν ἡμεῖς ἴδμεν, Αἰγύπτοι λέγονται θεῶν τε ἐννοίην λαβεῖν, χαὶ ἱρὰ ἴσασθαι — πρῶτοι δὲ χαὶ οὐνόματα ἱρὰ ἔγνωσαν, χαὶ λόγους ἱρούς ἔλεξαν. Lucian. *de Syria Dea* c. 2.

r. In *1. Mos.* 12, 2 Jehovah promises Abraham to make him a great people or nation and to make his name great.

s. For the moment, for we hope later to return to this, I refer—regarding the pre-Homeric age of the Cyclopean works in Greece—to my treatise delivered in the Academy of Science in Munich, and which appears in excerpt in its *2nd Annual Report* (1829-1831).

t. Οὐδ ἀλλήλων ἀλέγουσιν. *Odyss.* IX, 115.

LECTURE SIX

a. *On the Essence and Treatment of M[ythology].* p. 37.

b. *Storehouse of the Orient*, B. III, p. 279.

c. Val. Löscher, in the well-known work *De causis linguae Hebraeae* had long ago already led the way.

d. For example, see in *Creuzer*, in the preface to the first part of *Symbolism and Mythology* (2nd Ed., p. 2): "I adhere to my main thesis in its entire extent. It is the basis of an *initially purer* veneration and *knowledge* of One God, to whose religion all following ones are related *like broken and pale light rays to the source light* of the sun." Compare another passage from the *Letters on Homer and Hesiod* (p. 95): "I would like to compare my view of mythology with the hypothesis of the astronomers, who perceive in the newly discovered planets Pallas, Ceres, Vesta the *dispersed* parts of a scattered primordial planet."—whereupon he remarks further: the original unity, at which alone one must look, supposedly is a *purer primordial religion* that was monotheism, and, no matter to what extent it was splintered through the torn polytheism, has at no time entirely passed away.

e. We will return to this striking passage subsequently, and thereby at the same time have opportunity to show that it can be understood literally and materially in no other way than in the manner assumed above.

Lecture Seven

a. V. 25. 26.

b. On account of the linguistic use, c.f. *Jer.* 43, 1; it is not stated בְּשִׁמְךָ ךְ ֿקְרָאמִ֣ ' but rather only קְרָאמִ֣ ' בְּמִשֻּׁךְ.

c. *5. Mos.* 31, 19–21.

d. *1. Chron.* 29 (28), 9. The books of *Chronicles*, in matters religious, also go back readily to the oldest types of expression.

e. Ibid., 30 (29), 18.

f. *J. D. Michaelis*, in his comments to *Gen.* 6, 2, says: "Hitherto, the human species had divided itself into two large parts: the better, which believed in one God, named itself, by the true God, sons of God; the rest, who were not sunk in *superstition—for we find no trace of that prior to the great flood—but rather in complete unbelief*, Moses names the sons of men." As shown, for all that the missing trace was already to be found at *Gen.* 4, 26, where the Chaldean translators and the oldest Jewish interpreters—who had no interest to have successive polytheism to begin so early—also had found it, even if owing to an incorrect interpretation.

g. The latter stands, explicitly, in *Gen.* 7, 1.

h. *1. Mos.* 8, 21; compare with 6, 5.

i. One finds the passages in brevity together in *Rosenmüller's Old and New East*, Part. I, p. 23. (Also in *Stolberg's History of the Religion of Jesu Christi*, Part. I, p. 394.)

j. Compare *Eichhorn* in the *Repertory for Biblical and Eastern Literature*. V, p. 216.

k. *1. Mos.* 9, 20.

l. *Jerem.* 35.

m. *1. Mos.* 14, 1. To take *gojim* itself as the name of a people, *gojiten*, of which one otherwise knows absolutely nothing, is no reason, and equally unnecessary is every other artificial explanation. The appellative meaning is fully justified by the view above.

n. See *Gesenius, History of the Hebrew Language and Writing*, p. 11.

o. *1. Mos.* 12, 6, where it is used by Abraham himself; 37, 28, then 2, *Kings* 4, 8. 9, passim.

p. *1. Mos.* 17, 8. 35, 27. 37, 1. Jehovah's promises to give to him and his descendents perpetual ownership of the land in which he is as a foreigner thereby receive a more definite meaning.

q. Compare *1. Mos.* 47, 9. The only one of the above presented explanations that perhaps could be drawn for the name Hebrew would be that of *Wahl*, who, supported in this way—that עֲרָבָה, for which also a plural עֲרָבוֹה

(*Jer.* 5, 6., *2. Kings* 25, 5) meaning desert, is written—advances the clever conjecture that *Ibrim* (Hebrew), *Arabim* (Arab), and *Aramim* (Aramaic) are simple yet analogically conceivable variants of the same name. In the matter with which it is concerned nothing would be otherwise changed.

 r. *1. Mos.* 25, 27.
 s. *1. Sam.* 8, 5.
 t. Ibid., v. 8.
 u. See Gibbons, *History*, c. X.
 v. *J. Grimm* sees an intensifying prefix in this. *Göttingen gelehrte Anzeigen* 1835, p. 1105.
 w. *Ammian. Marcell.* L. XVI, c. 2.
 x. *1. Mos.* 12, 7. 17, 1. 18, 1. 26, 2. 28, 12. But chapter 35? Elohim appears here, but only in order to recall (v. 1) the God that *"appeared"* and to confirm (v. 11) his blessing.
 y. *1. Mos.* 12, 8. 13, 4. 21, 33. 26, 25.
 z. *1. Mos.* 20, 13.
 aa. Compare, for example, 35, 7.
 bb. *1. Mos.* 12, 1. 24, 7.
 cc. Compare **Storrii** *Obss.* p. 97. Examples: *jamim* means the great sea (p. 46, 3), *thanim* = *draco sed grandis*, *schamaim* = *altitudo, sed grandis*.
 dd. *1. Mos.* 20, 11.
 ee. *1. Mos.* 20, 6. 31, 24.
 ff. *1. Mos.* 20, 17.
 gg. *1. Mos.* 17, 9; from 1–8 Jehovah spoke. That this is not accidental is illuminated by 21, 4, where mention is again made of the command, and it runs: as *Elohim* had commanded him.
 hh. The main passage, of course, *1. Mos*, 22, 11. The angel Jehovah not differentiated from Jehovah himself: *Judg.* 6, 12, and compare 14, 16, 12. Where Jehovah and the angel Jehovah, there is of course also Elohim; Ibid., 13, 21, and compare with 22.
 ii. *Jerem.* 5, 15.
 jj. *Jos.* 24, 2.
 kk. *5. Mos.* 32, 17.
 ll. *1. Mos.* 24, 3.
 mm. Apparently, in this sense also is *saddik* in *1. Mos.* 6, 9 to be taken.
 nn. *1. Mos.* 5, 22. 6, 9.
 oo. Additionally, just Abraham, not Melchizedek also, names Jehovah the God of heaven and of the earth. *1. Mos.* 14, 22. Compare 19, 20.
 pp. *1. Mos.* 17, 1.
 qq. 6, 2f.
 rr. If one wanted—for which incidentally there is no reason—to explain (cf., *Storrii, Obss.*, p. 454) the ב in בְּאֵל as the well-known ב *praedicati*, although it would hardly occur in this construction, then it would amount to the same; it would be as if one said, "I appeared to them as El Schaddai."

ss. 1. *Mos.* 22, 1 with 22, 12 and 15–16.
tt. 2. *Mos.* 3, 14.
uu. 1. *Mos.* 18, 18–19. 26, 4.
vv. 1. *Mos.* 15, 6. Abraham *believed* Jehovah; Jehovah credited it to him as *righteousness*.
ww. 1. *Mos.* 20, 7.
xx. All thoughts in the O.T. are thus so directed toward the future that the devout narrator in *1. Mos.* 4, 1 already suggests of Eve a prophecy (moreover, by virtue of a much sought explanation of the name of Cain, which according to the same etymology admits of one much closer): "I have the man, Jehovah." With the continuation of the human race, which is guaranteed through the first human birth, the true God, which it does not yet have, is secured for humanity. —I prevent no one who has the desire to do so from seeing in the words the actual words of Eve; but then, however, he would also admit as proven historically that the true God was only a future one for the first humans.
yy. 2. *Mos.* 33, 11.
zz. 4. *Mos.* 12, 8.
aaa. 5. *Mos.* 34, 10.
bbb. To consider possible that superstitious customs—like the Mosaic ceremonial law prescribes—were still perhaps able to emerge in times like those of David or his successors presupposes an ignorance of the general path of religious development, an ignorance that could be excused 40 years ago. For at that time the opinion to be able to judge about an appearance, like the Mosaic law, outside of the larger and general context was pardonable. Today, however, it is no undue demand that everyone first strive for a greater education before he undertakes to speak about objects of such high antiquity.

LECTURE EIGHT

a. Θεὸς ἔνεμεν αὐτοὺς, αὐτὸς ἐπιστατῶν νέμοντος δὲ ἐκείνου πολιτεῖαί τε οὐχ ἦσαν. *Polit.* p. 271, E.
b. See: p. 141.
c. For comparison, some of his passages may be offered. *C'est un fait incontestable, qu' en remontant au-delà d'environ 1700 ans on trouve tout le Genre humain idolâtre. On ne saurait nous objecter ici ni les doutes et les principes sceptiques d'un petit nombre de Philosophes, ni le Théisme d'une ou de deux nations tout au plus, Théisme encore, qui n'était pas épuré.* (In this way Hume seems to intend to set aside the fact of the Old Testament or, really, Mosaic religion, instead of using this itself as proof for the priority of polytheism). *Tenons nous-en donc au témoignage de l'histoire, qui n'est point équivoque. Plus nous perçons dans l'antiquité, plus nous voyons les hommes plongés dans l'Idolatrie* (now, in any case, also disregarding the word *Idolatrie*, which is in no way synonymous with polytheism, this is too much said,

and not in accordance with the history), *on n'y aperçoit plus la moindre trace (?) d'une Religion plus parfaite: tous les vieux monumens nous presentent le Polythéisme comme la doctrine établie et publiquement reçue. Qu' opporesat-on à une vérité aussi évidente, à une verité également attestée par l'Orient et par l'Occident, par le Septentrion et par le Midi?*—*Autant que nous pouvons suivre le fil de l'histoire, nous trouvons livre le Genre humain au Polytheisme, et pourrions-nous croire que dans les temps les plus reculés, avant la découverte des arts et des sciences, les principes du pur Théisme eussent prévalus? Ce serait dire que les homes decouvrirent la verité pendant qu'ils etaient ignorans et barbares, et qu'aussitôt, qu'ils commencèrent à s'instruire et à se polir, ils tombèrent dans l'erreur etc. Histoire naturelle de la R.* p. 3. 4.

d. *Joh.* 4, 23. 24.

e. I borrow this expression from the well-known *Coleridge*, the first of his fellow countrymen who has understood and meaningfully used German poetry and science [*Wissenschaft*], especially philosophy. The expression is found in an otherwise singular essay in the *Transactions of the R. Society of Literature*. This essay has particularly pleased me because it showed me how one of my earlier writings (the text on the *Deities of Samothrace*)—whose philosophical content and importance was little, or, rather, not at all understood in Germany—has been understood in its meaning by the talented Brit. For the apposite expression mentioned, I happily let him have the borrowings from my writings, the borrowed writings sharply, all too sharply, criticized by his own countrymen, in which my name was not mentioned. One should not charge that to such a truly congenial man. The severity of such censures in England proves, however, what value is laid there on scientific propriety and how strictly the *suum cuique* in science [*Wissenschaft*] is observed. In other respects Coleridge uses the word *tautegorical* as synonymous with *philosophem*, which would admittedly not fit my meaning, but perhaps he only means to say mythology must likewise properly be taken just as one usually takes a philosophem, and this he has sensed completely correctly from the above mentioned essay. I have called the essay singular on account of the language, for if we are at pains to relinquish a part of earlier technical expression, or would happily relinquish if the matter allowed it, then he gives unhesitatingly to his fellow countrymen unfamiliar with it—if with some irony—expressions to be enjoyed, like *subject-object* and others similar.

Lecture Nine

a. P. 100.
b. P. 111.
c. This "without" is added here because it seems necessary to the meaning; in the text it is missing.
d. Lecture 3.

e. According to Ovid and Plutarch, the *household gods*. The passage in Plutarch reads (*Quaestiones Romanae*, ed. Reiske, p. 119): Διὰ τί τῶν Λαρητῶν, οὕς ἰδίως, πραιστίτας χαλοῦσι, τούτοις χύων παρέστηχεν, αὐτοὶ δὲ χυνῶν διφθέραις ἀμπέχονται; ἡ πραιστίτης μὲν οἱ πρεστῶτές εἰσι, τοὺς δὲ προεστῶτας οἴχου φυλαχτιχοὺς εἶναι προσήχει, χαὶ φοβεροὺς μὲν τοῖς ἀλλοτρίοις (ὥσπερ ὁ χύων ἐστὶν), ἡπίους δὲ χαὶ πράους τοῖς συνοιχοῦσιν· ἢ μᾶλλον, ὃ λέγουσιν ἔνιι Ῥωμαίων, ἀληθές ἐστι· χαί, χαθάπερ οἱ περί Χρύσππον οἴονται φιλόσοφοι, φαῦλα δαιμόνια περινοστεῖν, οἷς οἱ θεοὶ δημίοις χρῶνται χολασταῖς ἐπὶ τοὺς ἀνοσίους χαὶ ἀδίχους ἀνθρώπους οὕτως οἱ Λάρητες ερινυώδεις τινές εἰσι χαὶ ποίνιμοι δαίμονες, ἐπίσχοποι βίων χαὶ οἴχων διὸ χαὶ νῦν δέρμασιν ἀμπέχονται, χαὶ χύων πάρεδρός ἐστιν, ὡς δεινοῖς οὖσιν ἐξιχνεῦσαι χαὶ μετελθεῖν τοὺς πονηρούς. In *Gruter, Inscript.* p. 22. n. 1. p. 1065. n. 2. *Jovi praestiti*.

f. The Greek word mythos does not necessarily include in itself the corollary concept, with which the word fable is bound up for us.

g. *System of Transcendental Idealism*. Tübingen 1800.

h. Stuttgart and Tübingen 1807.

i. Part One, Leipzig 1803.

j. A minor text from W. *Menzel* is historically noteworthy to the extent that Voss met his match in it and was completely silenced by it.

Lecture Ten

a. See the statements in the first preface to the *Ideas on Philosophy of Nature*.

b. *Letters on Homer and Hesiod*, p. 67.

c. *Dissert. de Mythol. Graec.* p. X, On the Earth: "*in quo, senescente jam, nos medii inter duas ruinas aeternitatem, serius ocius novis fluctibus perituram, inani labore consectamur.*"

d. *Heerens Ideas on Politics and Trade of the Ancients Peoples*, Part. I, Division III, p. 311, note.

e. These lectures from 1803 are present completely in the handwritten literary estate. [D. H.]

f. Judges of art degrade *Platen* on account of his meager producing, as they called it. They did not know and will never know what was in him whose life-path was cut short so early and to whose memory I gladly for the meantime devote these lines, since I do not know if I will be permitted time for a more complete explication.

g. *Rom.* 11.

h. *Eph.* 2, 12. If ἐν τῷ χόσμῳ does not mean anything in itself, then it is the emptiest addition, because in the sense that it then has, the Christians are also in the world.

i. *Eph.* 2, 17. 18.

Translators' Notes

Lecture One

1. *Wissenschaft* can equally be translated as "knowledge" or "science." There is a historical context to the word, particularly when translated as "science." Although it indeed means science in the ordinary sense of the word, in German Idealism from Kant to Fichte to Hegel to Schelling *Wissenschaft* can also have the distinction of meaning philosophy in general, and particularly in the mode of the "queen of the sciences." Interestingly, with a clear view toward the etymological content of the word *historia*, in several places in his earlier works Schelling refers to *Wissenschaft* as *historia*. This usage indicates that Schelling clearly accounts for knowledge's (i.e., science's) aspect of narration, of the inescapability of the interpenetration of subjective and objective, and of its historical-contextual situatedness.

2. The important verb in this sentence is *erkennen*, which commonly means "to cognize" or "to know" but also has a colloquial variant meaning "to be alive to." Moreover, "knowledge," which precedes "discern" in the passage, is *Erkenntnis* instead of *Wissenschaft*. *Wissenschaft* and its variants denote often an organized system of research. Variations of the verb *erkennen* speak to a knowledge that is slightly less abstract and slightly more object involved. The translation as "to discern" is partly to be read in light of this consideration, and partly from the word's etymology, whose meaning beginning in thirteenth century German designates *erkennen* as the activity of a judge who discerns and passes judgment.

3. The phrase reads *"von der besonders die horazische Regel gelten sollte."* An alternate translation would read "to which Horace's law should be applied."

4. The German reads "*dem Forscher hervortraten,*" literally, "stepped forth to the researcher." This makes obvious Schelling's epistemological concern for understanding the interrelation between the researcher qua subject and the object being investigated.

5. The German for "tales" is *Sagen*, which is also denoted as "myths," "fables," "legends."

6. The German here is *hinausgehen*, a word frequently employed by Schelling. It means "to transcend," but the prepositional phrase *über etwas hinaus zu gehen* implies a going-through in order to get beyond.

7. Schelling's employment of the words *Dichtung* and *Poesie* presents translation headaches. As a rule, both mean "poetry." With respect to etymology, *Dichtung* implies, however, two particular characteristics. *Dichtung* and the related *Dichter* (poet) contain the root *dicht*, which means "compress(ed)" or "pack(ed) closely," which metaphorical language characteristic is often ascribed to the work of the poet (and also to the effects of symbolism, metaphor, allegory, etc.) and gives rise to the words *dichten* (to "compose" a literary work, etc.) and *Gedicht* (poem). At the same time *Dichtung* implies more than mere poetry, insofar as it also implies the creative impulse or inspiration behind the work. Problematically, this typology describing the creative impulse or inspiration corresponds to what in English is also called "poesy" (which, of course, also loosely means simply "poetry" or "poetic work"), and "poesy" (and Schelling's frequently employed German cognate *Poesie*) stems from the Greek *poiēsis* (to "create," "make," "invent," "fabricate") and its cognates. This last point comes often into play when Schelling plays with the idea of *Dichter* as "creators," "founders," "makers," or "inventors" of mythology. With all this taken into consideration, it is impossible to be perfectly consistent with respect to when *Dichtung* should be translated as "poesy" and *Poesie* as "poetry," and vice-versa. As a general rule, *Dichtung* is translated as "poesy" and *Poesie* as "poetry"; when the context seems unclear the German original is given in brackets.

8. The German here is *Götterlehre*, which could also translate as either "doctrine" or "teaching" of the "gods"/"deities," or even simply as "mythology." "Mythology" is not a good option as a translation for *Götterlehre* because Schelling employs the word *Mythologie* as the general term designating the topic of these lectures. A strictly consistent translation is impossible, moreover, insofar as '*Götterlehre*,' as a concept, takes on various meanings in different contexts of these lectures. The choice here to employ the slightly less literal "system" comes from Schelling's remark on the fact that the mythological gods, as multiplicitous, initially are found historically as existent in a set of relations. The task of the lectures, then, is to develop and make sense of the determinations of those relations. One might profitably think of the relation of the various translations of '*Götterlehre*' as developing the idea that "system" is the least determinate concept, while "doctrine" and "teaching" imply a more determinate concept of mythology. Generally, in the first part of the text

the translation "system" is retained, in part because of the importance of this set of lectures to Schelling's larger concerns with the difficulties of delineating the features and fissures of systematic thinking.

9. Broadly put, theogony is an account of the origin of the gods. It particularly deals with the genealogy of the gods. It is unknown exactly when the *Theogony* of Hesiod was written. It is known that Hesiod almost assuredly lived after Homer, most likely sometime around 700 BCE, and that he lived in Boeatia. Lore has it that Hesiod received his poetic gifts directly from the Muses of Mt. Helikon while tending sheep. The prelude to the *Theogony* consists of praises for the inhabitants of Mt. Helikon.

10. In this context, the choice of "sublation" to translate *Aufhebung*, in all its tripartite Hegelio-dialectical glory, is interesting because at this point in his career Schelling was long past his days of doing only "negative philosophy," which conceptually is defined significantly by sublation. Nonetheless, as Schelling mentions in the following parenthetical cause, the *preliminary* task requires the negative philosophy, and thus requires sublation. This becomes particularly evident with the procedure in lecture 3, where Schelling uses the valuable portions of the poetic and philosophical views of the genesis of mythology, discards their chaff, and combines them into a third. It also is worth mentioning that Schelling refers farther down in this paragraph to "another historical dialectic" in such a way that he clearly indicates that dialectics is not simply to be abandoned. Although Schelling was, at the writing of these lectures, invested in the "positive" philosophy, he never abandoned many of the procedures of the negative philosophy, continued to insist that all life "must pass through the fire of contradiction," and consistently stressed similarities between his work and that of Hegel.

11. The word for "entangles" here is *verwickle*, which is related closely to the word for development, *Entwicklung*. The science with which Schelling is dealing relies on the understanding that questioning the object on its own terms may naturally lead to mistakes and entanglements, that knowledge is not a mere development of what is preordained and known in advance.

12. Presumably Schelling is referring to the *Götterlehre oder mythologische Dichtungen der Alten* (1791), a text by the scholar and philologist Karl Philipp Moritz (1756–1793). In addition to being a teacher of Alexander von Humboldt, Moritz was a friend of Goethe, Schiller, and Jean Paul.

13. The Aeolian harp was an ancient instrument consisting of an open wood box over which strings are stretched. When the wind blows, the strings produce a tone. The instrument is named for Aeolus, the god of the winds.

14. Briefly, the story of Ixion and Juno (Hera) is as follows: Ixion attempted to seduce Juno, but Zeus discovered the seduction in advance. In order to foil the seduction he created a phantom of Juno, and when Ixion mated with the phantom Juno the centaurs were born. For his impiety Ixion was chained for eternity to a fiery wheel in Tartarus, the lowest level of hell and the abode of Sisyphus, the banished Titans, and others.

15. Schelling is referring here to Sir Francis Bacon, the Renaissance English statesman, scientist and philosopher who in 1609 wrote the *De Sapientia Veterum* and in 1620 the *Organum Novum*, the inductive empiricism of which was to replace the Aristotelian model of scientific knowledge.

16. The word here is *Entstehung*, which has consistently been translated as either "emergence into being" or "emergence." An alternate, essentially synonymous translation is "genesis," which is employed when necessary to smooth out sentence structure, particularly when there is the danger for an awkward set of possessive prepositions.

17. Little is known of the Pelasgians, the autochthonous inhabitants of the Peloponnesus and most likely some of the surrounding lands. What is known is that they probably migrated there from the north and that their presence in what is now modern Greece dates back to at least 7000 BCE. The name *Pelasgian* means "people from the sea." The contemporary knowledge of the Pelasgian relation to the Hellenic mythology is limited, but it does seem that the Pelasgians espoused an already extant Hera worship (attested to by a ruined Pelasgian temple dedicated to Hera), and the myth of Helios yoking his chariot to the sun seems to have begun with the Pelasgians.

18. Like Sappho, Alkaios was a poet from the Aeolian island of Lesbos. He lived most likely around 620 BCE and wrote monodic lyric poetry. Tyrtaios was an elegiac poet from Sparta. He lived during the Spartan conversion to a more militarized social structure, and many of his poems were marches and other military poems.

19. Although it is not totally clear here, it is very likely that Schelling is referring to the, for the nineteenth century, very new hypothesis of geological uplift [*Erhebungstheorie*]. In Scotland in 1785 Hutton had made a series of observations about how igneous rock was the mechanism for pushing up and elevating soil. From this he drew conclusions about geological forces, uplift, and the mechanisms for natural landscape alteration through geological time. He also hypothesized that the earth is immeasurably older than the approximately six thousand years that the competing geological ideas of diluvial theory granted. That is, Hutton was the father of modern geology, and his work, although at first treated as heretical, was the breakthrough in sweeping away the biblically inspired Mosaic time line of the earth, as well as the immediately forerunning geological theories of Neptunism and Vulkanism. As is well known, for his part, Goethe was extremely interested in natural science, even producing a theory of optics. He spent significant time doing geological studies and was one of the first discoverers of the ice age. *Faust*, of course, has references to geology buried in it.

20. The word *Entscheidung*, translated as "decision," contains the root *Scheidung*, which translates as "cision" or "crisis" (or, humorously enough for any who have lived through one, it also means "divorce"). One notices that Schelling employs this affinity in the following sentence, as well as in the earlier discussion of the "mythological crisis" taking place in the poets.

Lecture Two

1. "Proper and authentic" is the translation of *eigentlich*, which also means "true," "real," "actual." Schelling's language in this set of passages is very oblique, but, with respect to his adjective choice, what is at stake is that the poetic view and explanation, in not touching the universality of mythology, do not really tell us about the determinations that mythology takes on—knowledge of which determinations is necessary if one is to understand mythology in its specificities. In turn, if one thinks back to Schelling's thought experiment in lecture 1 (where he considers what questions a novice to mythology would pose: How do I take it? What does it mean? How has it emerged?), what this fact means for Schelling's analysis is that the poetic view does not tell us much about the origin, emergence, and coming-to-be of mythology.

2. The German here is *Eigentlichkeit*. Readers of Heidegger will recognize the difficulty of translating this word. The translation choice here is "that which is proper and authentic" (in part because of the reasons listed in translators' note 1 of this lecture, and also because *eigen* refers to "property" or "that which belongs" to a thing)—but "authenticity" here has nothing to do with the Heideggerian term. Throughout the beginning of lecture 2 and for most of lecture 1 Schelling has been toying with the notion of what a proper, real, actual, authentic meaning of mythology in the most expansive sense would be.

3. These rather obscure references are to (a) the Cambridge Platonist Ralph Cudworth (1617–1688), whose antiatheism text *The True Intellectual System of the Universe* (1678) was probably the most important text by the Cambridge Platonists; (b) the Swiss theologian Johannes Clericus (aka Jean Le Clerc, 1657–1736), who in 1703 also published some extracts of the *True System* and brought it to the attention of the Continent (the translators have been unable to specify precisely to which of Clericus's texts Schelling refers); and (c) J. L. von Mosheim, who in 1733 published a translation of the *True System* under the title *Systema intellectuale hujus Universi*, as well as notes intended as an introduction.

4. See translators' note 15 to lecture 1.

5. Schelling's allusion here is to *El mágic prodigioso* [*The Wonderful Magician*], the most well-known philosophical drama by Pedro Calderón de la Barca (1600–1681), the last and perhaps greatest dramatist of the golden age of Spanish baroque theater. Schelling was perhaps introduced to Calderón's work by Schlegel or the other German critics who had been looking back to the past for paths out of the neoclassicism of French drama. Calderón's influence on German Romanticism was surprisingly pronounced.

6. The reference here is to a philologist of ancient languages, Christian Gottlob Heyne (1729–1812), who was Professor for Poetry and Rhetoric at the University of Göttingen. A relatively important figure in the German Enlightenment, he was instrumental in spurring the development of Egyptology

and Etruscanology, in part through his work in writing for and publishing the journal *Göttingen Gelehrte Anzeigen*.

7. Schelling is playing here off of the double meaning of the German word *handelnde*, which means "acting" in the senses of both drama and general human activity, particularly trading or socioeconomic activity. Schelling intends here to reinforce the notion of personification that is at work as a principle of this manner of interpretation.

8. In addition to philology, Gottfried Hermann (1772–1848) was an expert scholar of the ancient world at the University of Leipzig. Achieving a degree of contemporary fame through *On the Essence and Treatment of Mythology* and the *Letters on Homer and Hesiod*, he advanced the position that the modern world's only real access to the intellectual life of the ancient world was through language study. Based on this he founded a sort of grammatico-critical school or research program that was in opposition to K. Ottfried Müller's and Burckhardt's historico-antiquarian school.

9. This is, of course, Phoebus Apollo, the god of the sun and grandchild of Phoebe the Titan; he is also referred to as "the radiant one."

10. This allusion to Thamyras is well known from the *Iliad* (Book II, lines 595–600), where the fabled minstrel of Thrace claimed to be able to outplay the Muses themselves in a harp-playing contest. For his hubris he lost both his eyesight and his ability.

11. Linus was the music teacher of Heracles and Orpheus. Heracles murdered Linus with Heracles's lyre when Linus reprimanded him for making an error while playing. Orpheus was the son of Calliope (a Muse) and the world's greatest musician. He was so good that his music could animate inanimate objects. The story of Orpheus and Eurydice is, of course, one of the most famous in all of Greek mythology. As for Olen(us), legend holds it that he lived with his wife on Mt. Ida. Because his wife boasted that she was more beautiful than any goddess he and his wife were turned into stone.

12. In this passage Schelling draws his genealogy from lines 147–63 of the *Theogony*. Born of Prime Matter (Gaia, and later Earth) and Heaven (Uranus, himself the offspring of Gaia), Kottus, Briareus and Gyes (otherwise known as the Hecatoncheires) are described as having one hundred arms and fifty heads each. Their stubborn personalities and presumptuousness made them "not to be neared," and they are referred to as being "horrible" and "hated" by their father from the very beginning. Thus Heaven locked them away in a secret part of Gaia, and refused them access to the light. Although resentful Gaia was pained by this act, Hesiod notes rather pithily that "Heaven took joy in his evil act" [159]. Perhaps this helps explain why Gaia conspires with another son, Kronos ("the devious, the youngest and most horrible of Earth's children, the Kronos who hated his lustful sire" [137–38]), to cut off Uranus's genitals with a sickle. Uranus's severed genitals produced Aphrodite [at line 196], and his blood [at lines 187–92] produces the Erinyes, the Giants and the Nymphs of Meliae. Prior to this wounding, however, "lusty" Uranus still had time to father the Cyclopes.

13. This is a reference to Pierre Simon de Laplace (1749–1827), a French mathematician and philosopher whose strict determinism and mechanism, derived from mathematical and cosmological study, are evidenced in his *Exposition du Systèm du Monde* [1796], an introductory text to his more mathematically oriented works on Newtonian mechanics, probability theory, and the stability of orbits in the solar system (thereby making unnecessary a divine intervention into the universe). In the *Exposition* he posited the hypothesis of a huge gas nebula as the origin of the universe.

14. This, of course, is a reference to the myth of Hades and Persephone.

15. Semele was the daughter of Cadmus and Harmonia and the mother of Dionysus (whose father was Zeus). The story runs basically as follows. Zeus and Semele had fallen in love, and Semele had become pregnant; the oft (and oft justifiably) enraged Hera discovers the pregnancy and through an elaborate set of ruses forces Zeus to reveal himself to Semele as he does to Hera, as thunder and lightning. Semele is instantly killed, but Zeus manages to rescue Dionysus; he sews the child into his thigh until he is born (hence Dionysus is called "the twice born"), and when Dionysus is mature he goes to Hades and rescues Semele.

16. See *Theogony* 116–38 for the first set of mythological figures following from chaos. The beginning [116–20] of this section is: "Right at the first came chaos to exist, and next broad-bosomed Gaia, the certain foundation of every immortal in the snowy Olympian peaks, and dark Tartarus deep in the Earth full of broad paths, and Eros, the most beautiful of the immortal gods." Presciently, and consistent with both contemporary scholarship and the *Theogony* itself, Schelling leaves ambiguous whether or not Gaia and Eros were considered *born* of chaos or simply as *appearing* after chaos. This ambiguity is present with Tartarus (Underworld) as well. However, as we see in the next paragraph, Schelling recognizes that it is absolutely clear that Erebus (Darkness) and Nyx (Movement downward) were considered children of chaos [122–123].

17. Here Schelling means the void, the empty space, referred to above as chaos.

18. This, of course, is an account of the birth of "day." See *Theogony* 122–24 for the genealogy running from: chaos→Erebus and Nyx→Aether and Hemere.

19. Here Schelling means Gaia, *prima materia* or the "primordial substance of all becoming." It is important to remember here the ambiguity as to the question of whether or not Gaia (as the "second element") was *born* of chaos or simply *appeared* after chaos.

20. Not only is it the case that Gaia gives birth to Uranus asexually, but Hesiod at 124–25 makes explicit that Uranus was "equal" to Gaia.

21. See *Theogony* 128–29, where Hesiod describes how after giving birth to Uranus (as Heaven, a place for the gods) Gaia gave birth to the "great mountains" (where the goddess-Nymphs "find abode in the dells") and then to the "violent swelling" of the "fruitless abyss," also asexually.

22. See *Theogony* 129–30. Also, as a translation note, in everyday German there is no difference between the words *Ozean* and *Weltmeer*: they both mean "ocean." Schelling makes a distinction because he is calling attention to the etymological connection of *Ozean* to *Oceanos* and *ochus*.

23. See *Theogony* 133–38 for the listing of the birth of the Titans. Their further offspring are: from Oceanus and Tethys were born the River gods and the Oceanids (including Electra and Styx); from Iapetus follow Atlas, Prometheus, Epimetheus, and Menoetius; from Mnemosyne (and also from Zeus) come the Muses; from Krius come Perses, Astraeus, and Pallas; from Themis come the Moerae; from Coeus and Phoebe come Leto and Asteria; from Hyperion and Theia follow Selene, Helius, and Eos; and, of course, from Rhea and Kronos come the Olympians.

24. Schelling employs the interesting word *hyperphysisch*, which is translated as "extra-physical" but which could just as well be "super-natural."

25. Azara (1746–1821) was a Spanish army officer sent to South America from 1781 through 1801 as member of a group doing cartographic work to solve a border dispute between Spanish Paraguay and Portuguese Brazil.

26. The word here is *Götterdiener*, which is translated as "polytheists," although a more literal translation would be "servers of many gods." This is worthy of attention because it is one of the many words Schelling uses to convey the idea of polytheism.

27. This passage is from *Theogony* [line 124], where she (Gaia) "bore in love by union with Erebus."

28. Although Schelling is unclear here, it is highly likely that he is also referring at least to Nyx's asexual offspring, a group that includes Philotes, Thanatos, Hypnos, and Nemesis.

29. With respect to this "it," the German original is—ironically (given the content of this paragraph) and despite the power of the German language's sexed and neuter articles and pronouns—as ambiguous as the English. Probably this "it" refers to the "sign of repudiation," but it could refer to "interpolation."

30. The first thing one should note is the untranslatable pronoun usage Schelling employs. When Schelling quotes the first line of the *Theogony*, "chaos" is mentioned without a pronoun; the sentence's second mentioning of "chaos" uses the neuter pronoun (as correct German does); the third instance, which Schelling is concerned to show as incorrect, refers to a male-gendered "chaos," *der Chaos*. There is no adequate way to relate this in English. At any rate, the point in this instance is precisely that such a gendering of "chaos" is unlikely by virtue of the deduction Schelling provides of the concept. As a second translation note, the fact that Schelling indicates that "chaos" was not a personality should now make clear why, unlike the other entities listed, the term has been left consistently uncapitalized (except in the very first allusion to Hermann's personification). Strangely enough, in this instance the translators have an advantage over Schelling, who, consistent

with standard German, has the confusion inducing obligation to capitalize all nouns (including *chaos*). This revelation by Schelling of nonpersonification in some instances of the *Theogony* is also the reason why the translators have opted to switch from a capitalized "Aether" (when spoken of in Hermann's potentially personified sense) to the uncapitalized "aether" (after Schelling's analysis).

Lecture Three

1. Schelling employs the word *beurteilen*, which carries the sense of "judgment" in several ways: the tension here is whether Schelling means it in the sense of a judge passing judgment or more in the sense of the objective process of evaluation (weighing and adducing evidence without regard to proclaiming a conclusion).

2. The word Schelling uses is *Wesenheiten*. Its meanings are myriad: "spirits," "essences," "substantialities," "substances," "decisive factors." Essentialit(y)(ies), a sort of neologism, has been selected because "essences" comes closest in tone but is misleading semantically, while "substances" would remind one too much of the general metaphysical category (which Schelling expressly claims he is attempting to avoid).

3. Here Schelling is referring to the special ability of the modal verb *können* to take on an elliptical grammatical characteristic in some instances. Normally this modal verb is paired with a second verb, which describes the action taking place in the sentence. In some instances, however, '*können*' does not require the second verb, as the meaning of the sentence is implicitly contained in '*können*,' which moreover takes the accusative case instead of the nominative. As a side note, of all the interesting biographical information about Schelling, one of the most precocious facts is that already as a teenager Schelling tutored Arabic and Hebrew (learned from his father) for pocket change.

4. Schelling employs the word *wirken* here. '*Wirken*' is a very versatile verb in both its transitive and intransitive forms. Transitively it means "to cause," "to bring about," "to work" (as in miracles), and "to produce." Intransitively, as is the case in this passage, it means "to be active," "to be effective," and "to operate." Its cognates *Wirkung* (effect), *Wirklichkeit* (actuality, reality), and *wirklich* (actual, real) are significant philosophical terms in general and in German Idealism in particular.

5. The word translated as what "emerges into being concomitantly" is *das Mitentstehende*. The sense is of a cöemergence or a cögenesis defined by necessarily implicated mutuality.

6. This discussion of the dream state [*Traumzustand*], and to an extent also of clairvoyance [*Hellsehen*, literally "to see clearly," or "to see the light"], reprises a topic that Schelling deals with in various forms throughout his

corpus. One of the most prominent iterations of these homologous discussions is found in the third draft of *Die Weltalter* [*The Ages of the World*] under the rubric of "magnetic sleep," to which we now refer as hypnosis. Bearing in mind that Schelling explicitly states that he is attempting to account for the "mythological crisis" that generates poets, philosophers, representations of the gods, the people(s) in which all of the above have their abode, and indeed the entire discursive domain relevant to mythology, it is also the case that Schelling is trying in his explanation to avoid the—above all Hegelian—mistake of presupposing the effects he is looking for as the causal or positing agent. One cannot argue that poetry and/or philosophy is the *intentionally* and *discursively* proximate cause of the crisis that produces mythology if poetry and philosophy have their conditions of possibility in what can only be a result of mythology. To do so is to fall victim to the epistemological variant of the problem of the serpent with its tail in its mouth. Schelling mentions the temptation of invoking such dream states or clairvoyance in part because they highlight the problem of circularity by appealing to a middle ground between intentionality/discursivity and mindless mechanism (both of which Schelling rejects), and in part because they highlight on the one hand the end of the "idealist" (and, frankly, rationalist) explanation and on the other hand the resultant necessity of proceeding to a historical and materialist account of the emergence of mythology. As a general historical note, this shift in grounding—whose Schellingian origins as a critique of idealism date back at least to the *Freiheitschrift* and is fully in play in the middle-period works such as the *Weltalter* and *The Deities of Samothrace*—was well known during Schelling's Berlin years and attracted to his lectures Kierkegaard, Friedrich Engels, Michael Bakunin, and Arnold Ruge (who attended at Marx's prodding). One hopes it is clear by Schelling's weighing and adducing of arguments and evidence that he is not advocating a mystical *Schwärmerei* in the place of reason. And as is particularly noticeable in the sarcastic word-play he uses to describe the temptation of clairvoyance, Schelling is even polemicizing against such a mystical flight. For a discussion of magnetic sleep and its relation to this issue of discursivity, see *Die Weltalter*. Jason Wirth's marvelous translation of the *Weltalter* has a particularly excellent note on magnetic sleep and its conceptual relation to both Indian mythology in particular and Schelling's *Philosophie der Mythologie* in general [Wirth 2000, 142–43]. Wirth's introduction to the text contains an excellent discussion of the larger issue of Schelling's movement toward the notion of a historical critique of idealism [Wirth 2000, viii–xxx].

7. "Historical" is the translation of *geschichtlich*, which along with its cognate *Geschichte* (which means "story," "tale," and, above all, "history"—in both the sense of past events and, more recently with respect to scholarship, of their narration, particularly disciplinary academic narration) stems from the quotidian verb *geschehen* (to happen, to occur), which itself is

derived from the old High German *giskiht* (ca. 1000 CE). At any rate, when Schelling determines a domain as *geschichtlich*, this refers to the primacy of the concrete, real, and material happenings, occurrences, and events of the domain under examination—as opposed to an investigation that inquires after phenomena according to a preordained, ideal structure wherein there always lies the danger of discovering only what was posited in the object by the form of questioning itself. At the same time, however, when referencing a phenomenon as *geschichtlich* Schelling is well aware that the word also implies that the *subjective* discursive act of narrating the events of history is inseparable from their apprehension as *objective*.

8. Within the scope of dealing with the continuity between lectures 2 and 3, it is noteworthy that here Schelling denotes Oceanus as the World-sea, which he expressly rejects doing in lecture 2.

9. To complete the synopsis, the Argive princess Io was the daughter of the river god. After Zeus turns her into a cow the ever-suspicious Hera demands the cow as a gift, which she receives and turns over to the watchman, Argus. Eventually Hermes arrives and saves her, but Hera dispatches a no doubt incredibly aggravating cow fly to torture Io. Wandering to escape the cow fly, she runs upon bound Prometheus and relates her tale of woe. Prometheus prophecies that she will reach the Nile River, where Zeus will restore her and she will become pregnant with his child, Epaphus. This comes to pass, making Io the (admittedly removed) ancestor of Heracles, who frees Prometheus. As an interesting side note, Ionia (the western part of Asia Minor) was named after Io because the legend holds that she flees toward the Nile (and away from Hera's cruel cow fly) in this direction (the Bosporus strait dominating this area between the Mediterranean and Black Seas means "the ford of the cow"). In the process of saving Io Hermes kills Argus, whose many eyes become the eyes in the peacock feathers (a bird associated with Hera). This story shows up, among other places, in *Prometheus Bound*, by Aeschylus.

10. The word translated as "affinity" is *Verwandtschaft*, which, as constructed around the root *verwandt* (belonging to the same family, ancestry, origin, extraction, or linguistic etymology) denotes familial relation in the largest sense of "family" and connotes a homological (instead of merely analogical) relation. Schelling makes this absolutely explicit at the end of the paragraph, where he refers to the type of relation of the various mythologies as a *Blutverwandtschaft* (a blood relation, consanguinity).

11. Briefly put, Isis (the daughter of Seb and Nut) was the wife of Osiris. She went off searching for Osiris's body, after he had been slain by her brother Seth. Isis impregnates herself with Osiris's body and gave birth to Horos in the Nile delta. Demeter was the goddess of the earth (and thus in part of fertility) and the mother of Persephone, who was abducted by Hades. In the myth Demeter wandered the earth searching for Persephone.

Lecture Four

1. Voss (1751–1826) was a classicist and philologist who lectured at the University of Heidelberg, among others. He translated many of the ancient classical texts from Homer, Hesiod, Ovid, Horace, Virgil, and others. Late in his life he was known chiefly for opposing the mythological research of Friedrich Creuzer, as well as of the Heidelberg romanticists.

2. The word here is the now obsolete *ahnden*, which carries the sense of having a premonition of something shrouded, hidden from discursive apprehension.

3. As a British import, Robert Wood's (1717–1775) 1769 *Essay on the Original Genius and Writings of Homer* had a special place of influence in the formation of the Storm and Stress movement that appeared after Weimar Classicism and then gave way to German Romanticism. Similar is the case of the strange and mysterious Celto-Gaelic-Scottish legend cycle *The Works of Ossian, the Son of Fingal* (1765), published by James Macpherson. Although no one actually knows the origin of the verse tales (as there was no manuscript found—and there is significant evidence that they are forgeries), a 1773 revised and published version (*The Poems of Ossian*) of the legend cycle influenced Goethe (who translated part of it into German) and German Romanticism as a whole. Napoleon carried it into battle with him; the book made it as far as Moscow.

4. Oreads (mountain and grotto nymphs), Dryads (forest nymphs), and Oceanids (water nymphs) were minor female deitylike beings who were attached as retinue to a deity.

5. One can think of *Potenz* as marking the "actual potential," to borrow a distinction found in, among other places but different contexts, Aristotle's works and Hegel's *Logik*. That is to say, *Potenz* in part describes what at every instance, in its potential-to-be or capacity-to-be (in its role as *das Seynkönnende*), actually *is* or *has being* or *participates in being*, even if it is not fully articulated. Seen in this way, *Potenz* would thus also be in a relation with the "potential actual," a generative ground or articulated principle whose status as the explicated *Potenz* does not consign that explicated *Potenz* to an actuality without dynamic possibility (that is, to a life of rigidity, an "actual," determined life devoid of *potentia*). The differential relations of *Potenzen* [potencies], as a framework for articulating the life-world's determinate relationships to both itself and the divine, are central to Schelling's understanding of the unfolding of time and thus of history. One might say that the temporal unfolding of *Potenzen is* the movement of history. *Potenz* is also "power" in the mathematical sense, as in to "raise to a power." Schelling toys with this notion in the following sentence.

6. With respect to the issue [n. 5 above] of the *Potenzen* (qua historical circulation of the "actual potential" and "potential actual"), and with respect to the issue of the mythological consciousness as the initiation of conscious-

ness *freely* related to the gods, and keeping in mind the previous lectures' movement away from the poetic and scientific drives and toward the religious drive as the effectual (*wirkende*) cause(s) of mythology qua *historical phenomenon*, *actus* takes on special significance here. Jason Wirth's remarks on Schelling's constellation of some of these concepts in the *Weltalter* are noteworthy: "*Actus*, what Schelling translates as *Wirkung*, is the past participle of the Latin *agere* (to drive, to do). *Actus*, in this sense, suggests something done or something driven in a particular way. When freedom does not come to act (*actus*), it does not come to pass, it does not happen, it does not actualize itself. It remains a force or δύναμις (*potentia*, *Potentialität*) or possibility (*Möglichkeit*) irreducible to actuality. It is always still to happen, *ein unendlicher Mangel an Seyn*" [Wirth 2000, 141, n. 57]. This last phrase translates as "an infinite lack of Being," which lack qua historical motor force temporally manifests itself in the continually circulating becoming of the *actus* out of the *Potenzen*. The fundamental "search for the object," the initial polytheistic "grasping and reaching for the vaguely demanded God" (mentioned in Schelling's immediately subsequent statements), and the fundamental development of the *Notitia Dei insita* (mentioned here) into its manifest, determinate forms are moments of this economy of lack and actuality, qua development of mythology, peoples, religion, and so on. This all comes into play as background for Schelling's statement at the beginning of the following paragraph, where "God is only the dark, vague goal that is *strived* for," "which is *sought* in nature" (and thus is lacking, in some sense) and which God qua dark, religious moment is the goal of peoples (themselves historical phenomena) [italics in this sentence were added by the translators.].

7. Constantin François de Chasseboeuf comte de Volney (1757–1820) traveled in Egypt and Syria in the 1780s. His travelogues, later useful to Napoleon during his Egyptian campaign, led to his 1791 philosophical work *Les Ruines, meditations sur les revolutions des empires*, which garnered him some fame. Charles François Dupuis (1742–1809) was a French scientist, man of letters, and member of the Academy of Inscriptions. His *Sur tous les Cultes* proposed an interpretation of myths as early astronomical theory.

8. The word *Vielgötterei* will become increasingly important in this text, particularly as it takes on a meaning differentiated from *Göttervielheit*. Both literally denote polytheism, in the sense of the existence of multiple gods. Later in the lectures, however, *Vielgötterei* will come to denote what Schelling refers to as "successive polytheism" (referring to the historical succession of multiple "One" "highest" or "true" God[s]), while *Göttervielheit* will come to denote a *mere* multiplicity of gods without there being any claim to a status of exclusivity. Since the lectures have not yet reached this point, and since Schelling is still merely foreshadowing this development, *Vielgötterei* is presently translated simply as "polytheism." Naturally, it is also to be kept in mind that Schelling has heretofore employed the more general word

Polytheismus to denote polytheism. One might thus reasonably argue that *Vielgötterei* and *Göttervielheit* are more specific determinations or typologies of a general *Polytheismus*. For the moment, when Schelling deploys these terms in an ambiguous way the German will be given in brackets.

9. The word Schelling uses here is *angebetete*, which through its root carries the connotation of being prayed to.

10. The highly influential and extremely modern Gotthold Lessing (1729–1781) was a playwright and dramatist (*Nathan der Weise*), aesthetician (the treatise *Lacöon, or On the Limits of Painting and Poetry*), philosopher (*On the Education of Man*, which argued for ethical freedom and human perfectibility), and an anticipator of the Storm and Stress movement and German Romanticism.

11. Among other passages, Schelling is referring here to an introductory statement from lecture 1: "To the extent that it is then seen that there are many of these religiously venerated beings, mythology is polytheism, and we will name this moment that initially offers itself for contemplation the *polytheistic* moment. By virtue of this, mythology is in general the *system of the gods* . . . The full concept of mythology is for this reason not to be a mere system of the gods, but rather the *history of the gods*." The involvement of mythology in teachings and/or doctrines is a further, historical determination of the "generality" of mythology, but because Schelling here explicitly seems to be alluding back to a comparatively indeterminate form of mythology, the translators have chosen to select "system of the gods."

12. The Mosaic writings are, of course, the Pentateuch ("the five-volumed book"), the first five books of the Bible (Genesis, Exodus, Leviticus, Numbers and Deuteronomy). Historically, Christians as well as Jews have accepted that Moses is the author, or at least the compiler, of the Pentateuch. Even over and above temporal and geographical considerations, for reasons that should be incredibly obvious (the account of the genesis of heaven and earth, the lineages of individuals and tribes and peoples or nations, supernatural events, the giving of laws, etc.) the scholarship linking the Pentateuch to mythology is myriad. With respect to the question of authorship, within the translations of the Bible itself at Acts 15:1 there is a statement that circumcision was "the practice taught by Moses," an illusion to Gen. 17, whereby it is generally inferred that intratextually the Bible takes the position that Moses was the author of the Pentateuch. Some more modern scholarship over the last few centuries has argued inconclusively that four essentially independent sources are coalesced into the Pentateuch, which if true would disprove Mosaic authorship. If Moses was the author or compiler, then—given the archeologico-historical data on migratory movements from Egypt to Israel—the Pentateuch would date from roughly 1450–1400 BCE. The documents supposed to prove the multiple authorship argument are listed as J, E, D, P. Interestingly for the scope of Schelling's argument, the J and E documents

are so designated according to the name employed to designate God (J for Jahweh/Yahweh, the tetragrammaton, the voweless and more personal Old Testament name for God; and E for Elohim, the generic name for God).

13. Japeth, Shem, and Ham (in descending order of birth) were three sons of Noah. The basic version of the story from Gen. 9:18–11:9 runs as follows: Noah, as "a man of the soil," planted a vineyard and, enjoying the fruits of his labor, became drunk in his tent one day. In addition to proving that such behavior is not confined to college students, he was also naked. Ham, upon seeing Noah's condition, informed his brothers, who in turn placed garments over Noah, although being careful to do so without "seeing their father's nakedness." When Noah awakened from his drunken slumber and discovered that his youngest son had contributed to Noah's dishonor in the eyes of his other sons, Noah cursed Ham and his descendents to be slaves to the other brothers and their descendents. Interestingly for Schelling's project, particularly with respect to the understanding of what a *Volk* is, Gen. 9: 18–19 names the three sons of Noah, each of whom survived the Flood in the Ark, as spreading out across the lands and as being they "from whom came the people who were dispersed over the earth." With reference to the "heathens" Schelling mentions, presumably he is alluding to the fact that Ham's descendents, the Hamites, are supposed to have become the nations or peoples of southwestern Asia (Canaan or modern day Palestine, Mizraim or modern lower Nile Egypt, Cush or modern southern Nile Egypt, and Put or modern northern Lybia), the peoples or nations often referred to in the Bible as "heathens" (to the extent that they were not members of the divinely blessed Israelite nation). Whatever else is the case with respect to the comparison of Kronos and Ham, there are at least two similarities: both Kronos and Ham are the youngest born, and both stories refer to the youngest son's encounter with the genitalia of the father.

14. Throughout the text Schelling hones in on the question of what a "people" is. "People" has been the consistent translation of *Volk*, but *Volk* is also often translated as "nation." Generally speaking, *Volk* will be translated as "people," with one major exception being in the (primarily subsequent) places where Schelling directly is working with biblical passages whose traditional English language translations employ "nations" (as in "host of nations") instead of "peoples." At this particular passage in lecture 4 Schelling employs intentionally the word *Nationen*, instead of *Volk*, presumably to emphasize the biblical notion of the various nations.

15. Gerhard Voss (1577–1649) was one of the first to handle theological dogmas historically. He also wrote on the relationship of this topic to the controversy surrounding the role of Pelasgians.

16. The French scholar Samuel Bochart (1599–1667) was the author of *Phaleg and Chanaan*. He was intensely learned and steeped in Oriental languages (Hebrew, Arabic, Syraic, Chaldaic), so much so that he was well

known for seeing the Phoenician in just about everything (including Celtic gods and myths). The French scholar, philosopher, Jesuit bishop, and Apologist Pierre Daniel Huet (1630–1721) worked and traveled some with Bochart; he wrote the *Demonstratio* in 1679 and *De la situation du paradis terrestre* in 1692. As a skeptic, Huet was a decisive opponent of Descartes (and thus of rationalism) and a proponent of the belief in revelation. The Phoenician Taaut is in some sense analogical to Kronos or Saturn, but with his four eyes (described in the *Sanchoniathon* as two front-facing, two rear-facing, à la the Roman Janus) seeing both past and present, he was associated with the Eternal Now. The Syrian Adonis (the Semitic analogue is Tammuz, and the Etruscan Atunis) carries a name that is a variation on Adonai (lord). He was a cult god of vegetation and the death-renewal cycle and was later imported into Greek mythology. A symbol of kingship, Osiris was the Egyptian god of the underworld and death and was known as civilizing the previously uncivilized Egyptians. Zoroaster (Zarathustra) was a Persian prophet (ca. 1000 BCE) and founder of Zoroastrianism, which fell into decline after Islamic conquests. The founder of Thebes, Cadmus was the father of Semele, a brother of Europa, and the son of the king of Phoenicia. Possibly a mythical representative of the Egyptian Pharaoh Akhenaton, Danaus was held as a brother of Aegyptus and son of Belus, a mythical Egyptian king. Danaus was linked to the foundation of Argos.

17. What Schelling is getting at here, of course, already in the first moves of Western and west Asian thought and religion takes on at least the aspect of the argument between monism and dualism.

18. The reference here is to Jean-Sylvain Bailly (1736–1793), a French astronomer, calculator of the orbit of Halley's comet, member of the French Academy of Sciences, friend of Laplace, and leader of the early part of the French Revolution. He met his end when he met Madame Guillotine.

19. A jurist by trade, Sir William Jones (1746–94) was an English philologist famed for his understanding of Oriental languages. Via both publications and the Society he exerted a large influence on Asian literature and language study in England and the Continent; he virtually created the disciplines of modern comparative philology and linguistics. Jones was among the first to indicate that Sanskrit was related to Latin and Greek through a common root: as he lauds, "the Sanscrit language, whatever be its antiquity, is of a wonderful structure; more perfect than the Greek, more copious than the Latin, and more exquisitely refined than either, yet bearing to both of them a stronger affinity, both in the roots of verbs and the forms of grammar, than could possibly have been produced by accident; so strong indeed, that no philologer could examine them all three, without believing them to have sprung from some common source, which, perhaps, no longer exists."

20. Georg Friedrich Creuzer (1771–1858) was professor at the University of Heidelberg from 1804 through 1845. He advanced the controversial

claim that the myths of Hesiod and Homer were a) traceable back to an Eastern source and b) mediated to the Greeks by the Pelasgians. More generally, he claimed c) that these myths were the remaining symbols of a primordial revelation.

21. See the translator's note 8 of this lecture for information on the translations of *Polytheismus*, *Vielgötterei*, and *Göttervielheit*.

LECTURE FIVE

1. *Vandiemensland* is an obsolete name for modern day Tasmania.

2. The word *Geschlecht* presents translation headaches. Its translations include "species," "race," "lineage," and "genus." To avoid confusion when Schelling elaborates his breathtakingly prejudiced view on "races" [*Racen*], generally the translators have opted to translate *Geschlecht* as "species," but there are many instances where "species" is employed in conjunction with the adjective "human," and in these instances one could just as well say "human race." The problem becomes more acute in subsequent passages, when Schelling's references to biblical *Geschlechter* demands the translation option "lineage." When there is potential confusion the German is given in brackets.

3. The reference here is to the German traveler Carsten Niebuhr (1733–1815), who was the sole survivor of an ill-fated scientific expedition through the middle east. He appears to have survived by adopting indigenous practices that saved his health.

4. Schelling's word here is *Affection*, which one is tempted to translate as "modification." Readers of Spinoza, and particularly his *Ethics*, will recognize *Affection* as one of Spinoza's central concepts. In Definition 5 of Part 1 of the *Ethics* Spinoza defines the "modes" of Substance as "the modifications [*Affectiones*] of Substance, or that which exists in, and is conceived through, something other than itself" [Elwes's translation]. Since for Spinoza there is only one Substance (God or Nature, *Deus sive Natura*, the unconditioned *causa sui* exhibiting infinite attributes modified by affections, a Substance "by nature prior to its modifications" but only distinguishable and thus only knowable through them), one can see the parallels between this Spinozistic monism (of the implicitness and explication of the *hen kai pan*) and the Schellingian understanding of the substantial unity of consciousness made graspable by the multiple modifications of language, by the splitting of peoples, by the emergence of varying mythologies, etc. This is certainly the case with respect to the paragraphs immediately preceding and following this one. Indeed, Schelling himself certainly had much to say about Spinoza. To this end, one of the best places to start is Schelling's essay "Leibniz, Spinoza and Wolff," found in English translation in Andrew Bowie's translation of Schelling's *On the History of Modern Philosophy*. Quite apropos the content of Schelling's investigation

into the unprethinkable ground of human consciousness and its modes, in the third draft of the *Weltalter* Schelling asserts that "[p]erhaps, of all the modern philosophers, there was in Spinoza a dark feeling of that primordial time of which we have attempted to conceptualize so precisely" [Wirth 2000, 104].

5. Many translations of the passage refer to "nations" instead of "peoples." Because there is no loss in meaning, the translators here and in most of the immediately following biblical references have chosen to employ "peoples" for the sake of continuity. The prophet is, of course, Jeremiah, and the passage Schelling takes from Jer. 51 is in the following context of divine judgment (the prophetic theme of Jeremiah), beginning at verse 6: "Flee from Babylon! Run for your lives! Do not be destroyed because of her sins. It is time for the Lord's vengeance; he will pay her what she deserves. Babylon was a gold cup in the Lord's hand; she made the whole earth drunk. The nations drank her wine; therefore they have now gone mad" [this citation from the NIV]. Earlier in the Old Testament, at Jer. 25, 15 the prophet Jeremiah claims that God told him to grasp God's cup filled with the wine of vengeance and wrath and make all the earth's nations drink from it and become mad. The context indicates that God was passing a divine judgment on some nations—curiously and famously enough, considering they were chosen people, God's wrath extended also to the nations of Judah (who had angered God not least of all due to their associations with the Babylonians). Jeremiah, whose name translates roughly as "hurled down from God," was tasked with orating this message of divine displeasure and coming woe to a Jewish people already splintered, relatively weak, currying disfavor with God, and subject to the political machinations of neighboring power states in Egypt, Assyria, and Babylon. As ironic proof thereof, the book following Jeremiah in the Bible is the poetic book known as Lamentations (traditionally considered authored by Jeremiah), which as one can easily surmise is wholly a series of laments by the communities of the believers. The laments primarily concern the God-ordained (and Babylonian executed) fall and destruction of Jerusalem in general and Solomon's temple in particular in 586 BCE. Coming on the heels of the Nebuchadnezzar-era Babylon's crushing of Egypt at Carchemish in 605 BCE, which augered a revolutionary shift in the regional power structure of ME nations (thus forcing the Jews to side with Babylon in the regional political structure, a shift in policy symbolic of the Jews having fallen away from the covenant), the result of the sacking of Jerusalem was a forced temporary exile (to Babylon, cf. the books of Daniel and Ezekiel) and diaspora of the nations of Judah, which only began to ebb with the fall of Nebuchadnezzar's Babylon to Cyrus's Persians and the rebuilding of the temple. Since Schelling is in part claiming that human peoples have a long memory for these types of events of dispersal and destruction, and that this long memory is a continually renewed traumatic relation of past and present, it is worth noting that Lamentations, the poetic reflection

on such events, is still read every week at the Wailing Wall in Jerusalem, and that Catholic doctrine requires the reading of Lamentations during the High Holy Week.

6. Pentecost is the fiftieth day after the Sabbath falling during the week of Passover. The highly significant Pentecost mentioned by Schelling is at Acts 2: "When the day of Pentecost came, they were all together in one place. Suddenly a sound like the blowing of a violent wind came from Heaven . . . They saw what seemed to be tongues of fire that separated and came to rest on each of them. All of them were filled with the Holy Spirit and began to speak in other tongues, as the Spirit enabled them" [translation from NIV]. In addition to a hysterically comedic portion wherein a crowd speculates on the drunkenness of the tongue speakers (and an even funnier response from Peter: "These men are not drunk . . . It is only nine in the morning!"), the rest of this section of Acts 2 goes on to a) list the wide array of home nations of the tongue-speaking visitors in Jerusalem, b) describe the bewilderment of the many Jews in Jerusalem, who were astonished that they each heard the tongue-speaking God praisers in their own language, and c) transcribe Peter's address to the crowd. For Schelling's point, there are several things going on in this passage. One aspect is that through the language of tongues the manifested God (qua Holy Spirit) temporarily reunites people from the lands of the empires of Parthia (stretching from the Tigris to India), Egypt, Arabia, Rome, Asia Minor, and Crete. Second, occasioned by this, Peter's address speaks to the prophetic notion of God refolding the peoples of the earth into his unity. As a side note with respect to the interrelationship of languages, it is interesting that the Holy Spirit (*der Heilige Geist, spiritus sanctus, hágion pneuma*) is described as a "wind." Spirit or *Geist* has a long etymological tradition incorporating the Latin words *spiritus* and *anima*, which functionally translate as "breath of God." In this context this significance should be clear. Moreover, the etymological relation and history extends to the Greek *psyche* and *pneuma* (a blowing, as in "pneumatic" or "pneumonia"), which, farther back still, relate to the Sanskrit *atman*, which is related to all these terms at least in the sense of implying a blowing or a wind (*atman* is the progenitor, for example, of the German word for "to breathe," *atmen*).

7. The word here is *ausscheiden*, which—in a physical, particularly chemical, context—means to "excrete," "exude," "precipitate (out)." "Extrude" in this instance and "precipitate" in the next paragraph have been retained precisely because a) there is probably not a better choice in English, and b) Schelling's thinking in the philosophy of nature, particularly with respect to the importance of analyzing fundamental occurrences, plays a background role in his discussion here.

8. A port city on the Saronic gulf, Megara is one of the oldest cities in Greece. Nauplia, a port city in southern Greece, is named in Strabo in reference to catacombs called the Labyrinth of the Cyclops.

Lecture Six

1. The distinction is between, respectively, *Göttervielheit* and *Vielgötterei*, seen within the larger scope of *Polytheismus*. Both literally denote many gods, a multiplicity of gods. As much as possible *Göttervielheit* will be translated as "multiplicity of gods" or "simultaneous polytheism," and when *Vielgötterei* is used it will be translated as much as possible as "successive polytheism." See the translators' note 8 in lecture 4 for a summary of these terms' relations and their relation to the more general *Polytheismus*. One thing to bear in mind with the relation of *Vielgötterei* qua successive polytheism to *Polytheismus* is that Schelling, confusingly, also sometimes employs *successiver Polytheismus* to denote successive polytheism. When there is ambiguity the German is given in brackets. This lecture also features the maddening problem of deciding when to capitalize "*God*" and when to leave it in lowercase letters. All gods that are explicitly mythological and polytheistic are left lowercase. When it is explicitly monotheistic, nonmythological, and/or "absolute" or "unconditioned," then "it" retains uppercase. Part of this lecture is devoted to breaking down this dichotomy, so in those instances the translators frankly have relied on context and intuition in order to determine if the divinity in question is more involved in exclusivity (= God) or in mythological systems with multiple gods (= god).

2. The sentence here reads: *Dass es die wirkliche Geschichte ihrer Entstehung ist, welche die Mythologie in der Aufeinanderfolge ihrer Götter bewahrt hat, wird vollends unwidersprechlich, wenn man die Mythologien verschiedener Völker vergleicht.* Thus an alternate translation could be: "That it is the actual history of its emergence that has preserved mythology in the sequentiality of its gods becomes fully incontestable when one compares the mythologies of different peoples with each other."

3. A northwest Semitic god, the reference here is to Beelsamen, the Phoenician "lord of the heavens." Referred to by Sanchuniaton as Uranus, Syrian writing identifies Beelsamen as Zeus Olympios.

4. The word here translated as "unconditioned" is *unbedingt*, which could also be translated as "absolute" or "absolutely." *Das Unbedingte* in German Idealism is often translated as "the Absolute." Part of the reason for translating *unbedingt* and *das Unbedingte* as respectively "unconditioned" and "the unconditioned," instead of variants of "absolute," is that Schelling also employs the terms *absolute* and *das Absolute*. Broken down into its elements, *unbedingt* is literally the *un-be-ding-t*, or the "un/non"-"thing" (*Ding*=thing), the "non-thing." Philosophically, metaphysics spent a tremendous amount of time and energy dealing with what it would mean to apprehend the unconditioned insofar as it is that which is uncaused, and therefore not a thing, that is, that which otherwise went under the name of the "Absolute," the uncaused cause, the prime mover, and so on. Andrew Bowie makes this point in his excellent *Schelling and Modern European Philosophy*: For Schelling "[e]ach object is part of a chain of ob-jects (*Gegen-stände*), which 'stand against' each other. Objects, then, are not absolutely real

because they only become themselves by not being other objects ... German Idealism demands an account of what makes these interrelated moments intelligible as objects, which cannot therefore be an object. They therefore term it the 'Absolute' because it cannot be understood in relation to something else" [Bowie 1993, 20]. The "Absolute" is not some mystical hocus-pocus force fit for contemplation by intellectually lazy Star Wars fans; rather it is a provocation for discursive thought brought about by the philosophically unavoidable demand to know how it is that understanding is possible in the first place. With respect to Schelling's discussion here, the notion of the unconditioned God A plays a similar role as the Absolute of the succession of Gods B, C, etc.—that is, they are to an extent understandable only by virtue of his being the ungrounded ground of their comprehensibility.

5. With "ethno*gony*" Schelling is referring to a theory of the emergence of peoples, which theory Schelling argues is necessary for a study of the characteristics and features of peoples. The use of the *sperrschrift*, which the translators indicate with italics of emphasis, indicates that Schelling is at least loosely alluding to a parallel to theo*gony*.

6. The Japhethites are thought to have spread, in the ancient world, to Tiras (modern Italy), Gomer (the western and northwestern Black Sea area), Javan (the Peloponnesus and the Hellespont), Meschech and Tubal (central and southern Anatolia), and Madai (modern northeastern Iraq and northwestern Iran). C.f. translators' note 13 in lecture 4 for the synopsis of the story of Noah's sons and information on the dispersal of the Hamites.

7. "Substantiality," the translation here of *Substantialität*, is—particularly given the context's discussion of mobility, determinations, and accidents—presumably to be contrasted with "subjectivity," perhaps in the sense that both Schelling (particularly in the period beginning with the *Freiheitsschrift*) and Hegel (in the *Logik*) criticize Spinoza's monism of "Substance" (the *Deus sive Natura* of the *Ethics*) as lacking subjectivity qua freedom.

8. Jean-Pierre-Abel Rémusat (1788–1832) was chair of Chinese at the Collège de France and founder of the Paris Asiatic Society.

9. Although from the context it is most likely that Schelling here means the roots, there is some ambiguity, in that he could be referring to the language(s).

10. The word here is *Zeitwörter*, which literally means "temporal-words."

11. The word here is *actuelle*, which means "actual" or "real" but also "topical," "present," "pertinent" or "up to date" (and in the physical or chemical context, it means "kinetic").

Lecture Seven

1. Schelling notes in the third draft of the *Weltalter* that these two designations can more accurately be broken down into Elohim, the universal "God" (the "I am who I am" speaking to Moses at Exodus 3:14), and Elohim's

"expression" (the Romanized name for Elohim, the unpronounceable tetragrammaton) *YHWH*, which means LORD and has been linguistically corrupted into the pronounceable Jehovah. YHWH as a name is actually nothing more than the "name of the LORD," "the expressing" of the name of Elohim, and as verb translates as *"He* is" or *"He* will be," which is an obvious third-person counterpart to Elohim as the *"I* am." The two terms often occur together (as in, "I am the LORD God" of Genesis 2:4), and, as Schelling states, "Jehovah was in an equally originary way posited as Elohim in this relationship of the expressing, of the *name* or the word." Essentially, the God denoted by these terms is the same, in that although there is differentiation, this differentiation of the One God is not polytheistic in orientation. If one views the relationship of monotheism and polytheism as one between what is primordial and what is derivative, then one might view the nominal distinction perhaps as the beginning of the end of the beginning, as Schelling seems to indicate later with respect to what the lineage of Enosh means. For Schelling's elaboration on the relation of Elohim and Jehovah, see Jason Wirth's translation of *Die Weltalter* [Wirth 2000, pp. 51–53].

2. Seth was born to Adam and Eve in part to fill the spot left by Abel, who was killed by Cain. Seth's son was Enosh, which means "man," just as the name Adam. Enosh begat Kenan (and was thus the father of the Kenites), and Enosh's descendents are contrasted in the first genealogical sections of Genesis with the cursed lineage of Cain.

3. At this point in the text the translators have opted to switch to "race," instead of "species," as the translation for the term *Geschlecht*. For many of the biblical references Schelling makes, *Geschlecht* could be translated both as "race" and "lineage" (both taken in the biblical sense). This term is further complicated by the fact that in some instances in this lecture "race" is essentially equivalent to "species"—as in the "human race" = the "human species."

4. The German word Schelling here employs is *Riesen*, which means "giants." An alternate and more metaphorical translation, which actually stands out within the context of Schelling's subsequent reference to "men of renown," would be "giants of history" or "heroes." This alternate translation is also vouched by the Hebrew word *Nephilim* (which Schelling translates as *Riesen*), found at the relevant passage of Genesis 6:4. *Nephilim* literally denotes "people/beings of enormous size and strength," but also "the fallen ones" or "sinners," an especially important connection given Schelling's concern with dealing with the early biblical passages about the fall of man and Schelling's point about the transition occurring through the generations.

5. This is an extremely obscure passage, both in Schelling and in the Bible. First, the reference to "sons of God" and "daughters of men" has in various contexts and permutations been read as indicating either/or as well as both/and angels and human beings. At Job 1: 6; 2: 1 and Jude 6–7 and possibly Psalms 29:1 it indicates angels (and at the reference in Ps. is translated as "the mighty ones," thus indicating a further reference to the *Nephilim*).

Second, for a further indication of Schelling's subsequent claim that this passage is related to mythology, some scholars assert that these phrases are references to intermarriage and corelationships of divine beings (e.g., angels, in this context) and humans, which certainly was a prevalent belief in ancient mythologies. Third, with respect to Schelling's concern to deal in part with the early biblical genealogical lines, it may also be the case that "sons of God" means godly men and "daughters of men" means descendents of the "sinful" line of Cain. If this is the case, then this set of references would connect with Schelling's note six in this lecture: "'Hitherto, the human species had divided itself into two large parts: the better, which believed in one God, named itself, by the true God, sons of God; the rest, who were not sunk in *superstition—for we find no trace of that prior to the great flood—but rather in complete unbelief*, Moses names the sons of men'." That is, "sons of God" would be the descendents of the Sethite lineage (via Enosh and his son Kenan) and the "daughters of men" the Cainites, thus alluding to a breakdown of the sterility between the two tribes and an unraveling of the divinely commanded exclusion and cursing of Cain's lineage and blessing of Seth's (whose name means "man," like that of his father, Adam). With respect to Schelling's points in this context, this version would explain how Enosh and thus Seth were responsible for a second, profane humanity establishing itself in the world. Of course, at the same time, this would also dovetail with Schelling's comments that the religious interpretation being employed indicates that only this second mankind can usher in the actual, true, One and eternal God of monotheism, the one in contrast to the "wicked" polytheism that has to exist as its contradiction such that it be known in consciousness. Last, a different explanation might be that "sons of God" refers to the Near East royalty who were held essentially as gods and who, in their establishment of harems, were responsible for a "profanely" distorted life in the manner of Lamech, the son of Cain.

6. The phrase translated here as "the disposition or composition" is *das Gebilde oder Gedicht* (*Gebilde* = disposition, *Gedicht* = composition). The general sense of the phrase is "the motivation or disposition" of "the thoughts of . . ." In its relation to *figmentum*, as well as in its more common meaning "poetry/poesy," *Gedicht* carries the sense of imagination or productive source of thoughts and actions. *Gebilde* denotes "product," "creation," "form," and "shape." The connotation here is of the status of the heart and mind, but the meaning runs much deeper when one considers the relation of *Gebilde* (and its root *Bild*) to the notions of the formed image, the icon (and thus of iconography), and idols. Through its etymological relation to *das Bild* (a formed, usually artistic image) and also *das Gebildete* (a figure that has been formed or shaped), one arrives at the association of *das Gebilde* with idols (and thus of the Greek *eidos* = the outward shape of something). Schelling seems explicitly to be alluding to this association, in that he subsequently repeatedly cites biblical verses dealing with the Mosaic tradition's prophecy

that the Israelites will become wicked in their hearts and express this in the creation of idols (thus breaking God's covenant with the Israelites: that is, the Second Commandment explicitly and the First Commandment implicitly). In this sense, '*Gebilde*' ("disposition" or "figure" metaphorically and "idol" literally) is a double *entendre*. With respect, then, to Schelling's larger point about the emergence of successive polytheism (and in the images or idols of God thereto appertaining) this *Gebilde* of the mind represents the attempt of mankind to form the image of God, to distinguish or differentiate God. But as Schelling points out, the mankind in a position to do so, in a position to become discursively aware of its relation to the Absolute God, is always already in a relation of separation to that God and thus thwarts its own enterprise at the same time that it establishes both the very *idea* ($=eidos$) of the Absolute God and the polytheism to which that God must stand in a contrasting relation. Hence, again, curiously, the discursive notion of the monotheism of the one, true, eternal, absolute God is in a relation of mutual presupposition with polytheism.

7. Hierapolis is located in northern Syria, near the confluence of the Euphrates and Sajur rivers. There were natural springs at this ancient Commagenian sanctuary. A native rhetorician and satirist in Commagene, Lukiano (Lucian) wrote *Dialogues of the Gods,* and his *De Dea Syria* mentions phallic worship of Derketo (Atargatis), a Syrian mermaid goddess of nature.

8. A Sumerian god imparting wisdom to mankind, Oannes was the mythical being—arising from the Persian Gulf—who introduced humans to science and the first written language (cuneiform).

9. The Recabites were a nomadic tribe closely related to the Kenites. Many of the Recabites, through a series of politico-historical causes involving the pressures of the large "heathen" kingdoms on the borders of Palestine, lived among the Israelites and were on good terms with them. Jonadab, one of the patriarchs of the Recabite tribe, living approximately 250 years prior to Jeremiah, aided King Jehu of the Israelites in his drive to extirpate Baal worship in the Northern Kingdom. Essentially, the passages by Jeremiah about the Recabites are intended to contrast the obedience of the Recabites with the disobedience of the tribes of Judah.

10. Diodorus was the Greek writer of the *Bibliotheca historica*, which combines observations on war, geography, and history in the ancient world.

11. The translators opt for "nations" here because the standard English translations of the Bible do so.

12. The rather awkward usage "peoples or nations" as the translation for *Völker* is simply meant to a) capture the fact that Schelling is still referring to "peoples" in a sense consistent with the rest of the text and b) remain faithful to biblical translations wherein "nations" are often employed instead of "peoples." Maintaining both consistency and readability in these passages is difficult, so some places in the text will include only one of the two choices. In those places the German is inserted in brackets.

13. The text here is either illegible or a misprint.
14. It is worth pointing out what Genesis says here. Remember that at the age of ninety-nine, and on the occasion of the covenant of circumcision, Abram's name is changed to Abraham. One recalls that *Abram* means "exalted father," and *Abraham* means "father of many." With respect to the name, there is no mention of peoples or nations, but the traditional translation of the content of God's covenant with Abraham [at Gen. 17:2–8] has God promising Abraham that he will make him "fruitful," "make peoples or nations of [him]," make "kings come from [him]." In short, God pledges to make him "father of many peoples or nations." Ignoring for the moment the birth of Ishmael by Abraham's slave-wife, Hagar, God's covenant is held in that at the age of one hundred Abraham's wife, Sarah, gives birth to Isaac, who in turn (and years after a rather harrowing near death incident at Mount Moriah) fathered Jacob, who in turn fathered the twelve tribes of Israel. The relevant question, then, is to what extent the "tribes" are "peoples or nations," or, more accurately, to what extent the twelve tribes constitute a people or nation.
15. This is a reference to one of the Semitic descendents. The passage is at Gen. 10:21. Eber is often considered the ancestor of the Hebrews, to the extent that research shows that the word "Eber" is taken by Hebrew to be the origin of 'Hebrew.' The clay tablets of Ebla (at modern Tell Mardikh in northern Syria), dating from ca. 2500–2300 BCE, mention a king or ruler called Ebrium, who ruled in Ebla for approximately thirty years. It is possible that Ebrium and Eber refer to the same person. Schelling's subsequent point is that this association is questionable, and most likely a retrospective interpolation of the origin of the Hebrew.
16. Dorus was the son of Hellen, father of Xanthippe, and proverbially the ancestor of the Dorians. Ion was the son of Xuthus and Creusa and the mythical ancestor of the Ionians.
17. With "Hus" Schelling presumably intends "Cush," the far southern Nile region. Ham (brother of the blessed Shem and Japhet), whose lineage was cursed by God, was the father of Canaan (which Canaan, of course, would then be associated with the land conquered by the Semite Israelites after their flight from Egypt and wandering through the Sinai). See translators' note 13 in lecture 4 for the genealogy of Ham's descendents.
18. In at least three ways *Israel* is another name for Jacob, who along with Esau was a son of Isaac and grandson of Abraham: 1) there is the sense of the "tribes of Israel" being called also the "tribes of Jacob" (in that Jacob was the father of the twelve sons forming the nation of Israel); 2) the poetically styled sense derived from Gen. 32, where Jacob literally wrestles with the incarnate God at Peniel, resulting in God telling Jacob that his name will become Israel ('Israel' means "wrestles with God"); 3) the destiny of the Israelites (both its positive side qua the fulfillment of the divine Abrahamidic covenant through Jacob's offspring, and the less pleasurable aspect of repeated wandering and diaspora qua divine punishment for unfaithfulness)

is prefigured by Jacob's journeys throughout the Near East. Hence Schelling's opaque transition from discussing Jacob's wandering to discussing Israel's settling.

19. The Alemanni (meaning "all men"), a Germanic tribe composed of various warbands living south of the Main River, were continually in conflict with the Romans. They launched many invasions, controlled parts of Roman territory (Alsace), and were eventually incorporated into the Frankish kingdom. In 213 CE they are mentioned by Caracalla (Roman Emperor Marcus Aurelius Antoninus, 211–217 CE), with respect to their adversarial role.

20. The Marcomanni (meaning "frontier men") were a German tribe that formed alliances with other German tribes against the Roman Empire, notably against Marcus Aurelius in the second century CE.

21. In 98 CE Tacitus wrote the early ethnography of Germanic peoples, the *De Origine et situ Germanorum*, where he dealt with religious beliefs of the tribes. He was partially working in the mold of Julius Caesar, who documented aspects of the German tribes in his *Gallic Wars*.

22. As is known, Abraham is a very important religious figure for Jews, Christians, and Muslims. As examples, Gen. 18:17–19, 2 Chr. 20:7, and Isa. 41:8 refer to the friendship of God and Abraham.

23. It is worth noting that this passage is followed by Gen. 1: 27 ("So God created man in his own image/ in the image of God he created him;/ male and female he created him."), which is the first Old Testament passage written in verse (the OT is approximately 40 percent poetry).

24. "Jehovah" (LORD) and "Elohim" (God) occur thousands of times in the Old Testament, and are often coupled together as particular and generic respectively such that the translation of the Hebrew is the "LORD God."

25. Remembering that in Hebrew "Adam" means "man" (in a generic sense), and the focus Schelling places on the narrative of the descent of humanity from general to particular, this clause could be translated as mankind "differentiated in itself" and "[a mankind wherein man is] opposed one to another."

26. For the brief synopsis on the authorship of the Pentateuch, see translators' note 12 in Lecture 4.

27. The pronouns here are unclear. Possibly Schelling means "time" instead of "humanity" here.

28. The passage from Jos. 24:2–3 deals explicitly with Abraham's separation from his polytheistic family. "Long ago your ancestors . . . lived beyond the Euphrates and worshipped other gods. But I took your father Abraham from that land beyond the River and led him throughout Canaan and gave him many descendents." This translation is from the NIV.

29. "Salem" is a shortened form of "Jerusalem" and, as should be obvious, is related to the Hebrew word for "peace." In that Abraham gives Melchizedek 10 percent of all he owns, Abraham acknowledges that they both serve the same LORD. See Gen. 14:18–20 and Heb. 7. Sanchuniaton is

the pre-Homeric age author of works in Phoenician, but fragments are only found in Philo of Byblos.

30. In light of traditional English translations of the Bible, alternate translations of "justice" and "just" would be "righteousness" and "righteous." "Melchizedek" is often translated as "king of righteousness" or "my king is righteousness."

31. The word here is *umstürzende*, which carries the sense of political "overthrow" or "upheaval."

32. Abraham, when Sarah was still barren and thus prior to his fathering Isaac through Sarah, fathered Ishmael through Hagar, Sarah's maidservant. Although Isaac received the Lord's covenant blessing, at Gen. 17 Ishmael was also blessed by the Lord to be the "father of many," of "twelve rulers," of "a nation." At Gen. 25 Ishmael has twelve sons, many of whom have Arabic names—thus supporting the Arab tradition that Ishmael is their ancestor.

33. The literal translation of *El Schaddai* is "Lord Almighty" or "God, the Mountain One," with both indicating insurmountable strength.

34. God says this to Moses at Ex. 6:3. The name *El Schaddai* appears rather seldom in the Bible (fewer than fifty times, and thirty-one of those in Job), and is the special name by which God reveals himself to the patriarchs. The implication is that the patriarchs did not fully comprehend God as the One who was to redeem the Israelites.

35. This is of course a reference to God's testing of Abraham at Mount Moriah.

36. Macrobius (395–423 CE) was a Roman grammatician and philosopher whose most famous work *Saturnalia* contains many religious, mythological, and cultural discussions. Macrobius (Iao), Diodorus (Iao), and Sanchuniaton (Jevo) all refer to the same god, the mythical symbol of the Supreme Being, "the light conceivable only by intellect." The pronunciation is related to that of the tetragrammaton.

Lecture Eight

1. The German word here is *die Enge*, which also means "narrow space" (in the sense of, say, a mountain pass) or "straits" (in both literal and metaphorical senses) as well as "dilemma" or "difficulty."

2. Schelling employs here the technical composition term *Grundton*, the basic note or key of a composition. The word also means "undertone" or "prevailing mood (or sentiment)."

3. The phrase *"crisis* of the peoples" is the translation of *Völker*krisis. It is noteworthy to recall that Schelling often mentions the "separation" (translated as *Trennung*) of the peoples as a "cision" (*Scheidung*), which is a word closely related to "crisis."

4. The word for "fanatical" is *schwärmerisch*, which is the adjective form of *Schwärmerei*, which is usually thought of as a form of "religious frenzy."

5. The verse Schelling refers to as "the context" reads: "Believe me, woman, a time is coming when you will worship the Father neither on this mountain nor in Jerusalem. You Samaritans worship what you do not know; we worship what we do know, for salvation is from the Jews" [NIV translation]. It is worth noting that the Samaritan holy book was only the Pentateuch, so to this extent the Samaritans were seen as failing to accept or realize the central (futural) part of God's covenant, as failing to adequately "know" God.

6. "Holding for true" is the translation of the now essentially obsolete word *Fürwahrhalten*. The sense is of considering something as "real" or "actual."

LECTURE NINE

1. Müller (1797–1840) was a historian and the author of the *History of the Literature of Ancient Greece*.

2. The word here is *Kunst*, but given the context and Schelling's own self-reference to this text's earlier passages, particularly those in lecture 3 and those on poetry as "creative" drive, the translation "art" has been passed over in favor of "creative."

3. The reference here is to Chryses's outrage over his daughter's kidnapping by Agamemnon. Chryses offers a ransom, which is spurned, and then turns to Apollo to avenge him, which Apollo does by plaguing the Greek army. Achilles obtains a prophecy from Calchas, which indicates the origin of the plague in Agamemnon's obstinacy. Agamemnon eventually gives in and returns the daughter but demands Achilles's battle prize (a woman) in return. Achilles, the best Greek warrior, then refuses to fight the Trojans until the death of Patroclus.

4. The *Legio fulminatrix* is the "thundering legion" of Roman soldiers that battled the Marcomanni in 174 CE; they were supposedly saved by a miracle thunderstorm after Christian prayers.

5. The translators have chosen to capitalize "Philosophy of Mythology" at this point because Schelling is beginning to operate with the term as an articulation of a philosophical discipline like the Philosophy of Nature, the Philosophy of Art, the Philosophy of Language, and so on.

6. At this juncture in Schelling's life and career this point in part takes on a personal dimension. Schelling's Berlin period was marked by the publication (in 1843) of the so-called *Paulus-Nachschrift*, Dr. H. Paulus's transcription of (and polemic against) Schelling's winter semester 1841–1842 Berlin lectures on the Philosophy of Revelation. Schelling fought the *Nachschrift*'s publication but failed legally to prevent it.

7. The word here is *Verrückung*, which suggests "madness" or "going crazy."

8. The word here is *Attractions-Sphäre*. The concepts of attraction and contraction have a history in Schelling's corpus, particularly in their origin in Schelling's Philosophy of Nature. Contraction (or attraction) is coupled together with expansion, its opposed principle. In the Philosophy of Nature the principle of contraction (or attraction) of the divine can be imagined to the mind's eye as operating like a black hole: it is force without dimension, noticeable only in its effect. It is nothing without the expansive principle, which without contraction can be considered like an infinite, infinitely accelerating breaking apart of everything. The two forces or principles are in a tension productive of the observable world. In the *System of Transcendental Idealism* contraction (or attraction) and expansion play an analogous role in the production of self-consciousness. Kyriaki Goudeli's excellent *Challenges to German Idealism: Schelling, Fichte, and Kant* captures the heart of the point: "Self-consciousness results as the outcome of two infinite, mutually contrasted activities; one expansive, which is a pure producing out towards infinity and is called *real*, and a second contractive, which infinitely limits the first activity . . . and is called ideal. The reverting, intuitant activity is conceived as an act of absolute freedom, which, in its continuous limitations of the producing activity, builds the infinity of limitations and differentiations in the whole of reality" [Goudeli 2002, 148–49]. Given the partial critique to which the concept of the *Attractions-Sphäre* is submitted here, it is worth considering that Schelling may be in part criticizing his own earlier philosophical work. For a discussion of these terms in their later Schellingian usage, see Slavoj Zizek's introductory essay in *The Abyss of Freedom/The Ages of the World* (Ann Arbor: University of Michigan Press, 1997); see also Slavoj Zizek, *The Indivisible Remainder: An Essay on Schelling and Related Matters* (London: Verso, 1996).

9. The rather awkward phrase "polytheism of a simple series of a multitude of gods as such" is the translation of *Vielgötterei*, which has usually been translated as "successive polytheism," but which obviously cannot in this passage be so translated. The distinction Schelling is making is between *successiver Polytheismus* as successive polytheism taken in its whole course, in its entire *process*, and *Vielgötterei* as successive polytheism qua the multitude of gods *abstracted from the process* in which they each have their positional significance. As Schelling points out, the *Vielgötterei* is properly understood actually as part of the whole of *successiver Polytheismus*, which fits in with the notion of *Polytheismus* forming the role of a more universal, holistic determination of which *Vielgötterei* is a part.

10. Thurn and Taxis founded the German postal system.

11. The French chemist Antoine Fourcroy (1755–1809) helped develop plant and animal chemistry.

12. Joseph II was HRE (1765–1790) and an "enlightened monarch" with his seat in Austria. After trying to trade Belgium for Bavaria, his massing

of troops in the East—to support other campaigns—allowed the Belgians to revolt, an act that his administrators were unable to hinder.

13. The phrase reads "*Ein Drittes, worin sich die Philosophie nicht finden und erkennen kann*" . . . An alternate translation would be: "A third matter to which philosophy cannot reconcile or accommodate itself and in which it cannot know or perceive itself."

14. Kanne was a professor of Oriental languages in Erlangen from 1819 through 1824; Schelling was also at Erlangen during this period.

Lecture Ten

1. The interesting word here for "events" is *Ereignisse*. It is a misconception that the word's root stems from *eignen* (to be characteristic of, or suitable to). Rather, the etymological history of the word indicates that it stems from the eighth century Old High German *ouga* and *ouga*'s derivation *Auge* (eye), which word descended into the Middle High German *erougen*, *eröugen* (to place before the eyes) and their Early Lower High German relation *eräugnen* (to place before the eyes). *Eräugnen* remained standard as the word for "event," but by the middle of the eighteenth century had mutated to *ereignen*, the root of *Ereignis*. The sense of "event" in German thus carries the strong connotation of something empirical, which of course fits nicely with Schelling's understanding of the reality and truth content of mythology and its respective events and causes.

2. The word here is *Rechtsverfassung*, which carries along with it the denotation of a "constitution" but also of a judiciary or specifically legal system.

3. *Historie* stems from the Greek ἱστορία, a word that means "historical representation" and is related to ἱστορεῖν (to research, to observe, to report what has happened or an event). As much as possible, the word *Historie* will thus be translated as an appropriate variant of "history as an account," while *Geschichte* will be translated simply as "history." This translation is in part warranted by the fact that later in this lecture Schelling makes the same distinction.

4. The most reasonable assumption here is that Schelling is referring to Hegel and his late writings and lectures on the Philosophy of History. Although it is the case that Hegel's many pre-*Logik*, *Realphilosophie* writings (i.e., the *Phenomenology*, the *Lectures on Fine Art*, etc.) contain a logical structure whose dialectical kernel is expounded in pure form in the *Logik*, Schelling would most likely have had in mind the lectures and writings beginning from around the time of the *Philosophy of Right*, which makes explicit reference (particularly in the Preface) to the role of the dialectical structure of the Concept in both the objective occurrences of the emergence and functioning of the state and the subjective *account* of the emergence and functioning of the notion of the state. This emphasis remains in Hegel's thought until his death in Berlin.

5. Baron Georges Cuvier (1769–1832) was a French naturalist and comparative anatomist. A founder of functional anatomy, he expanded on Linneaus's work on classes, systematized fossils, and was the father of paleontology. His "Essay on the Theory of the Earth" was influential on theories seeing life as arising from the sea. The translators have been unable to locate the reference to Ballenstädt.

6. In the seventh and eighth centuries CE the Pallava kings in India built the structural temples, bas-relief, and rock cut temples at Mavalpuram (Mamallpuram), of which the most famous is the bayside located Dravidian style Shore Temple. The hewn granite cave temples of Ellore are stunning architectural work done by generations of Buddhist, Hindu, and Jain monks. The largest monolith in the world, the Kailasa temple was carved to represent the home of Shiva.

7. This is probably a misprint or some other mistake; "forty" years should have been written.

English-German Glossary

Absolute, the: *Absolute, das*
Abyss: *Tiefe, die*
accept: *annehmen*
Act, the: *That, die*
Activity: *Thätigkeit, die; Handlung, die*
actual: *eigentlich, reell*
Actuality: *Wirklichkeit, die*
Advance, the: *Fortgang, der*
Affection: *Affection, die*
Affinity: *Verwandtschaft, die*
Age (of the world): *Weltalter, das; Zeit, die*
ancient time: *Vorzeit, die*
Antiquity: *Altherthum, das; Vorzeit, die*
Antithesis: *Gegensatz, der*
Appearance: *Erscheinung, die*
Apprehension: *Auffassung, die*
arbitrary: *willkürlich*
Art: *Kunst, die*
articulated: *ausgesprochen*
artificial: *künstlich*
assume: *annehmen*
Attraction: *attraction*
Attunement: *Stimmung, die*
authentic: *eigentlich*
Author: *Urheber, der*
Basis: *Grundlage, die; Grund, der*

221

be effective: *gelten, wirken*
be in force as: *gelten*
become prominent: *hervortreten*
Beginning, the: *Anfang, der*
Being: *Seyn, das*
Being, a/the: *Wesen, das*
Belief: *Glaube, der*
Belief in many gods: *Götterglaube, der*
Blood relationship: *Blutverwandtschaft, die*
Bond, the: *Band, das*
Boundary: *Beschränkung, die*
bring forth: *hervorbringen*
Capacity to be: *Seynkönnende, das*
Cause: *Ursache, die*
cause: *wirken*
Christianity: *Christenthum, das*
Cision, the: *Scheidung, die*
Clan: *Stamm, der*
cognize: *erkennen*
Coherence: *Zusammenhang, der*
Communality: *Gemeinschaft, die*
Community: *Gemeinschaft, die; Gesellschaft, die*
comprehend: *begreifen, auffassen*
comprehensible: *begreiflich*
Comprehension: *Auffassung, die; Begreifen, das*
Concept: *Begriff, der*
Conception: *Vorstellung, die*
conceptualizable: *begreiflich*
Conclusion: *Schluss, der*
concrete: *reell*
Condition, the: *Bedingung, die; Verhältnis, das* (in the sense of state or status)
Confusion: *Verwirrung, die*
Connection: *Verbindung, die; Zusammenhang, der*
Consciousness: *Bewusstseyn, das*
Consciousness of G/god: *Gottesbewusstseyn, das*
Consequence: *Folge, die; Wirkung, die*
Content, the: *Inhalt, der; Gehalt, der*
Contradiction: *Widerspruch, der*
Contrast, the: *Gegensatz, der*
count (as), to: *gelten*
create: *ershaffen*
Creation, the: *Schöpfung, die; Gebilde, das*

Creator: *Urheber, der*
Culture: *Bildung, die*
Customs: *Sitten, die*
Decision: *Entscheidung, die*
Deduction: *Schluss, der; Deduktion, die*
Deep, the: *Tiefe, die*
define: *bestimmen*
deform: *entstellen*
Degeneration: *Entartung, die*
Deification/Deifying of nature: *Naturvergötterung, die*
deify: *vergöttern*
Deities: *Gottheiten, die*
Deity: *Gott, der*
Descent (in the sense of origin or lineage): *Abkunft, die*
desire, to: *begehren*
determinate being: *Dasein, das*
determine: *bestimmen*
Development: *Entwicklung, die*
Dialectic(s): *Dialektik, die*
differentiate: *unterscheiden*
Discovery: *Entdeckung, die*
Discussion: *Erörterung, die*
Disfiguring, the: *Entartung, die*
Disintegration: *Auflösung, die*
Dispersal/dispersion: *Zerstreuung, die*
disperse: *auseinandergehen*
Disposition: *Stimmung, die; Gemüt, das*
Dissolution: *Auflösung, die*
distinguish: *unterscheiden*
distort: *entstellen*
diverge: *auseinandergehen*
Divinity: *Gottheit, die*
doctrinaire: *doctrinelle*
doctrinal: *doctrinelle*
Doctrine: *Lehre, die*
Doctrine of the gods: *Götterlehre, die*
Drawing into one, the: *Ineinsziehung, die*
Dream state: *Traumzustand, der*
Drive, the: *Trieb, der*
East, the: *Morgenland, das*
effect: *wirken*
Effect: *Wirkung, die*
Embryo: *Keim, der*

emerge (into being): *entstehen*
Emergence (into being): *Entstehung, die*
Entity: *Wesen, das*
Epoch: *Zeit, die*
Era: *Zeit, die*
Error: *Irrthum, der*
Essence: *Wesen, das*
Ethics: *Sitten, die*
Event: *Ereignis, das*
Examination: *Erörterung, die*
Expanse: *Raum, der*
Experience: *Erfahrung, die*
explicit: *ausgesprochen*
Expression: *Ausdruck, der*
extraphysical: *hyper-physisch*
Fact: *Thatsache, die*
Faith: *Glaube, der*
Fate: *Schicksal, das*
Figure, the: *Gestalt, die*
Force, the: *Kraft, die; Gewalt, die; Macht, die*
Force of attraction: *Anziehungskraft, die*
Force of nature: *Naturkraft, die*
Form, the: *Gestalt, die; Gebilde, das*
Formation: *Bildung, die*
Foundation: *Grundlage, die; Grund, der*
Founder: *Urheber, der*
Freedom: *Freiheit, die*
General, the: *das Allgemeine*
Genesis, the: *Entstehung, die*
Goal: *Zweck, der*
G/god: *Gott, der*
grasp: *begreifen*
graspable: *begreiflich*
Greeks: *Hellenen, die*
Ground, the: *Grund, der*
Heathendom: *Heidenthum, das*
Hellenics: *Hellenen, die*
hidden: *verborgen*
historical account: *Historie, die*
History: *Geschichte, die; Historie, die*
Human race: *Menschheit, die*
Humanity: *Menschheit, die*
Idea: *Idee, die; Vorstellung, die*

ideal: *ideell*
Idol: *Gebilde, das*
Idolatry: *Abgötterei, die*
idolize: *vergöttern*
illusory being: *Schein, der*
Image: *Bild, das*
immediate: *unmittelbar*
Immobility: *Unbeweglichkeit*
Impulse: *Anwandlung, die*
Inclination toward: *Anwandlung, die*
Independence: *Unabhängigkeit, die*
Individual, the: *Einzelne, das*
inner substance/concept: *Inbegriff, der*
interact: *durchwirken*
Interpenetration: *Durchdringung, die*
Interpretation: *Deutung, die*
Interrelation: *Zusammenhang, der*
Intuition: *Anschauung, die*
invent (poetically): *erdichten*
Invention: *Erfindung, die*
Judgment: *Urteil, das*
know: *erkennen*
Knowledge: *Wissenschaft, die; Erkenntnis, die*
Lack, the: *Mangel, der*
Law: *Gesetz, das*
Legend: *Sage, die*
Liberation: *Befreiung, die*
Limit: *Beschränkung, die*
limit, to: *beschränken*
Lineage: *Geschlecht, das*
Line of descent (lineage): *Abstammung, die*
Link, the: *Band, das*
Lordship: *Herrschaft, die*
Madness: *Wahnsinn, der*
Manifestation: *Offenbarung, die*
Mankind: *Menschheit, die*
Mastery: *Herrschaft, die*
Material: *Stoff, der; Materie, die*
Matter, the: *Materie, die; Stoff, der*
Meaning: *Bedeutung, die; Sinn, der*
mediate, to: *vermitteln*
Mind, the: *Gemüt, das; Geist, der; Verstand, der*
Model: *Vorbild, das*

Moment, the: *Augenblick, der*
Motion: *Regung, die*
Movement: *Bewegung, die*
Multiplicity of the gods: *Göttervielheit, die*
mutually act: *durchwirken*
Myth: *Mythe, die; Sage, die*
Myth of the gods/deities: *Göttersage, die*
Mythology: *Mythologie, die; Götterlehre, die*
Nation: *Volk, das; Nation, die; Völkerschaft, die*
natural: *physikalisch*
Nature: *Natur, die*
Necessity: *Notwendigkeit, die*
Neediness: *Bedürftigkeit, die*
Note: *Bemerkung, die*
Object, the: *Gegenstand, der*
Observation: *Bemerkung, die; Beobachtung, die*
Oneness: *Einheit, die*
Opinion: *Meinung, die*
Opposition: *Entgegensetzung, die; Widerspruch, der*
Orient, the: *Morgenland, das*
Origin: *Ursprung, der*
original people/nation: *Urvolk, das*
originate: *entstehen*
Particular: *Besondere, das*
Past, the: *Vergangenheit, die*
People: *Volk, das*
perceive: *erkennen, wahrnehmen*
Period (in history): *Weltalter, das; Zeit, die*
Phenomenon: *Erscheinung, die*
physical: *physikalisch*
Poem: *Gedicht, das*
Poesy: *Dichtung, die; Poesie, die*
Poetry: *Poesie, die; Dichtung, die*
Polytheism: *Polytheismus, der; Vielgötterei, die; Göttervielheit, die*
posit: *setzen*
Possibility: *Möglichkeit, die*
Potency: *Potenz, die*
Potential, the: *Potenz, die*
Power, the: *Macht, die; Gewalt, die; Kraft, die*
pre-historical time: *Vorzeit, die; vorgeschichtliche Zeit, die; vorhistorische Zeit, die*
present: *vorhanden*
present, to: *darstellen*

present existence: *Dasein, das*
presuppose: *voraussetzen*
primal substance: *Urstoff, der*
prime/primordial matter: *Urstoff, der*
primordial law: *Urgesetz, das*
primordial people/nation: *Urvolk, das*
primordial time: *Urzeit, die*
Principle, the: *Prinzip, das; Satz, der*
Proceeding, the: *Fortgang, der*
Procreation: *Erzeugung, die*
produce, to: *hervorbringen*
Producing, the: *Erzeugung, die*
Product: *Erzeugnis, das; Schöpfung, die*
Production, the: *Erzeugnis, das; Erzeugung, die; Zeugung, die*
proper: *eigentlich*
Proposition: *Satz, der*
Purpose: *Zweck, der; Absicht, der*
Quality, the: *Eigenschaft, die*
Race, the: *Geschlecht, das; Gattung, die*
ready to hand: *vorhanden*
real: *reell*
Reality: *Realität, die; Wirklichkeit, die*
Reason, the: *Vernunft, die; Grund, der*
reciprocal action/effectivity: *Wechselwirkung, die*
recognize: *erkennen*
Redemption: *Erlösung, die; Heil, das*
relate: *beziehen*
Relation: *Verhältnis, das; Beziehung, die*
Relationship: *Beziehung, die; Verhältnis, das; Verwandtschaft, die*
remember: *erinnern*
Representation: *Vorstellung, die*
Reproduction/reproducing: *Zeugung, die*
restrict: *beschränken*
retroactive: *rückwirkend*
Revelation: *Offenbarung, die*
Rigidity: *Unbeweglichkeit, die*
Salvation: *Erlösung, die; Heil, das*
Science: *Wissenschaft, die*
scientific: *wissenschaftlich*
Seed: *Keim, der*
Semblance: *Schein, der*
Sense: *Sinn, der*
Sentence: *Satz, der*

separate: *scheiden*
Separation: *Trennung, die*
Separation of the peoples/nations: *Völkertrennung, die*
Series: *Aufeinanderfolge, die; Folge, die*
Servers of many gods: *Götterdiener, die*
set: *setzen*
set in opposition: *entgegensetzen*
sever: *scheiden*
Singular, the: *Einzelne, das*
Society: *Gesellschaft, die*
Space, the: *Raum, der*
Species: *Geschlecht, das; Gattung, die*
Spirit: *Geist, der*
step back: *zurücktreten*
step forth: *hervortreten*
strive: *streben*
strive out beyond: *hinausstreben*
Structure: *Bildung, die*
Subject, the: *Subjekt, das*
sublate: *aufheben*
Sublation: *Aufhebung, die*
Substance: *Stoff, der*
Substantiation: *Begründung, die*
Succession: *Aufeinanderfolge, die; Folge, die*
successive polytheism: *Vielgötterei, die; successiver Polytheismus*
sunder: *scheiden*
Sundering, die: *Scheidung, die*
Superstition: *Aberglauben, der*
supra-/super-historical: *übergeschichtlich*
Syllogism: *Schluss, der*
System: *Lehre, die; System, das*
System of the gods: *Götterlehre, die*
Teaching: *Lehre, die*
Teaching of the gods: *Götterlehre, die*
Tension: *Spannung, die*
Time: *Zeit, die*
Traditions: *Überlieferungen, die; Sitten, die*
Transition: *Übergang, der*
Tremoring, the: *Erschütterung, die*
Tribe: *Stamm, der; Völkerschaft, die*
Truth: *Wahrheit, die*
Unconditioned, the: *Unbedingte, das*
understand: *begreifen*

understandable: *begreiflich*
Understanding: *Verstand, der*
Unity: *Einheit, die*
Universal, the: *Allgemeine, das*
unmediated: *unmittelbar*
unprethinkable: *unvordenklich*
Verb: *Zeitwort, das*
View, the: *Meinung, die*
Void, the: *Raum, der*
Wandering of the peoples/nations: *Völkerwanderung, die*
West, the: *Abendland, das*
Whole, the: *Ganze, das*
worship: *anbeten*

Index

Abraham/Abrahamites, 109–111, 113–121, 124, 136, 183n.r, 185n.oo, 186n.xx, 213n14, 213n18, 214n22, 214nn28–29, 215n32, 215n35
A/absolute, ix–x, 151, 208–209n4. *See also* universal relation (the universal)
Acts, 202n12, 207n6
actus, 56, 60, 100, 124, 129–130, 137, 201n6
Adam, 104–106, 114–115, 210n2, 211n5, 214n25
Adonai, 120, 204n16
Aeschylus, 45, 179n.t, 199n9
Aether, 30, 34–35, 195n18, 197n30
A/affection, 133–134, 205n4
Africa, 32, 69
Agamemnon, 140, 216n3
Ages of the World, The, vii, ix, xviii–xxiii, 198n6, 201n6, 206n4, 209–210n1
Aphrodite, 25, 194n12
Apollo, 140, 216n3
apologetics/apologists, 172, 204n16
Arab(s), 69, 106, 109, 118, 207n6, 215n32
Arabic (language), 39, 77, 79, 106, 114, 117, 182n.h, 183n.m, 185n.q, 197n3, 203n16, 215n32
Argus, 44, 199n9
Aristophanes, 34, 35

Aristotle, ix, 38, 152, 192n15, 200n5
art, xvii, 19, 46, 89, 166–168, 187n.c, 216n2
  P/philosophy of, 151, 167–168, 216n5
atheism, 14, 31, 55, 60, 99, 131, 180n.f, 193n3
Azara, D.F., 32, 48, 54–55, 82, 196n25

Babel, 76–77, 182n.j
  Tower of, xi, 83, 114
Babylonian(s), 76, 108–109, 167, 206n5
  Babylonian mythology, 21
Baco, 15, 24, 174, 192n15
Bailly, J. S., 64, 204n18
begin(ning), x, xviii, 21, 35–36, 40, 108, 117, 127–128, 155, 160–163, 165–166, 171, 210n1
Beginnings of Greek History, The, 23
Bochart, Samuel, 63, 203–204n16
Briareus, 194n12

Cadmus, 63, 195n15, 204n16
Cain/Cainites, 105, 186n.xx, 210n2, 211n5
Calderón de la Barca, Pedro, 24, 193n5
Canaan, 111, 203n13, 213n17, 214n28
Caracalla, 112, 214nn19–20
Castor, 27
Chaldean(s)/Chaldaic (language), 77, 109, 116, 184n.f, 203n16

231

C/chaos, 30, 35, 195n16, 195nn16–19, 196–197n30
Charites, 36
China/Chinese, 71, 95–97, 209n8
Christian/Christianity, 24, 27, 60–61, 78–79, 110, 117–118, 126, 128, 140, 148, 156, 167–168, 172, 188n.h, 202n12, 214n22, 216n4
Chronos. *See* Kronos
Cicero, 27, 54, 178n.b, 182n.g
Clericus, J., 23, 193n3
Coleridge, S. T., 187n.e
consciousness, xii, xxii, 17–18, 33, 38–40, 47–49, 52, 56, 58, 60–61, 64–65, 73, 75–76, 78–82, 84–85, 88–90, 93, 95, 97–99, 101, 103–104, 110, 113, 115, 119–120, 124–128, 131, 133, 135–137, 139–146, 148, 150, 155, 159, 162, 167, 169, 175, 200n5, 205–206n4
  God positing consciousness, 129–130, 132, 138, 170
  religious consciousness, xxi, 14, 17, 38–39, 47, 49, 56, 65, 77–78, 94, 100, 110, 113–116, 119, 124, 129–134, 138, 141, 145, 171, 173–174, 211n5
  self-consciousness, 155, 217n8
Corinth(ian), 78, 182n.k
cosmogony, 25, 30, 45, 61, 88
Creuzer, F., 64–67, 89, 98, 149, 157, 179n.s (chapter 2), 179n.b, 183n.d, 200n1, 204n20
Cudworth, R., 23, 62, 193n3
Cuvier, G., 164, 219n5
Cyclopes, 83–84, 183n.s, 194n12, 207n8

Danaus, 63, 204n16
De Dea Syria, 183n.q, 212n7
De natura Deorum, 178n.b, 178n.i
De origine et causis Fabularum Homericarum, 178n.f
De Origine et progressu Idolatriae, 63
De Sapientia Veterum, 24, 192n15
Demeter, 47, 199n11
Demonstratio Evangelica, 63, 204n16
Depuis, C. F., 57, 201n7

Derketo, 108, 212n7
Deuteronomy, 183n.n, 185n.kk, 186n.aaa, 202n12
dialectic(s), ix–xi, xviii, xx, 11, 153, 191n10, 218n4
Dike, 36
Diodor(us), 109, 120, 212n10, 215n36
Dionysus, 28, 106, 195m15
Dissertatio de Historiae Graecae, 179n.b
Dissertatio de Mythol. Graecorum antiquississima, 179n.l, 188n.a
di-syllabism, 95–96
di-theism, 95
doctrine:
  doctrinal character of specific mythologies/religions, 20–21, 41, 63, 65–66, 82, 89, 123–124
  meaning of mythology as, 12–14, 16, 21, 36, 37, 41–42, 50–53, 58–60, 63, 67, 88–90, 97–98, 136–137, 139, 149, 162, 172, 187n.c, 190n8, 202n11
Dryads, 55, 200n4

East, 28, 33, 44, 63–66, 113, 124, 187n.c, 205n20, 214n18
Eber, 111, 213n15
Egypt/Egyptian(s), 21, 44–45, 47, 49, 72, 78, 79–80, 82, 109, 111–112, 120, 166–167, 178n.e, 201n7, 202n12, 204n16, 206n5, 207n6, 213n15
  Egyptian mythology, 21, 44–45, 47, 49, 63–65, 178n.e, 204n16
El Eljon, 117
El Olam, 115–118, 211–212nn5–6. *See also* God
El Schaddai, 118–119, 132, 185n.rr, 215nn33–34. *See also* God
Elohim, 86, 101, 104, 113–115, 117–118, 185n.x, 185nn.gg–hh, 203n12, 209–210n1, 214n24. *See also* God
emanation theory, 65, 86
empiricism, xv, 157, 192n15
end(ing), x, 18–19, 21, 35–36, 127, 154–155, 160–161, 163, 210n1

Enosh, 104–106, 110, 210nn1–2, 211n5
Epaphus, 45, 199n9
Epicurus, 23–24, 27, 42
Erebus, 30, 34, 195n16, 195n18, 196n27
Erlangen lecture courses, viii
Eros, 30, 35, 195n16
error, xvi, xviii–xix, 55, 66, 147
Esau, 111, 213n18
essence, x, 129–133, 136, 142–143, 146, 153, 197n2
eternity, 100, 105, 117, 120, 127, 130, 133, 163–164
Ethics, The, 205n4, 209n7
ethnogony, 91, 209n5
ethnology, 91
eumeritic explanation of mythology, 23–24, 27, 62, 162
Eumeros, 23, 52, 149, 162
Eunomie, 36
Euphrates river, 108, 111, 116, 212n7, 214n28
Eurydice, 194n11
Eve, 186n.xx, 210n2
Exodus, 186n.ss, 186n.yy, 202n12, 209n1, 215n34
Exposition de Système du Monde, 30, 195n13

fall of man, 99–100, 103, 115, 143, 210n4
Far East. *See* East
5. *Mos. See Deuteronomy*
1. *Chronicles*, 105, 184nn.d–e
1. *Mos. See Genesis*
1. *Samuel*, 185nn.s–t
Fourcroy, A., 151, 217n11
4. *Mos. See Numbers*
freedom, ix–x, xvi–xvii, xix, 52, 99, 123–124, 132, 134, 160, 201n6, 202n10, 209n7, 217n8
 freedom of consciousness vis-à-vis mythology, 17, 21, 99, 123–124
 human freedom, vii, 99, 123–124, 132, 134, 202n10
Freedom essay (1809), vii–ix, 198n6, 209n7

Gaia, 31, 34, 36, 194n12, 195n16, 195nn19–21, 196n27
General Methodology of Academic Study, viii
Genesis, 63, 74, 100, 103–107, 111, 113–115, 119–120, 163, 183n.r, 184nn.f–h, 184n.m, 184–185nn.o–r, 185nn.ll–qq, 202–203nn12–13, 210nn1–2, 210n4, 213nn14–15, 213n18, 214nn22–23, 214n29, 215n32
God:
 absolute One God, 90, 103, 105, 115, 121, 127, 212n6
 divine Self. *See under* Godhead
 Divinity, the. *See under* Godhead
 eternal God. *See* El Olam
 Godhead, xxiii, 55, 59, 62, 65, 89, 101, 131–133, 143, 148, 173, 180n.f, 217n8
 O/one universal God, 80, 85, 91, 110–111, 114, 125, 127–128, 132, 134, 209–10n1, 211–212nn5–6, 215n34
 primordial God, 110, 114–115, 118
 relative One, 90, 103, 105–106, 110, 113, 115, 119–121, 124–125, 127, 128–130, 132, 134
 singularity of God, 61, 86, 90, 104, 121, 145
 ultimate One. *See under* O/one universal God
 unconditioned One, 90, 97, 103, 107, 209n4
Goethe, J. W., 13, 19–20, 178n.g, 191n12, 192n19, 200n3
Götterlehre oder mythologische Dichtungen der Alten, 191n12
Göttervielheit. *See* polytheism: simultaneous polytheism
Göttingen gelehrte Anzeigen, 180n.c, 185n.v, 194n6
great flood, 106–110, 113, 184n.f, 203n13, 211n5

Greek(s), 9–10, 15–21, 27, 36, 44, 47, 49, 55, 76–79, 83, 84, 87–89, 91, 93, 96, 105–106, 120, 134, 148, 161, 166, 168, 177–178n.g, 179n.d, 183n.s, 190n7, 192n17, 204n19, 205n20, 207n6, 207n8, 211n6, 212n10, 216n3
Greek mythology, xxiii, 15, 18, 21, 25, 28–29, 44–45, 47, 49, 53, 55, 62–66, 79, 86–88, 91, 93, 106–109, 111, 177–178n.g, 192n17, 204n16, 205n20, 216n
Guarani, 82

Hades, 195nn14–15, 199n11
Hagar, 117, 213n14, 215n32
Ham/Hamites, 62, 93, 111, 203n13, 209n6, 213n17
heathen(dom), 76, 110–111, 115–117, 121–123, 126, 135, 143, 148, 167–168, 171–173, 203n13, 212n9
Hebrew (language), 39–40, 76, 79, 96, 104, 106, 110, 119, 163, 179n.a, 183n.n, 184n.q, 185n.q, 197n3, 203n16, 210n4, 213n15, 214nn24–25, 214n29
Hebrew(s). *See* Jewish people
Hegel, G. W. F., vii–viii, xvii, xx–xxi, 189n1, 191n10, 198n6, 200n5, 209n7, 218n4
Helen, 25
Helios, 25, 192n17, 196n23
Hellenic people. *See* Greek(s)
Hemere, 34, 195n18
Hera, 14, 24, 44, 191n14, 192n17, 195n15, 199n9
Heracles/Hercules, 27, 194n11, 199n9
Herder, J.G., 160
Hermann, G., 28–29, 31–36, 41, 43–44, 47, 49, 51–52, 60, 90, 137, 149, 164–165, 169, 174, 179n.b, 179n.s (chapter 2), 182n.l, 194n8, 196–197n30
Hermes, 199n9
Herodotus, 15–18, 21, 35, 72, 78–79, 161, 177n.e, 183n.o

Hesiod, xxiii, 15–18, 21, 23, 28–31, 33–36, 38, 44, 83, 177n.e, 191n9, 194n12, 195nn20–21, 200n1, 205n20
Heyne, C. G., 25–29, 32, 38, 43–44, 49, 51–54, 137, 149, 178n.g, 193n6
Hierapolis, 108, 212n7
Hinduism. *See* India
history, ix, xvi–xvii, xix–xxi, xxiii, 10, 19, 23, 42, 49, 55, 62, 64, 66, 69, 72, 78–81, 83, 87, 103, 125–130, 132–133, 137, 155, 159–160, 162–166, 168, 187n.c, 189n1, 198–199nn6–7, 200n5, 208n2, 218n3
  of the gods, 10, 14–18, 23, 27, 37, 49, 51, 53, 62, 86–89, 91, 137, 140, 202n11, 208n2
  P/philosophy of, xvi, 49, 100, 125, 129, 151, 155, 158, 160–162, 165, 167, 218n4
  qua *historia/Historie*, xviii, xxi–xxii, 53, 161, 164, 189n1, 198–199n7, 218n3
History of Astronomy, 64
History of the Literature of Ancient Greece, 216n1
Homer, xxiii, 12–13, 15–16, 18, 26, 34–36, 46, 53–54, 83–84, 166, 177n.e, 183n.s, 191n9, 200n1, 205n20, 215n29
Horace, 8, 53, 70, 189n3, 200n1
Horai, 36
Horos, 199n11
Huet, Daniel, 63, 204n16
human race, 9, 15, 32, 59, 62, 64, 67, 70–76, 78–83, 85, 89–95, 97–99, 101, 103–106, 108–110, 112–117, 122–125, 127–131, 133, 135–136, 142–143, 145, 147, 150, 154–155, 157, 162–163, 165–166, 169–170, 184n.f, 186n.xx, 205n2, 210n3, 211n5, 214n25, 214n27
  as original man, 129–130, 137, 139, 144, 159
human species. *See* human race
humanity. *See* human race
Humboldt, A. von, 55, 191n12

Index

Hume, D., xxii, 52, 55–56, 58–61, 128, 137, 161, 186n.c
Hyperion, 31, 196n23

Iapetus, 31, 196n23
ideal relation (the idea), viii–x, xxiii, 65, 123, 139–140, 151, 174, 198–199nn6–7, 217n8
I/idealist, xv, xix–xx, 198n6
Ideas on Politics and Trade of the Ancient Peoples, 188n.d
idolatry/idols, 118, 186n.c, 211–212n6
Iliad, The, 46, 140, 194n10
Ilium, 25
Inachus, 44
India(n)(s), 19–21, 45, 65, 71–72, 78, 130, 148, 166–167, 177n.g, 182n.a, 207n6, 219n6
 Bhagavad Gita, xxiii
 Brahmanism, xxiii, 72
 Indian mythology, xii–xxiii, 19–21, 63, 65, 78, 148, 177n.g, 198n6
 Upanishads, xxiii
 Vedas, xxiii, 65
invention:
 mythology/religion not characterized by, xi, 16, 25, 32–34, 38, 41–45, 47–49, 51, 53, 60, 87–89, 116, 133, 134–136, 139–141, 154, 164–165
 poetic drive for in mythology, 13–15, 20, 32, 37, 41, 190n7
Io, 44–45, 199n9
Isaac, 113, 119, 213n14, 213n18, 215n32
Ishmael, 213n14, 215n32
Isis, 47, 199n11
Islam, 117, 204n16, 214n22
Israel/Israelites, 107, 109–112, 116, 122, 124, 202–203nn12–13, 212n6, 212n9, 213n14, 213–214nn17–18, 215n34
Ixion, 14, 191n14

Jacob, 111, 113, 119, 124, 213–214n14
Japheth/Japhethites, 93–94, 203n13, 213n17
Jaspers, Karl, x

Jehovah, 104, 107, 113–120, 124, 183n.r, 184n.p, 185nn.gg–hh, 185n.oo, 186n.vv, 186n.xx, 203n12, 210n1, 214n24
Jeremiah, 206n5, 212n9
Jeremiah, 109, 182n.f, 184n.b, 185n.q, 185n.ii, 206n5
Jerusalem, 109, 167, 206–207nn5–6, 214n29, 216n5
Jesus Christ, 123–125, 132, 173
Jewish people, 40, 63, 104, 110–111, 121, 123–124, 129, 132, 173, 184n.f, 202n12, 206n5, 207n6, 213n15, 214n22, 216n5
Jonadab, 109, 212n9
Jones, Sir William, 64–65, 149, 204n19
Joshua, 116
Joshua, 185n.jj, 214n28
Judaism, 117, 171
 and mythology, 21, 86
Julius (Caesar), 112, 214n21
Juno. *See* Hera
Jupiter, 27

Kanne, J. A., 156, 218n14
Kant, I., xxii–xxiii, 41, 103, 151, 178n.d, 189n1
Katater(s), 109
Kenan/Kenites, 210n2, 211n5, 212n9
King David, 107, 119, 186n.bbb
Koeus, 31
Kottus, 194n12
Krius, 31, 196n23
Kronos, 9, 26, 31, 36, 62, 86–88, 91, 108, 121, 137, 194n12, 196n23, 203n13, 204n16

Lamentations, 206–207n5
language(s), xi, 19, 26, 29, 32–33, 39–40, 43, 47–49, 73–74, 77–82, 94–97, 154, 182n.j, 194n8, 205n4, 207n6, 212n8
 confusion of, 74–79, 81, 83, 94, 106, 108, 114, 167
 language of tongues, 78, 207n6
 P/philosophy of, 8, 155, 216n5
Laplace, P. S., 30, 195n13, 204n18

Latin, 31, 39, 79, 148, 182n.g, 201n6, 204n19, 207n6
Legio fulminatrix, 140, 216n4
Leibniz, G., 40
"Leibniz, Spinoza and Wolff," 205n4
Lessing, G. E., 61–62, 202n10
Letters on Homer and Hesiod, 179n.b, 179n.s (chapter 2), 181n.t, 183n.d, 188n.b, 194n8
Letters on the Origin of the Sciences, 64
Linus, 28, 194n11
Löscher, V., 183n.c
Lucian. *See* Lukiano
Lukiano, 108, 183n.q, 212n7
Luther, Martin, 104, 108, 116, 182n.g

Macrobius, 120, 215n36
Mágic prodigioso, El, 24, 193n5
mankind. *See* human race
Marcomanni, 112, 214n20, 216n4
Melchizedek, 117–118, 185n.oo, 214–215nn29–30
Metaphysics, The, ix
Michaelis, J. D., 184n.f
Mizraim, 111, 203n13
Mnemonsyne, 31, 196n23
Mohammed, 117–118
monism, 204n17, 205n4, 209n7
monosyllabism, 95–96
monotheism, x, xxi, xxiii, 61, 65–67, 85, 90, 93, 97–99, 103–104, 106, 113, 115, 117, 119–120, 123–126, 129–133, 145–146, 148, 183n.d, 208n1, 210n1, 211–212nn5–6
absolute monotheism, 91, 122, 208n1
Christian monotheism, xxiii, 117–118
historical monotheism, 157
Islamic monotheism, xxiii, 117–118
Jewish monotheism, xxi, xxiii
relative monotheism, 90–91, 93–95, 97–101, 121–122, 125, 129, 148
supra-historical monotheism, 129
Moritz, K. P., 12, 191n12
Mosaic law. *See* Pentateuch
Mosaic writings. *See* Pentateuch

Moses, 63–65, 107, 118–121, 184n.f, 202n12, 209n1, 211n5, 215n34
Mosheim, J. L., 23, 193n3
Moslem. *See* Islam
Müller, K. O., 139–141, 194n8, 216n1
multiplicity, 61–62, 65–66, 76, 80, 86, 114, 125, 132, 201n8
multiplicity of gods. *See* polytheism
Munich lectures (1833–34), xviii–xix
Muse(s), 191n9, 194nn10–11, 196n23
Muslim(s). *See* Islam
mythological process, xxi–xxii, 134–135, 142–151, 154, 162, 167, 172.
See also theogonic process
Mythology of the Greeks, 156

Natural History of Religion, The, 180nn.f–g, 181nn.k–m
nature, ix, 27–29, 32, 56–57, 61–62, 65–66, 81, 143, 147–148, 150, 153–156, 168–170, 201n6
human nature, 23, 56, 129–130, 152
P/philosophy of, 8, 12, 151, 154–156, 160, 207n7, 216n5, 217n8
Near East. *See* East
Nebuchadnezzar, 109, 206n5
necessity, ix–x, 124, 132, 134, 136, 139, 141, 143–144, 149, 162, 168
negative philosophy, ix, 11, 191n10
Neoplatonists, 14, 27
New Testament, 76, 111, 112, 182n.h
Niebuhr, C., 72, 109, 205n3
Noah, 62, 93, 105, 108–110, 113, 203n13, 209n5
nomads/nomadism, 109, 111, 114, 118, 212n9
nominalism, 38
Notitia Dei insita, 56–58, 170, 201n6
Numbers, 186n.zz, 202n12
Nut, 199n11
Nyx, 30, 34, 195n16, 195n18, 196n28

Oannes, 108, 212n8
Obelus, 35
object(ivity), xviii, xx–xxi, xxiii, 7–9, 17, 56, 58, 134, 137, 141, 143–146, 148–150, 187n.e, 189n1, 190n4,

191n11, 199n7, 201n6, 208–209n4, 218n4. *See also* speculative relation; subject(ivity)
Occident(alism), xvi, 162, 187n.c
Oceanus, 31, 44, 70, 196n23, 199n8
Odysseus, 13
Odyssey, The, 46, 83, 177n.a
Old Testament, 62–64, 75–76, 79, 94, 100, 104, 106, 113–114, 126, 128, 186n.c, 186n.xx (chapter 7), 203n12, 206n5, 214nn23–24
Olen, 28, 194n11
Olympiador, 179n.k
On the Deities of Samothrace, viii, xxii, 177, 181n.q, 187n.e, 198n6
On the Education of Man, 61, 181n.p, 202n10
On the Essence and Treatment of Mythology, 179nn.m–p, 179n.r, 181n.n, 183n.a, 194n8
On the Original Genius of Homer, 54, 200n3
Oreads, 55, 200n4
Orient(al). *See* East
Orientalism, xvi, 162
Origine des tous les Cultes, 180n.h
Orpheus, 28, 53–54, 194n11
Osiris, 63, 199n11, 204n16
Ossian, 54, 200n3
Otto, Walter, vii–viii
Ovid, 77, 188n.e, 200n1

Pallas, 183n.d, 196n23
pantheism, 65, 147, 157
Pantheon of the Oldest Natural Philosophy, 156
particular relation (the particular/ particularity), xxiii, 110, 146, 167
Paul (the Apostle), 182n.g
Pelasgian(s), 17, 78, 93, 177n.g, 192n17, 203n15, 205n20
Pentateuch, 62–64, 74, 76, 103–109, 112, 114, 118–119, 121, 161, 181n.q, 183n.n, 186n.bbb (chapter 7), 186n.c, 202n12, 212n5, 214n26, 216n5
Pentecost, 78, 182n.j, 207n6

people(s), the, xi–xii, xxi, 15, 32–33, 37, 43–50, 54, 58–60, 62, 64–67, 69–74, 76, 79–82, 88–89, 91–94, 108–113, 116–118, 121–123, 125, 129, 135, 140, 147, 152, 162–163, 165–166, 184n.m, 198n6, 201n6, 203nn13–14, 206n5, 207n6, 208n2, 209n5, 212n12, 213n14, 215n3
  as biblical nations, 110–113, 114, 116, 118, 121, 166, 183n.n, 202–203nn12–14, 206n5, 212n12, 213n14, 215n32
  emergence of, 67–69, 72–74, 79–81, 84–85, 91–92, 94, 167, 209n5
  as primordial, 15, 19, 64
  separation of, 67, 70–76, 78, 83, 85, 91–92, 106, 108, 111–112, 114–115, 120, 127, 162, 205n4, 215n3
  wandering of, 78
Persephone, 63, 195n14, 199n11
Phaedrus, 27
Philosophy of Mythology (11–20), The, xxii, 198n6
Philosophy of Mythology and Revelation, vii, 97, 140, 151–154, 158–159, 165, 167, 174, 216nn5–6
Philosophy of Religion, 158, 169–170
Philosophy and Religion, ix
Philosophy of Revelation, 182n.j
Phoebe, 31, 194n9, 196n23
Phoebus, 28, 194n9
Phoenician(s), 21, 63, 88, 109, 166–167, 204n16, 208n3, 215n29
Plato, xxiii, 27, 123, 152, 182n.g, 183n.n
Pluto, 36
poesy, vii, 9, 12–18, 21, 41, 167–168, 190n7, 211n6
poetry, xii, xvii, xxiii, 14–21, 23–25, 27, 35, 37–44, 46, 51, 53, 64, 66, 74, 89, 111, 114, 149, 168–169, 187n.e, 190n7, 193n1, 198n6, 201n6, 211n6, 214n23, 216n2
poets (as creators of mythology), 15, 18, 21, 24, 26–27, 30, 33, 37, 40, 43, 51, 53, 136, 139–141, 190n7, 198n6

Politicus. See *Republic, The*
Pollux, 27
polysyllabism, 95–96
polytheism, x, xxi, xxiii, 9, 32, 52, 55–62, 64–67, 76–79, 85–86, 88, 90, 97–99, 106–111, 113–115, 117, 119–121, 124–125, 127–128, 131, 133–134, 136–137, 145–148, 183n.d, 186–187n.c, 196n26, 201n6, 201–202n8, 202n11, 205n21, 208n1, 210n1, 211–212nn5–6, 214n28, 217n9
   simultaneous polytheism, 86–87, 91, 134, 201–202n, 205n21, 208n1
   successive polytheism, 86–91, 93, 95, 97–98, 108–109, 113, 115, 118, 125, 127–128, 132, 134, 145–146, 149, 184n.f, 201–202n8, 205n21, 208n1, 212n6, 217n9
Poseidon, 36, 79
positive philosophy, vii, ix–x, 191n10
potency, xii, xx, xxii, 56–57, 88, 97, 115, 119, 125, 144–146, 150, 173, 200–201nn5–6
   as God positing, xii, 144–145
primordial time. *See* time: absolutely pre-historical time
Prolegomena to a Scientific Mythology, 139
Prometheus, 179n.t, 199n9
Pythagoreans, 38

Quaestiones Romanae, 188n.e

race(s) [*Geschlechter/Racen*], 46, 70–72, 80–81, 83–84, 107–110, 112, 121, 163, 170, 205n2, 210n3
rationalism/rationalist, xv, xx, xxiii, 126, 171, 174, 198n6, 204n16
real relation (the real), x, xxiii, 65, 87, 89, 123, 136, 139–140, 150, 155, 162, 170, 174, 208n4, 217n8
realism, 38
Recab/Recabites, 109, 118, 212n9
religion:
   meaning of mythology as, 23, 32, 51–52, 54, 55, 56, 61, 81, 85–86, 97, 100, 108, 145, 150, 211n5
   mythological religion, 170–171
   natural religion, 170–173
   primordial religion, 94, 117, 183n.d
   rational religion, 170, 172, 174
   revealed religion, 171, 173
   universal religion, 170
Rémusat, J. P. A., 95, 209n8
Republic, The, 178n.h, 182n.e, 183n.n, 186n.a
revelation, xxiii, 60–66, 85, 99–100, 103, 106, 108, 112–113, 116, 119, 122–123, 125–126, 133, 137, 139, 141, 166, 169–174, 204n16, 205n20
P/philosophy of, viii, 216n26
Philosophy of, xxiii
Rhea, 31, 196n23
Roman philosophy, 27, 148
romantic(s)/romanticism, xv, 168–169, 193n5, 200n1, 200n3, 202n10
Ruines, Les, 180n.i, 201n7

Salem, 117–118, 214n29
Samaritan(s), 123, 216n5
Samuel, 112
Sanchuniaton, 117, 120, 204n16, 208n3, 214n29, 215n36
Sanskrit, 19, 79, 96, 204n19, 207n6
Sarah, 213n14, 215n32
Saturn, 27, 204n16
science (*Wissenschaft*):
   natural science, 12, 27–33, 35, 39, 55, 149, 189n1, 192n15, 201n6, 212n8
   philosophical science, xviii–xxi, xxiii, 7–8, 11–12, 20, 42, 80, 100, 129, 133, 142, 151–153, 155–156, 158–159, 165, 169, 171, 187n.e, 189nn1–2, 191n11, 201n6
Seb, 199n11
2. *Kings,* 184n.o, 185n.q
2. *Mos.* See *Exodus*
Selene, 25, 196n23
Semele, 30, 195n15, 204n16
Semite(s), 93, 213n15, 213n17
Semitic language(s), 39, 79, 95, 114, 204n16, 208n3
Seth (biblical), 104–106, 210n2, 211n5
Seth (Egyptian), 199n11

Shem, 93, 110, 203n13, 213n17
Socrates, 27, 34–35
Solomon, 107, 119, 206n5
Sophocles, 166
South America, xii, xxiii, 32, 48, 80, 82, 196n25
speculative relation, xviii–xxi, 35, 59. *See also* object(ivity); subject(ivity)
Spinoza, B., xvi, xix, 205–206n4, 209n7
state of nature, 123
Stoicism, 27
Storehouse of the Orient, 183n.b
Strabo, 77, 207n8
subject(ivity), ix–xii, xviii, xx–xxi, xxiii, 39, 137, 142–144, 149–150, 179n.a, 187n.e, 189n1, 190n4, 199n7, 209n7, 218n4. *See also* object(ivity); speculative relation
sublation, xi, 8, 11, 65, 99, 120–121, 132, 134, 146–147, 150, 172, 191n10
S/substance, 94, 96, 116, 129–130, 132–133, 138, 197n2, 205n4, 209n7
Sur tous les Cultes, 201n7
Symbolism and Mythology of the Ancient Peoples, especially of the Greeks, 181n.r, 183n.d
System intellectuale, 23, 193n3
system of the gods, 9–10, 13–14, 16, 21, 43, 45, 62–66, 76, 78, 86, 91–93, 108, 124, 154, 162, 178n.g, 190–191n8, 202n11
System of Transcendental Idealism, The, xvii, 188n.g, 217n8

Taaut, 63, 204n16
Tacitus, 112, 214n21
Tartarus, 191n14, 195n16
tautegory, xii, 136, 187n.e
temporality. *See* time
Tethys, 31, 196n23
Thamyras, 28, 194n10
Theaetatus, 182n.g
Theia, 31, 196n23
theism, 31, 55, 58–61, 65, 130–131, 133, 150, 164, 186–187n.c

Themis, 31, 196n23
theogonic process, xii, xxii, 137–138, 142, 144–145, 150–151, 159, 169. *See also* mythological process
theogony, xxi, 10, 15–16, 86, 93, 137, 191n9
Theogony, The, xxi, 23, 28–30, 32–35, 89, 177n.e, 179n.d, 191n9, 194n12, 195n16, 195n18, 195–196nn20–23, 196n27, 196–197n30
Thucydides, 161
time, ix, xvii–xviii, xxi, 31, 43, 65, 75, 80, 86, 92, 110, 116–118, 123, 125, 127, 130, 134, 161–167, 170, 200n5, 206n4, 214n27
  absolutely pre-historical time, 127–128, 163–165
  historical time, viii, 9, 74, 116, 127–128, 143, 160–165
  pre-historical time, 9, 43, 59, 64, 79, 81, 83, 97, 107, 116–117, 119, 123, 124, 127, 133, 159–164
  relative pre-historical time, 128, 163–164
  supra-historical time, 128–129, 133–134, 143, 163
  ultimately pre-historical time. *See* absolutely pre-historical time
Titans, 18, 25, 31, 34, 107, 177n.e, 191n14, 194n9, 196n23
tribes, 32, 48, 55, 62, 67, 69, 72, 75, 81, 93–94, 109–110, 112, 123, 125, 202n12, 212n9, 213n14, 213n18, 214nn19–21
Trojan(s)/Troy, 25, 216n3
True Intellectual System of the Universe. *See System intellectuale*
truth, xvi–xvii, xxiii, 11–12, 23, 41, 50–51, 56, 61, 66, 87, 135, 143, 146, 148–153, 164, 168, 173–174
  relatively true, the, 98, 152

unisyllabism, 95–96
universal relation (the universal/universality), xxiii, 23, 25, 47, 61, 66, 78, 150–152, 167

unprethinkability, 65, 76, 117, 129, 170, 206n4
Uranus, 10, 27, 30, 34, 62, 86–87, 93, 108, 137, 194n12, 195nn20–21, 208n3

Vielgötterei. *See* polytheism: successive polytheism
Volk, das. *See* people; (people) as biblical nations
Volney, C. F., 57, 201n7
Voss, G., 63, 126, 203n15
Voss, J. H., 52–53, 149, 157, 188n.j, 200n1
Voyage dans l'Amerique méridionale, 179n.q

Wissenschaft. *See* science
Wonderful Magus. See *Mágic prodigioso, El*
Wood, Robert, 54, 200n3
Works of Ossian, the Son of Fingal, The, 200n3

Yahweh. *See* Jehovah

Zarathustra. *See* Zoroaster/Zoroastrianism
Zeus, 18, 26, 36, 44, 86–87, 93, 177n.e, 191n14, 195n15, 196n23, 199n9, 208n3
Zoroaster/Zoroastrianism, 63, 204n16

Printed in Great Britain
by Amazon